Possibilities, Challenges, and Changes in English Teacher Education Today

Possibilities, Challenges, and Changes in English Teacher Education Today

Exploring Identity and Professionalization

Edited by
Heidi L. Hallman
Kristen Pastore-Capuana
Donna L. Pasternak

ROWMAN & LITTLEFIELD
Lanham • Boulder • New York • London

Published by Rowman & Littlefield
An imprint of The Rowman & Littlefield Publishing Group, Inc.
4501 Forbes Boulevard, Suite 200, Lanham, Maryland 20706
www.rowman.com

6 Tinworth Street, London SE11 5AL

Copyright © 2019 by Heidi L. Hallman, Kristen Pastore-Capuana, and Donna L. Pasternak

All rights reserved. No part of this book may be reproduced in any form or by any electronic or mechanical means, including information storage and retrieval systems, without written permission from the publisher, except by a reviewer who may quote passages in a review.

British Library Cataloguing in Publication Information Available

Library of Congress Cataloging-in-Publication Data

Names: Hallman, Heidi L., 1976- editor. | Pastore-Capuana, Kristen, editor. | Pasternak, Donna L., editor.
Title: Possibilities, challenges, and changes in English teacher education today : exploring identity and professionalization / edited by Heidi L. Hallman, Kristen Pastore-Capuana, Donna L. Pasternak.
Description: Lanham, Maryland : Rowman & Littlefield, [2019] | Includes bibliographical references and index.
Identifiers: LCCN 2019003224 (print) | LCCN 2019010499 (ebook) | ISBN 9781475845464 (electronic) | ISBN 9781475845365 (cloth) | ISBN 9781475845457 (pbk.) Subjects: LCSH: English language—Study and teaching—United States. | English philology—Study and teaching—United States. | English teachers—United States—Attitudes. | English teachers—Training of—United States.
Classification: LCC PE1068.U5 (ebook) | LCC PE1068.U5 P67 2019 (print) | DDC 428.0071—dc23
LC record available at https://lccn.loc.gov/2019003224

For English teacher educators and their teacher candidates,
with whom we share the journey

Contents

Acknowledgments	xi
Introduction *Heidi L. Hallman, Kristen Pastore-Capuana, and Donna L. Pasternak*	xiii
Part I: English Language Arts Teachers' Professional Roles and Identities	**1**
1 Engaging Preservice Teachers in Productive Struggle Through Antideficit English Education *Amber Warrington and Michelle Fowler-Amato*	3
A Response to Chapter 1 *Melinda J. McBee Orzulak*	17
2 "It's Just Not What I Thought It Would Be": Teacher Candidates Navigating Tensions in Identity *Katharine Covino*	21
A Response to Chapter 2 *Amber Warrington and Michelle Fowler-Amato*	35
3 The Potential of Problematic Practice: Educating Teachers for the Secondary ELA Classroom *Melanie Shoffner*	39
A Response to Chapter 3 *Brandon Sams and Mike Cook*	51

Part II: External Pressures on Teachers' Professionalization — 55

4 Writing Problems and Promises in Standardized Teacher Performance Assessment — 57
Sarah Hochstetler and Melinda J. McBee Orzulak

A Response to Chapter 4 — 71
Connor K. Warner

5 Changing English: Technology and Its Impact on the Teaching of English Education — 77
Donna L. Pasternak

A Response to Chapter 5 — 91
Julie Bell

6 "We Need to Go Next Door and Talk About Our Lessons": One State's Context and Collaboration Around Standards-Based Reform — 95
Lara Searcy and Christian Z. Goering

A Response to Chapter 6 — 107
Jessica Gallo

7 Making Video Recording and Reflection Meaningful for English Teacher Candidates — 111
Julie Bell

A Response to Chapter 7 — 127
Christian Z. Goering and Seth D. French

Part III: Beyond English Language Arts: Challenges to Our Profession — 131

8 More Than Left, Right, Up, Down: Teaching Tensions in Non-ELA Literacy Methods Courses — 133
Jeff Spanke and Chea Parton

A Response to Chapter 8 — 145
Melanie Shoffner

9 Learning From Interns Who Leave the Profession: Emotional Labor and the Limits of the Methods Course — 149
Brandon Sams and Mike Cook

A Response to Chapter 9 — 161
Jeremy Glazer

10 Training for the Unsustainable: The Need to Consider Attrition in ELA Teacher Preparation — 163
Jeremy Glazer

A Response to Chapter 10 — 173
Jeff Spanke

Index 177

About the Editors and Contributors 181

Acknowledgments

This project started with a desire to unite those who teach the methods course in English language arts (ELA) teacher education programs. We recognized that there was a need to share what we refer to as *tensions* or *dilemmas* in teaching this course and to make these tensions visible for others in an effort to improve the practice of teaching the English language arts. The concept of tensions arises from the most recent study of English teacher education, *Secondary English Teacher Education in the United States*, and we are indebted to the work of Donna L. Pasternak, Samantha Caughlan, Heidi L. Hallman, Laura Renzi, and Leslie S. Rush for bringing these concerns to the field through their national study.

Through the National Council of Teachers of English's (NCTE) English Language Arts Teacher Educators' (ELATE) Commission on Methods Teaching and Learning, we encountered others who shared this vision to problematize practices currently taught through methods, or pedagogy, courses. In collaboration with members of this commission, this project was born. We are appreciative for the enthusiasm of all the commission members who contributed to this project—from senior scholars in the ELA field to graduate students.

First, we would like to thank those who have contributed their scholarship and expertise to this project. Both the chapter authors and respondents have fostered a rich dialogue about the teaching of ELA methods in today's context. The structure of the book, with responses following each of the chapters, intends to encourage ongoing discussion among readers of the book concerning the issues that are presented in the book.

Thank you to our editors, Sarah Jubar and Emily Tuttle, who assisted us in shaping this project and seeing it to completion. Thank you to Terri Rodriguez, Melissa Schieble, and Sarah Hochstetler, who offered initial feedback and drafts that focused this endeavor in its earliest stages.

Lastly, we would like to acknowledge our families for their support during this project: John Mattes and the Hallman Mattes children; Michael J. Capuana, Sophia M. Capuana, and Michael A. Capuana; and Stanley B. Shulfer.

It is our hope that projects such as this, which are possible only through a high level of engaged collaboration, continue in our field in order to foster vibrant scholarly conversation, advocacy, and change.

Introduction

Heidi L. Hallman, Kristen Pastore-Capuana, and Donna L. Pasternak

This book explores how many of the tensions that arise in the subject-specific methods course, such as the English language arts methods course, intersect with teacher identity and professionalization, issues that occur as teacher candidates move from university-based teacher education programs to middle and secondary school sites. Chapters in this book pay careful attention to how teacher candidates are socialized from residing in the space of preservice teacher to one of in-service teacher.

We begin this discussion on issues of professionalization by exploring the space of the methods course in teacher education. The methods course in English teacher education programs supports teacher candidates not only in learning pedagogy but also in addressing current issues in teaching English language arts (ELA). The methods course is sometimes referred to as the *didactics* or *pedagogy* course in other countries; in the United States, it is the course in which prospective teachers learn how to teach the school subject of English language arts: literature, composition, grammar, linguistics, speech, drama, and the multimodal/multiliteracies, as they emerge with literacy advances.

The methods course is typically taught alongside other courses in a teacher education program. We draw on Pasternak, Caughlan, Hallman, Renzi, and Rush's (2018) definition of the subject-specific methods course as

> primarily focusing on the representation and teaching of English language arts content. A methods course often also involves inquiry into the beliefs or opinions of participants regarding concepts of English language arts at the secondary level, the planning of lessons or courses of study, and classroom management related to content-specific methods. Courses providing background in

English content for teacher candidates should not be regarded as methods courses for the purposes of answering these questions if the focus is not on how to teach the content. (p. 25)

The tensions that teacher educators experience in teaching the methods course has been the catalyst for this book, and in the chapters that follow, English teacher educators hone in on themes that revolve around teacher identity and professionalization.

PROFESSIONALIZATION AND TEACHER IDENTITY: TENSIONS ACROSS THE FIELD

In our previous book, *Using Tension as a Resource: New Visions in Teaching the English Language Arts Methods Class*, we discussed changes to methods courses and field experiences in English language arts as the discipline educates English teachers for "doing tomorrow in today's classrooms" (Morrell, 2015, p. 312). In this book, we take a long look at English teacher educators' experiences concerning professionalization and teacher identity.

The term *professionalization* itself can be problematized (Popkewitz, 1994), as it connotes adherence to realities to professional norms that are based on particular histories. For example, teaching through "best practice," or even teaching with alignment to professional standards, is an idea that dictates what it means to be a teacher who is teaching within a certain era. Several of the chapters in this book ask questions about how *external pressures* play a part in shaping what counts in our profession today.

Yet teacher educators must confront how to mentor prospective teachers into the field and how changes to the field manifest changes to what it means to be a professional. In research about changes in English teacher education over the past 20 years, Pasternak, Caughlan, Hallman, Renzi, and Rush (2018) presented five distinct foci of ELA programs that have evolved: (1) changes to field experiences within teacher education programs, (2) altered conceptions of teaching literature and literacy within the context of ELA, (3) increased adherence to standardization, (4) changing demographics of students in K–12 classrooms, and (5) increased expectations for use of technology within ELA. These foci affect how professionals in ELA are viewed from both inside and outside the profession, and how they navigate these tensions in teacher education programs to define what it means to identify as an English teacher.

Throughout this book, chapter authors articulate dilemmas that revolve around professionalization and teacher identity, suggesting ways that teacher educators might productively work within these dilemmas. While some chapters suggest methods for increased awareness of tensions within practice, other chapters approach professionalization and teacher identity by asking what the limits of methods classes and teacher education might be in educating ELA teachers and supporting them to remain in the profession.

In today's political environment, teachers and teaching are often devalued, a situation that has critics deriding the educational standards at institutes of higher education while concurrently lauding alternative programs that do not have to adhere to the same rigorous teacher certification requirements. English teacher educators are now being asked to design programs, soften requirements, and recruit and mentor teacher candidates in a profession that, in the past, certified more new English teachers than it could employ (Borsuk, 2017). The chapters in this book explore what it means to educate and be an English teacher educator under these conditions.

Throughout the book, we invite readers into a conversation about English teacher education. The complexities that prompt each chapter are further problematized in the chapter responses as a way to underscore how intricate it has become to support and retain teachers. It is our hope that readers can apply the conversations within this book to their own program's context and consider possibilities, challenges, and changes in English teaching today.

OVERVIEW OF CHAPTERS

English Language Arts Teachers' Professional Roles and Identities

The opening section of the book raises questions about the intersection of English language arts methods classes and issues of teachers' roles and identities. Chapter 1, "Engaging Preservice Teachers in Productive Struggle Through Antideficit English Education," by Amber Warrington and Michelle Fowler-Amato, begins by describing the importance of working toward greater equity and social justice in ELA classrooms. The authors share ways to invite preservice teachers into embodying antideficit stances in teaching and learning. The chapter highlights some of the challenges the authors have experienced in asking preservice teachers to engage in this difficult work.

The response to Chapter 1, authored by Melinda J. McBee Orzulak, urges teacher educators to not only offer preservice teachers responses to so-called logistical questions but also assist preservice teachers in engaging in discussions about critical issues in teaching, including discussions of how instructional approaches differently value students' racial, gendered, classed, and linguistic identities.

The second chapter, "'It's Just Not What I Thought It Would Be': Novice Teachers Navigating Tensions in Identity," by Katharine Covino, explores how constructivist philosophies and stances highlight the importance of preservice teachers' voices, experiences, and perspectives. In preservice teachers' own words, this chapter underscores the importance of race/ethnicity, socioeconomic status, access, and equity to teaching practice.

The response to this chapter, written by Amber Warrington and Michelle Fowler-Amato, reiterates Covino's use of the idea of "tensions as teachable moments" (p. 31), thereby encouraging teacher educators to work with preservice teachers to name the tensions they experience as they move across the worlds of university methods courses and secondary classrooms.

Chapter 3, "The Potential of Problematic Practice: Educating Teachers for the Secondary ELA Classroom," by Melanie Shoffner, engages with how teacher candidates work with failure in the form of *practitioner problems*, the author's term for scenarios gleaned from actual classroom teachers' experiences.

The response to this chapter, written by Brandon Sams and Mike Cook, notes that teacher educators and preservice teachers may use the concept of *practitioner problems* to analyze how teachers instruct, think about, and position students. Therefore, *practitioner problems* become not only a site for thinking about teaching but also a site for thinking about both teachers and students.

The opening three chapters of the book foster discussion on the question of "what is professionalism?" in the space of teaching secondary English language arts. Each of these chapters, through being proponents of supporting critical teaching practice, advocates for a reflective stance on the part of teacher educators and teachers. Such a stance becomes a productive site for examining practice and, as Chapter 3 proposes, the *practitioner problems* that come with the practice of teaching.

External Pressures on Teachers' Professionalization

The second section of the book explores how external pressures affect teachers' professionalization. We see external pressures as forces outside of the discipline that provoke teacher education to adapt, adjust, or change curriculum and its assessments, licensure requirements, standards, and ELA content.

Chapter 4, "Writing Problems and Promises in Standardized Teacher Performance Assessment," by Sarah Hochstetler and Melinda J. McBee Orzulak, discusses the authors' experiences confronting an external pressure—teacher performance assessment—as an integrated part of their teacher education programs. The authors, as methods instructors, experience tension in preparing preservice teachers for standardized teacher performance assessments.

In his response to Chapter 4, Connor Warner argues that it is not just one standardized teacher performance that matters. Instead, it is the context of varied and competing teacher performance assessments that are more complex than the field often acknowledges. Warner asserts that a deeper understanding of this complexity will reinforce the gravity of the concerns Hochstetler and McBee Orzulak raise.

Chapter 5, "Changing English: Technology and Its Impact on the Teaching of English Education," by Donna L. Pasternak explores the pressures teacher educators face when integrating technology into the teaching of English. She reports that some English teacher educators see it as essential other content in the English language arts classroom while others struggle with learning the platforms that change how we communicate through it. She details the tensions some English educators feel about influences from people outside the field who feel that technology integration is *the* panacea for learning.

The response to Chapter 5, written by Julie Bell, underscores Pasternak's call for more understanding of how technology is integrated across K–12 partner school districts. Doing so will increase teacher educators' responsiveness to what preservice teachers will confront when in the field.

Chapter 6, "'We Need to Go Next Door and Talk About Our Lessons': One State's Context and Collaboration Around Standards-Based Reform," by Lara Searcy and Christian Z. Goering, discusses the influence that state standards have in teachers' conceptions of teaching a particular subject area. Searcy and Goering highlight the case of one state, thereby fostering a collective understanding of the role standards play in a state and in that state's teacher education coursework. They note the political challenges and potential drawbacks of a state-specific education system and argue for collaboration with teacher education programs within a state and with states next door.

In the response to Chapter 6, Jessica Gallo asserts the value of *everyday advocacy*, calling for "teachers who integrate an advocacy stance into their very busy daily routines and who, by doing so, play an important role in changing the narrative about teachers and teaching" (Fleischer, 2016, p. 19).

The final chapter of this section of the book, "Making Video Recording and Reflection Meaningful for English Teacher Candidates," by Julie Bell, addresses the use of video recording and reflection in preservice teachers' practice. Bell notes that teacher educators have frequently asked preservice teachers to videotape and analyze their own teaching over the past 40 years in an attempt to link theory and practice (Erickson, 2007). Now the ubiquity of mobile devices has made capturing teaching easier than ever, but such facility also necessitates careful thought about the purpose and intended outcome of preservice teachers' recording of teaching.

The response to Chapter 7, authored by Christian Z. Goering and Seth D. French, asks critical questions of the act of video recording teaching—stressing that video recording is often used in *gatekeeping* activities, such as teacher performance assessments. They prompt teacher educators to examine the purposes for the inclusion of video recording and reflection in teacher education programs.

The chapters and responses in this section of the book highlight the intertwined nature of external pressures and teacher education. While trying to articulate the complexities of this intertwining, authors and respondents call for a critical stance on the part of both teachers and teacher educators. From that critical stance, a position as an *everyday advocate* (Fleischer, 2016) can emerge.

Beyond English Language Arts: Challenges to Our Profession

The final section of the book begins with looking outside of the discipline of English language arts and toward a more expansive notion of what *methods* classes are today. Jeff Spanke and Chea Parton, in their chapter, "More Than Left, Right, Up, Down: Teaching Tensions in Non-ELA Literacy Methods Courses," discuss the concept of *literacy* as it may relate to preservice teachers in other disciplines. The authors discuss that, while English education programs continue to advance a broader and more inclusive framework for literacy education, the gap between English education's increasingly sociocultural literacy pedagogies and a more traditional, text-centric approach embraced by teachers in other disciplines continues to widen. Throughout their chapter, Spanke and Parton interrogate the tensions they encountered when working with preservice teachers outside the discipline of English language arts.

In the response to this chapter, Melanie Shoffner notes the pedagogical discomfort that both teachers of other disciplines might encounter when thinking about how *literacy* relates to them. Shoffner also discusses the pedagogical discomfort that Jeff Spanke and Chea Parton may have experienced in working outside of their discipline. In both cases, Shoffner notes the power of revision and seeing a situation from another vantage point.

Chapter 9, "Learning From Interns Who Leave the Profession: Emotional Labor and the Limits of the Methods Course," by Brandon Sams and Mike Cook, reflects on the purpose and limits of the English methods course, in light of preservice teachers who have left teacher education programs before completing their final internship/student teaching experience. The authors ask how the methods course could have better prepared teacher candidates to succeed, and at the heart of the chapter is the question, In what way could the methods course ever have met the needs of preservice teachers who did not finish the program? Pursuing this question exposes the potential limits of method and, possibly, of teacher education.

Jeremy Glazer, in his response to Chapter 9, reiterates that teacher education must take, as Sams and Cook note, emotional labor seriously. Teacher education must treat the preparation for such labor the same way we treat the preparation of making lesson plans, grading papers, or performing any other task we know that student teachers need to be prepared for. For Sams and Cook, this preparation must include a recognition that teacher interns will ultimately have to learn how to deal with the full range of teacher emotions and that these emotions will need a place for "honest expression and deliberation" (p. 152).

In the final chapter of the book, "Training for the Unsustainable: The Need to Consider Attrition in ELA Teacher Preparation," Jeremy Glazer focuses on a group he calls *invested leavers*: experienced, fully credentialed teachers who leave the classroom after making it through the induction period but before reaching midcareer. Glazer notes that there is a tension inherent in studying teachers who leave while preparing teachers about to begin. As Glazer notes, this tension was exacerbated when he identified that the very ways he was preparing teacher candidates for life as an English teacher perhaps ran them directly into many of the same issues and conflicts enumerated by teachers choosing to exit the classroom.

Framing his response through Albert Camus's *Myth of Sisyphus*, Jeff Spanke reminds us that Glazer's work highlights the degree to which all teachers—not just the invested leavers—must grapple with becoming the rocks they themselves push up the hill. Spanke writes,

> As both Glazer and Camus suggest, we must teach our future teachers that there is, indeed, "no sun without shadow, and it is essential to know the night" (p. 123). As Glazer rightfully suggests, simply finding *another district* is often not (and perhaps should never be) an option. Sisyphus can't choose another hill. "One always finds one's burden again" (p. 123). And yet Camus suggests that "the struggle itself towards the heights is enough to fill a man's heart" (p. 123). (p. 174)

The struggle is in the tensions that this book outlines. It is in the bridge between theory and practice and in the partnerships between universities and schools. It is between the external pressures and the internal workings of the field. Supporting preservice teachers to navigate these tensions is an important part of our work as English teacher educators.

REFERENCES

Borsuk, A. J. (2017, July 15). How ACT10 contributes to teacher shortages—and how it does not. *Milwaukee Journal Sentinel*.

Camus, A. (1955/1991). *The myth of Sisyphus, and other essays*. New York: Vintage.

Erickson, F. (2007). Ways of seeing video: Toward a phenomenology of viewing minimally edited footage. In R. Goldman, R. Pea, B. Barron, & S. Derry (Eds.), *Video research in the learning sciences* (pp. 145–155). Mahwah, NJ: Lawrence Erlbaum.

Fleischer, C. (2016). Everyday advocacy: The new professionalism for teachers. *Voices From the Middle, 24*(1), 19–23.

Morrell, E. (2015). The NCTE presidential address: Powerful English at NCTE yesterday, today, and tomorrow; Toward the next movement. *Research in the Teaching of English, 49*(3), 307–327.

Pasternak, D. L., Caughlan, S., Hallman, H. L., Renzi, L., & Rush, L. S. (2018). *Secondary English teacher education in the United States: Responding to a changing context*. New York: Bloomsbury.

Popkewitz, T. (1994). Professionalization in teaching and teacher education: Some notes on its history, ideology, and potential. *Teaching and Teacher Education, 10*(1), 1–14.

Part I

English Language Arts Teachers' Professional Roles and Identities

Chapter One

Engaging Preservice Teachers in Productive Struggle Through Antideficit English Education

Amber Warrington and Michelle Fowler-Amato

Historically, English language arts (ELA) classrooms have failed to recognize and value the language and literacy practices of students of color and students from working-class and poor communities (e.g., Heath, 1983; Michaels, 1981; Smitherman, 1977). Oftentimes, this failure to recognize students' out-of-school literacy practices in the classroom stems from deficit thinking, which links school failure to perceived internal deficits, such as "limited intellectual abilities, linguistic shortcomings, [and] lack of motivation to learn" (Valencia, 1997, p. 2).

Additionally, deficit thinking discounts communal funds of knowledge and cultural assets (Moll, Amanti, Neff, & Gonzalez, 1992; Yosso, 2005) and assumes white, middle/upper-class ways of knowing and being as the standard (Paris, 2012). Paris (2012) states, "Simply put, the goal of deficit approaches was to eradicate the linguistic, literate, and cultural practices many students of color brought from their homes and communities and to replace them with what were viewed as superior practices" (p. 93). Past deficit instructional approaches that position students' languages and literacies as "problems to fix" continue to appear in ELA classrooms (Alford, 2014; Aukerman, 2015; Dudley-Marling, 2007; Dyson, 2015; Michaels, 2013).

Language and literacy scholars have countered deficit-oriented ELA teaching by demonstrating students' cultural and linguistic strengths and showing ways that teachers can draw upon students' strengths in the classroom (e.g., Ladson-Billings, 1994; Lee, 2007; Moll et al., 1992). This body of work termed by Paris and Ball (2009) as *resource pedagogies* "repositioned the linguistic, cultural, and literate practices of poor communities—

particularly poor communities of color—as resources to honor, explore, and extend" (Paris, 2012, p. 94).

As methods instructors prepare predominately white, English-speaking preservice teachers (PTs) (Aud et al., 2011) to enter culturally and linguistically diverse classrooms, they must consider that "how teachers . . . respond to this diversity will depend on whether they view students' languages and cultural experiences as assets on which they can draw in support of school learning or deficiencies that must be overcome—or 'fixed'—before students can succeed academically" (Dudley-Marling & Lucas, 2009, p. 362). The ELA methods course is an important space in which methods instructors can work alongside PTs to disrupt deficit thinking and promote antideficit English education (Fowler-Amato & Warrington, 2017), an approach to curriculum, instruction, and assessment that (1) recognizes and draws on students' literacies, languages, and resources; (2) positions students as knowledgeable participants through inquiry and dialogue; and (3) counters oppressive systems, ideologies, and structures.

PRODUCTIVE STRUGGLE IN THE ENGLISH LANGUAGE ARTS METHODS CLASS

The ELA methods class serves as a space for PTs to make meaning of past and current classroom experiences and explore the enactment of pedagogies learned in university courses, as these courses are often structured to be taught in tandem with a field experience. When PTs face challenges in their implementation of pedagogy, they sometimes blame their students rather than turning the reflective lens on their own assumptions and instructional approaches. When debriefing PTs' classroom fieldwork, methods instructors often hear statements such as, "The kids don't read outside of school," or "They can't even write a complete sentence." This kind of deficit thinking (Paris, 2012; Valencia, 1997) provides methods instructors with opportunities to work toward greater equity and justice in ELA classrooms. As methods instructors investigate PTs' assumptions underlying such statements, they have the opportunity to promote antideficit teaching that recognizes and values secondary students' cultural, linguistic, and community resources.

These opportunities for antideficit work are filled with challenges for methods instructors (Cochran-Smith, 1995; Gort & Glenn, 2010), as they mediate the discomfort that PTs often feel in reflecting on their own positionality and privilege. Additionally, methods instructors engage PTs in productive struggle to recognize common school practices as inequitable and rooted in racism. Instructors also negotiate PTs' resistance to reenvisioning traditional ELA curriculum and instruction, particularly when that instruction led to PTs' own success as secondary students.

This complex work in methods classes involves tensions for PTs as well, as they reflect on their own positionality and privilege and take up an antideficit stance toward their secondary students' cultural and linguistic resources (Amatea, Cholewa, & Mixon, 2012; Cochran-Smith & Lytle, 1992; Glenn, 2012; Johnson, 2012). That self-reflection and shift in stance can be a challenging journey of learning and growth, and methods instructors will likely see only part of that journey in the span of a one-semester methods class. PTs may resist course content, failing to see the relevance of power, privilege, and racial, cultural, and linguistic diversity to their learning in a methods class. This learning can be particularly difficult in predominantly white spaces, such as teacher education programs and suburban field placements, where all too often white PTs do not interact with colleagues or students of color.

Alongside the development of an antideficit stance, methods instructors and PTs must explore pedagogical approaches that embody and carry out that theoretical stance (Athanases, Wahleithner, & Bennett, 2012; Durden & Truscott, 2013). This work involves recognizing the deficit ideologies underlying traditional approaches to ELA instruction and reorienting classroom practice around resource pedagogies. Methods instructors ask PTs to not only accept new approaches to teaching ELA but also push back against practices rooted in deficit thinking once they enter secondary classrooms. The following sections examine ways that instructors have navigated these tensions in methods classes and offer possibilities for engaging in this challenging work with PTs who are preparing to teach ELA.

ANTIDEFICIT APPROACHES IN PRESERVICE ENGLISH LANGUAGE ARTS TEACHER EDUCATION

Research has shown ELA methods instructors respond to the tensions described above by inviting preservice ELA teachers to explore counternarrative texts in order to better understand characters and communities whose lived experiences seemed to contrast with their own. Schieble (2011) and Glenn (2012) found that as PTs interacted with counternarrative texts, they engaged in important conversations about race, power, and identity.

Recognizing the role that counternarrative texts can play in rethinking teaching and learning in ELA classrooms, methods instructors have often drawn on digital tools to invite PTs to tell new stories about teaching and learning in ELA classes. For example, Skerrett, Warrington, and Pruitt's (2014) case study described a PT who composed her own counternarrative texts within an ELA methods course, linking antideficit theory to practice as she blogged in response to the course readings and conversations. In doing so, this PT demonstrated her own racial literacy, positioning racism as a structural, rather than an individual, concern and noting how race has the potential to affect individuals and groups as they participate in schools.

Methods instructors have also drawn on digital tools to increase opportunities for PTs to interact with young people in the ELA methods course. Focusing specifically on teacher/student relationships formed through e-mail interactions, McGuinn and Naylor (2009) argued that alternative spaces for teaching and learning available through the use of digital tools encouraged PTs to try on new identities, considering how dialogic and appreciative stances compared to authoritative and deficit positions.

In addition to forming relationships over e-mail, PTs have been invited to use video in the ELA methods course, revisiting critical moments to consider whether the identities that the PTs took on aligned with their own beliefs about teaching and learning (Schieble, Vetter, & Meacham, 2015) as well as to reflect on PTs' implementation of a dialogic curriculum (Caughlan, Juzwik, Borsheim-Black, Kelly, & Fine, 2013). Schieble, Vetter, and Meacham (2015) argued that inviting PTs to engage in discourse analysis upon revisiting teaching and learning through video supported one PT in understanding how the power structures within education, and therefore within her school, seemed to limit the kind of teacher she was becoming.

Some of the lessons described above have been learned in face-to-face interactions in "unofficial" settings in which teaching and learning occur as well. For example, when PTs engaged in service learning as part of their ELA methods class, taking on the role of tutor in after-school programs (Hallman & Burdick, 2011) and mentoring homeless youth (Hallman, 2012), they began to question their biases about students and their literacies. In doing so, PTs began to rethink the roles they might eventually take on in the classroom, recognizing the importance of building on strength and working toward equity.

The interventions highlighted in these research studies, all of which were facilitated in the ELA methods class, have supported PTs in (1) rethinking assumptions they had about communities with which they have had limited interactions, (2) examining and wrestling with their own privilege, (3) considering the role that racial literacy might play in the classroom, and (4) reflecting on whether PTs' actions in the classroom aligned with their beliefs about teaching and learning.

Despite the growth that individual PTs demonstrated, these studies also serve as reminders that there is plenty of work to be done in the ELA methods class, particularly in thinking about the role that racism plays in our society and, therefore, our schools (Schieble, 2011; Skerrett et al., 2014). For example, while some PTs began to consider their own privilege and the role that it has played in how they see the world (Glen, 2012), others failed to recognize racism as a structural issue (Schieble, 2011) and racial literacy as strength in the classroom (Skerrett et al., 2014). As a result, it is likely that some of the participating PTs in these studies remained unaware of how institutional racism in education affects the design and implementation of curriculum, instruction, and assessment in the secondary ELA class. Without this understanding, it can be difficult for PTs to recognize the importance of countering deficit instructional approaches.

IMPLEMENTING AND ADVOCATING ANTIDEFICIT ENGLISH EDUCATION IN THE METHODS CLASS

Methods instructors can learn from and build on the research that has been done in the ELA methods class, making a conscious effort to implement and advocate antideficit English education (Fowler-Amato & Warrington, 2017), an approach to curriculum, instruction, and assessment that (1) recognizes and draws on students' literacies, languages, and resources; (2) positions students as knowledgeable participants through inquiry and dialogue; and (3) counters oppressive systems, ideologies, and structures.

It is necessary that teacher educators intervene early in PTs' journeys of becoming teachers, making efforts to challenge and to offer support to PTs whose deficit ideologies have limited their ability to recognize the resources that individuals bring to the learning communities in which they are participating. The following sections break down the components of antideficit English education and provide additional examples of invitations that instructors might make in the ELA methods course, encouraging PTs to embrace the productive struggle that is an important step in learning to implement antideficit English education.

Recognizing and Drawing on Students' Literacies, Languages, and Resources

In their call to educators to expand understandings regarding what counts as literacy and literacy teaching in order to better prepare students for public, community, and economic life, the New London Group (1996) defined literacy in schools as "a carefully restricted project" (p. 61), one in which particular practices and text forms have been valued, while others have not. In this piece, the New London Group argues, "to be relevant, learning processes need to recruit, rather than attempt to ignore and erase the different subjectivities, interests, intentions, commitment and purposes that students bring to learning" (p. 61). Teachers might begin this work in the ELA course by making efforts to understand what students do as readers, writers, and users of language across diverse spaces and places, positioning variety and flexibility as a strength that will allow students to negotiate a wide range of rhetorical situations.

Methods instructors committed to preparing PTs to implement resource pedagogies in the secondary ELA class must take on a similar stance in the ELA methods course, modeling what this might look like in practice and demonstrating the importance of creating space for this work. This might be done through inviting PTs to engage in ethnographic investigations of their literate lives, exploring their histories as readers, writers, and users of language (Bomer, 2011; Bomer & Fowler-Amato, 2014).

In order to develop new understandings about the journey that has led PTs to have the literate lives that they do, methods instructors might invite PTs to create maps or timelines (Bomer, 2011; Bomer & Fowler-Amato, 2014); make metaphorical drawings of their experiences with reading, writing, and language (Bomer, 2011; Bomer & Fowler-Amato, 2014); or compose literacy and language narratives (Clark & Medina, 2000; Goodman, 2006), sharing their observations with their learning community. Bomer (2011) provides additional invitations that can be made in secondary ELA classrooms in an effort to better understand what students know and do.

An inquiry into the literate practices of a learning community can provide PTs with an opportunity to learn from the practices and processes of others, better preparing them to meet the needs of the diverse group of learners that PTs will, one day, interact with and support in the secondary ELA class. In addition, this class inquiry creates an opportunity for methods instructors to draw on what they learn about the participating PTs' literate lives to support them in their growth, not only as teachers, but also as readers, writers, and language learners. Methods instructors can consider the data the PTs collect when they plan for whole-class instruction, individualize reading and writing conferences, and support PTs in choosing texts, topics, and genres to explore across the various teaching and learning experiences within the methods course. In doing so, methods instructors have opportunities to engage in teacher-to-teacher conversations with PTs, explaining how the data that PTs collected informs the choices that methods instructors make in designing and implementing instruction.

After engaging in this inquiry as university students, PTs can practice naming what young people know and do, ensuring they will not rely on their own assumptions or information passed on to them in the teachers' lounge, upon taking on the role of teacher. Methods instructors might invite PTs to interview adolescents about their literacy and language histories, composing case studies that can be shared in the methods course to support PTs in better understanding the diversity of the literate practices of young people. At the end of the semester, methods instructors might invite PTs to return to the data they collected and the case studies they composed, drawing on what they have learned through their participation in the methods course to discuss how they might differentiate instruction to support individual students in their growth as readers, writers, and users of language.

In addition to the experiences previously discussed, teacher educators might plan opportunities for PTs to engage in appreciative assessment and response (Bomer, 2011; Warrington, Graeber, White, & Saxton, 2018), looking at student writing or facilitating conferences with adolescent learners in an effort to name what students know, rather than correct what they do not yet understand. With the support of a methods instructor and the learning community, PTs will have opportunities to consider how they might build on these strengths in the secondary ELA class, as their methods instructors have modeled throughout the semester.

Positioning Students as Knowledgeable Participants Through Inquiry and Dialogue

While discussing what it means to take on an inquiry stance (Ray, 2006) in the classroom, learning with and from secondary students, it is not uncommon for PTs to resist the notion that curriculum might grow out of the questions students pose, the observations that they share, and the knowledge that they bring with them to the ELA class. PTs often argue, "Students have to know the rules before they can break them," and question, "What about the students who need more structure than this?" These responses grow out of PTs' struggle to envision a learning environment in which the teacher is not the only "expert," the sole decider of what counts as knowledge.

Recognizing the opportunities missed when teachers see students as "receptacles to be filled" (Freire, 2007, p. 73), PTs must learn to create a culture of "collaborative knowledge building" (Wells, 2001), developing a community of inquirers who work together to explore the questions that teachers and students pose and the topics that the community sees as meaningful and worthy of their time and efforts.

To engage in this work, methods instructors might implement a workshop structure (Atwell, 1986; Bomer, 2011) within the ELA methods class, ensuring that the work of the class is focused on the literacy practices of the readers, writers, and language learners participating in the learning community. Though a workshop typically begins with a teacher-led mini-lesson created in an effort to support the participants in the work they will do across their literate lives, most of the time is dedicated to participants engaging in the inquiry to which the learning community has committed (a language study, an author study, an independent or shared reading experience, etc.).

While individuals delve into the inquiry, the teacher has the opportunity to confer with individuals and small groups, offering strategies to support learners in the choices they are making as readers, writers, and thinkers. Workshops typically conclude with an invitation to the learning community to think together about what they have come to understand as they have engaged in the inquiry. Similar to what students might experience in the secondary ELA class, PTs might participate in book clubs, genre studies, craft studies, and so forth, within the ELA methods course in order to consider how they might implement these kinds of student-centered experiences in their own classrooms.

Methods instructors might also invite PTs to engage in an inquiry in response to a question that the learning community has posed. For example, a community of preservice ELA teachers might explore the practices and processes of published writers through familiarizing themselves with different texts in which writers reflect on their writing lives (Lamott's *Bird by Bird*, Dillard's *Writing Life*, King's *On Writing: A Memoir of the Craft*, etc.), coming together during workshop to consider how these understandings might inform the choices they make as writers and teachers of writers.

To ensure that participants collect and grow their own thinking while engaging in the different inquiries the learning community pursues across a methods course, methods instructors might introduce the notebook, a tool for self-sponsored thinking (Bomer, 2011). Readers, writers, and language learners might make use of notebooks to (1) collect ideas, observations, and wonderings; (2) gather information on topics of interest; (3) return to past entries to build on these ideas; and (4) reflect on practices and processes while engaging in independent literate practice as well as the inquiries the learning community pursues together.

It is important to note that the experiences highlighted in this chapter are included because they invite PTs to collect and make sense of their own observations, sharing them with the learning community, in hope that these observations will support their classmates in their growth as readers, writers, and users of language as well as future teachers of ELA. The conversations that PTs engage in throughout the process are just as important as the reading, writing, and thinking that they do, as PTs will continue to draw on the understandings that grew out of the class inquiry when they engage in future literate activity, both inside and outside of the classroom. The understandings PTs develop through participating in the experiences and engaging in the conversations will simultaneously support them in their future work with secondary students.

Countering Oppressive Systems, Ideologies, and Structures

While preservice ELA teachers may come to appreciate young people's varied languages and out-of-school literacies, engaging in antideficit classroom practices remains difficult, particularly when those practices run counter to department or school culture (Smagorinsky, Gibson, Bickmore, Moore, & Cook, 2004; Smagorinsky, Wright, Augustine, O'Donnell-Allen, & Konopak, 2007). Antideficit practices draw on resource pedagogies (Paris & Ball, 2009). In order to build on and extend previous conceptualizations of resource pedagogies, Paris (2012) examined the three tenets of culturally relevant pedagogy and noted the challenge of reaching Ladson-Billings's (1995) third tenet related to developing an antideficit stance. Paris states: "We must ask if a critical stance toward and critical action against unequal power relations is resulting from ... research and practice" (pp. 94–95).

Therefore, to help PTs develop a critical stance toward inequitable and oppressive curriculum and instruction, methods instructors and PTs can critically examine traditional, teacher-centered approaches to teaching reading, writing, speaking, and listening; for example, teaching a whole-class novel, teaching canonical texts, correcting sentence-level errors in student writing, providing skill worksheets on grammar and usage, and giving writing prompts and templates that remove student choice and decision-making. Methods instructors and PTs can inquire into the assumptions underlying each traditional approach, with questions such as, (1) What messages does this instructional approach send to students about what is valued in terms of their racial, cultural, gendered, classed, and linguistic identities? (2) How does this instructional approach build on students' linguistic, racial, and cultural knowledge? (3) How does this instructional approach position students as capable and knowledgeable readers, writers, speakers, or listeners? and (4) How does this instructional approach position students as active participants and decision-makers in the classroom? These questions can lead methods instructors and PTs to explicitly name deficit ideologies underlying common methods of teaching ELA.

Methods instructors can provide opportunities for PTs to create curriculum and instruction that counters deficit approaches. For example, PTs might curate a list of books that addresses students' racial, cultural, and linguistic diversity for independent reading, book clubs, reading partnerships, or whole-class reading (Garcia & O'Donnell-Allen, 2015). PTs could also develop writing units in which students write about self-selected community issues, interview community members about the issues, and present to local audiences (Bomer & Bomer, 2001; Kinloch, 2010).

To develop the practice of turning classroom challenges back on the practitioner rather than blaming students and their communities, PTs can engage in teacher research, developing inquiry questions about instructional challenges. To explore each challenge, PTs can collect data, including interviews with students and parents/caregivers; student surveys; classroom observations; home visits; community observations; instructional artifacts; and student work. In reporting their research, PTs can provide the students' perspectives on the instructional challenge and explain how they could revise their practices in response.

Methods instructors can build critical reflection and self-reflexivity into the methods course by providing opportunities for guided reflection on each major assignment, asking PTs to create inquiry questions from their fieldwork to facilitate class discussion and explicitly linking theory to practice in lesson plan reflections. PTs might also critically reflect on reading and writing pedagogies that worked well for them as secondary students as a way to investigate oppressive ideologies shaping ELA curriculum. PTs can explain why they found those particular pedagogies to be enjoyable and effective and can then engage in critical dialogue, examining why those pedagogies may not be enjoyable and effective for learners with different interests, cultural and linguistic backgrounds, and learning styles. These reflections give PTs opportunities to make assumptions about teaching and learning visible, and they give methods instructors a space to speak into deficit thinking and offer antideficit perspectives.

REMAINING TENSIONS, CHALLENGES, AND QUESTIONS IN ANTIDEFICIT ENGLISH LANGUAGE ARTS METHODS

An ongoing tension methods instructors face is acknowledging the deficit ideologies that come into the methods course while meeting PTs where they are in order to build on what they think and know. While deficit stances may be expressed by individuals, they are rooted in systemic racism and inequities (Ladson-Billings & Tate, 1995; Solorzano & Yosso, 2001; Valencia, 1997). By naming deficit ideologies as systemic, methods instructors can work alongside PTs to identify deficit thinking and practices without pointing fingers at individual PTs, who are at different places on the journey to becoming antideficit English educators.

As ELA methods instructors engage in antideficit work with PTs, they support PTs in navigating countercultural practices that aim to transform teaching and learning beyond the methods course. A question with which teacher educators wrestle is how to educate PTs to push back against inequitable ELA practices and dialogue with colleagues about antideficit practices in ways that do not end in isolation or burnout. Methods instructors continually consider how to teach PTs to push against a system they must work within and how to practice that resistance in the safe space of a methods class.

REFERENCES

Alford, J. H. (2014). "Well, hang on, they're actually much better than that!": Disrupting dominant discourses of deficit about English language learners in senior high school English. *English Teaching: Practice and Critique, 13*(3), 71–88.

Amatea, E. S., Cholewa, B., & Mixon, K. A. (2012). Influencing preservice teachers' attitudes about working with low-income and/or ethnic minority families. *Urban Education, 47,* 801–834.

Athanases, S. Z., Wahleithner, J. M., & Bennett, L. H. (2012). Learning to attend to culturally and linguistically diverse learners through teacher inquiry in teacher education. *Teachers College Record, 114*(7).

Atwell, N. (1986). *In the middle: Writing, reading, and learning with adolescents.* Portsmouth, NH: Heinemann.

Aud, S., Hussar, W., Kena, G., Bianco, K., Frohlich, L., Kemp, J., Tahan, K., & National Center for Education Statistics. (2011). *The condition of education 2011 (NCES 2011-033).* National Center for Education Statistics, Institute of Education Sciences, U.S. Department of Education. Washington, DC.

Aukerman, M. (2015). How should readers develop across time? Mapping change *without* a deficit perspective. *Language Arts, 93,* 55–62.

Bomer, R. (2011). *Building adolescent literacy in today's English classrooms.* Portsmouth, NH: Heinemann.

Bomer, R., & Bomer, K. (2001). *For a better world: Reading and writing for social action.* Portsmouth, NH: Heinemann.

Bomer, R., & Fowler-Amato, M. (2014). Expanding adolescent writing: Building upon youths' practices, purposes, relationships and thoughtfulness. In K. A. Hinchman & H. Sheridan-Thomas (Eds.), *Best practices in adolescent literacy instruction* (2nd ed.). New York: Guilford Press.

Caughlan, S., Juzwik, M. M., Borsheim-Black, C., Kelly, S., & Fine, J. G. (2013). English teacher candidates developing dialogically organized instructional practices. *Research in the Teaching of English, 47*(3), 212–246.

Clark, C., & Medina, C. (2000). How reading and writing literacy narratives affect preservice teachers' understandings of literacy, pedagogy, and multiculturalism. *Journal of Teacher Education, 51*(1), 63–76.

Cochran-Smith, M. (1995). Uncertain allies: Understanding the boundaries of race and teaching. *Harvard Educational Review, 65*(4), 541–570.

Cochran-Smith, M., & Lytle, S. L. (1992). Interrogating cultural diversity: Inquiry and action. *Journal of Teacher Education, 43,* 104–115.

Dillard, A. (2009). *The writing life.* New York: HarperCollins.

Dudley-Marling, C. (2007). Return of the deficit. *Journal of Educational Controversy, 2*(1), Article 5.

Dudley-Marling, C., & Lucas, K. (2009). Pathologizing the language and culture of poor children. *Language Arts, 86,* 362–370.

Durden, S., & Truscott, D. (2013). Critical reflectivity and the development of new culturally relevant teachers. *Multicultural Perspectives, 15*(2), 73–80.

Dyson, A. H. (2015). The search for inclusion: Deficit discourse and the erasure of childhoods. *Language Arts, 92,* 199–207.

Fowler-Amato, M., & Warrington, A. (2017). Teachers as designers: Social design experiments as vehicles for developing antideficit English education. *Literacy Research: Theory, Method and Practice, 66.*

Freire, P. (2007). *Pedagogy of the oppressed.* London: Continuum.

Garcia, A., & O'Donnell-Allen, C. (2015). *Pose, wobble, flow: A culturally proactive approach to literacy instruction.* New York: Teachers College Press.

Glenn, W. J. (2012). Developing understandings of race: Preservice teachers' counternarrative (re)constructions of people of color in young adult literature. *English Education, 44*(4), 326–353.

Goodman, D. (2006). Language study in teacher education: Exploring the language in language arts. *Language Arts, 84*(2), 145–156.

Gort, M., & Glenn, W. J. (2010). Navigating tensions in the process of change: An English educator's dilemma management in the revision and implementation of a diversity-infused methods course. *Research in the Teaching of English, 45*(1), 59–86.

Hallman, H. L. (2012). Community-based field experiences in teacher education: Possibilities for a pedagogical third space. *Teaching Education, 23*(3), 241–263.

Hallman, H. L., & Burdick, M. N. (2011). Service learning and the preparation of English teachers. *English Education, 43*(4), 341–368.

Heath, S. B. (1983). *Ways with words: Language, life, and work in communities and classrooms.* New York: Cambridge University Press.

Johnson, J. D. (2012). "A rainforest in front of a bulldozer": The literacy practices of teacher candidates committed to social justice. *English Education, 44*, 147–179.

King, S. (2010). *On writing: A memoir of craft.* New York: Scriber.

Kinloch, V. (2010). *Harlem on our minds: Place, race, and the literacies of urban youth.* New York: Teachers College Press.

Ladson-Billings, G. (1994). *The dreamkeepers: Successful teachers of African American children.* San Francisco: Jossey-Bass.

Ladson-Billings, G. (1995). Toward a theory of culturally relevant pedagogy. *American Educational Research Journal, 32*, 465–491.

Ladson-Billings, G., & Tate, W. F. (1995). Toward a critical race theory of education. *Teachers College Record, 97*, 47–68.

Lamott, A. (2007). *Bird by bird: Some instructions on writing and life.* New York: Anchor Books.

Lee, C. D. (2007). *Culture, literacy, and learning: Taking bloom in the midst of the whirlwind.* New York: Teachers College Press.

McGuinn, N., & Naylor, A. (2009). Hesitantly into the arena: An account of trainee teachers' and sixth form students' preliminary attempts to enter into dialogue through e-mail. *English in Education, 43*(3), 211–225.

Michaels, S. (1981). "Sharing time": Children's narrative styles and differential access to literacy. *Language in Society, 10*, 423–442.

Michaels, S. (2013). Commentary. Déjà vu all over again: What's wrong with Hart and Risley and a "linguistic deficit" framework on early childhood education? *Learning Landscapes, 7*(1), 23–41.

Moll, L. C., Amanti, C., Neff, D., & Gonzalez, N. (1992). Funds of knowledge for teaching: Using a qualitative approach to connect homes and classrooms. *Theory Into Practice, 31*, 132–141.

New London Group. (1996). A pedagogy of multiliteracies: Designing social futures. *Harvard educational review, 66*(1), 60–93.

Paris, D. (2012). Culturally sustaining pedagogy: A needed change in stance, terminology, and practice. *Educational Researcher, 41*(3), 93–97.

Paris, D., & Ball, A. F. (2009). Teacher knowledge in culturally and linguistically complex classrooms: Lessons from the golden age and beyond. In L. M. Morrow, R. Rueda, & D. Lapp (Eds.), *Handbook of research on literacy and diversity* (pp. 379–395). New York: Guilford Press.

Ray, K. W. (2006). Exploring inquiry as a teaching stance in the writing workshop. *Language Arts, 83*(3), 238–247.

Schieble, M. (2011). A case for interruption in the virtual English classroom with the graphic novel *American born Chinese*. *Journal of Language and Literacy, 34*(2), 202–218.

Schieble, M., Vetter, A., & Meacham, M. (2015). A discourse analytic approach to videoanalysis of teaching: Aligning desired identities with practice. *Journal of Teacher Education, 66*(3), 245–260.

Skerrett, A., Warrington, A. S., & Pruitt, A. (2014). Tools and processes for building racial knowledge on teacher education blogs. In P. J. Dunston & S. K. Fullerton (Eds.), *63rd yearbook of the Literacy Research Association* (pp. 191–202). Oak Creek, WI: Literacy Research Association.

Smagorinsky, P., Gibson, N., Bickmore, S. T., Moore, C. P., & Cook, L. S. (2004). Praxis shock: Making the transition from a student-centered university program to the corporate climate of schools. *English Education, 36*, 214–245.

Smagorinsky, P., Wright, L., Augustine, S. M., O'Donnell-Allen, C., & Konopak, B. (2007). Student engagement in the teaching and learning of grammar: A case study of an early-career secondary school English teacher. *Journal of Teacher Education, 58*(1), 76–90.

Smitherman, G. (1977). *Talkin and testifyin*. Detroit, MI: Wayne State University Press.

Solorzano, D. G., & Yosso, T. J. (2001). From racial stereotyping and deficit discourse toward a critical race theory in teacher education. *Multicultural Education, 9*(1), 2–8.

Valencia, R. R. (1997). Conceptualizing the notion of deficit thinking. In R. R. Valencia (Ed.), *The evolution of deficit thinking: Educational thought and practice* (pp. 1–12). New York: RoutledgeFalmer.

Warrington, A., Graeber, L., White, H., & Saxton, J. (2018). Finding value in the process: Student empowerment through self-assessment. *English Journal, 107*, 32–38.

Wells, G. (2001). The development of a community of inquirers. In G. Wells (Ed.), *Action, talk and text: Learning and teaching through inquiry* (pp. 1–24). New York: Teachers College Press.

Yosso, T. J. (2005). Whose culture has capital? A critical race theory discussion of community cultural wealth. *Race Ethnicity and Education, 8*, 69–91.

A Response to Chapter 1

Melinda J. McBee Orzulak

In their chapter, "Engaging Preservice Teachers in Productive Struggle Through Antideficit English Education," Michelle Fowler-Amato and Amber Warrington extend understandings of how resource pedagogies enable teachers' abilities to enact more equitable, antideficit approaches. Their chapter provides key resources for teacher educators and preservice teachers to use the frame of engaging in productive struggle against racism and inequities.

In a conversation related to their chapter, the authors described how their work stems from the concept of countering the single story (see Chimamanda Ngozi Adichie's TED talk [2009]), that is, how methods instructors are tasked with opening up possibilities for how preservice teachers understand what it means to do English: How do we open up the possibilities for English language arts (ELA) teaching with multiple texts, genres, literacies, and language study—across multiple spaces? How do we open up possibilities for what it means to read and write?

CRITICAL ACTION: A REMINDER TO PUSH BACK

This chapter response was initiated at the beginning of a semester when the respondent's methods students were full of practical questions after being tasked with interpreting new teacher performance assessments, state mandates, and mentor teachers' scripted curriculum. Preservice teachers often bring many logistical questions to methods courses as they work through their understandings of many terms prioritized in schools and coursework, such as classroom management, academic language supports, and interactive methods.

Fowler-Amato and Warrington's chapter reminds teacher educators that enactment of antideficit English education should not be pushed to the side even in these conversations: There are high stakes for equity if methods courses run out of time to support teacher candidates with tangible ways to challenge the status quo of current power systems.

In particular, the authors elucidate the ways preservice teachers often remain unaware of institutional racism in education. In response, method instructors can consider how to integrate the following questions the authors introduced for analyzing the assumptions of traditional approaches (Fowler-Amato & Warrington, p. 11):

1. What messages does this instructional approach send to students about what is valued in terms of their racial, cultural, gendered, classed, and linguistic identities?
2. How does this instructional approach build on students' linguistic, racial, and cultural knowledge?
3. How does this instructional approach position students as capable and knowledgeable readers, writers, speakers, or listeners?
4. How does this instructional approach position students as active participants and decision-makers in the classroom?

Fowler-Amato and Warrington's discussion of extending critical understandings of literacy can inspire methods instructors to consider how to better model resource pedagogies, such as reflecting on how the selection of texts, authors, and voices in methods courses may also reflect realities of institutional racism. The authors further describe how attention to inquiry-based approaches encourage preservice teachers to move beyond assumptions based on their own experiences or lore from the teachers' lounge—and toward critical action. They discuss the value of teacher research as way of turning the challenge back on oneself as practitioner and looking at data to investigate future action steps. Additionally, they note that analysis and planning for next steps over a career trajectory need attention.

A CALL TO ACTION: ENGLISH TEACHER EDUCATORS PUSHING FORWARD

The authors inspire reflection on how preservice teachers' journeys simply start in our programs as they begin to expand their perspectives and recognize their positionality in the world. Fowler-Amato and Warrington's work informs discussion about preservice teachers' transitions beyond our programs and beyond a semester of methods courses throughout the teachers' life span and varied contexts. In turn, teacher educators are reminded to question our own teaching and learning, learning from the authors how this process needs to link to the concept of the *journey* over time.

Their work further inspires a deeper look at both the individual methods course and the overall institutional design. In a conversation I had with the authors, the authors discussed considering text selections as methods instructors and analyzing syllabi; this offers possibility for modeling faculty learning in relation to critical action and enactment over time in teaching. The conversation provided an opportunity to discuss how different methods instructors use work to diversify voices and foreground social justice in English methods courses, such as those scholars cited in the chapter (e.g., Garcia & O'Donnell-Allen [2015]; Glenn [2012]; Paris & Ball [2009]). The recent racial literacy dialogue from English Language Arts Teacher Educators' (ELATE) Commission on Social Justice is another example of how larger dialogue can inform practice and help us engage across school sites (Justice.education, n.d.). This website encourages teacher candidates to explore issues of equity and social justice across different contexts and experiences.

Fowler-Amato and Warrington can be applauded for drawing teacher educators' attention toward systematic, long-term views of antideficit approaches through embedded program review and planning across semesters. How might we better frame antideficit conversations with methods instructors, field instructors, and even content area instructors?

Questions to be explored might include some of the following:

- Across our programs, what does it mean to interact with or explore counternarrative text?
- Are we systematically providing opportunities for preservice teachers to understand those outside of their own communities and perspectives (through as the chapter suggests, accessing digital tools, revisiting critical moments, and engaging in work in unofficial settings)?
- In English departments, English educators serve as crucial go-between—what also are our roles in alternate spaces, continuing education, the National Writing Project, and other ongoing teacher inquiry communities?

Pushing back against inequities is a multifaceted journey. Teacher educators can model this for preservice teachers by making our own conversations more explicit and preparing them to see understanding and enactment of resource pedagogies as a long game that requires critical action, an ongoing journey that requires productive struggle in conversation with others.

REFERENCES

Adichie, C. N. (2009). *The danger of a single story* [Video file]. Retrieved from https://www.ted.com/talks/chimamanda_adichie_the_danger_of_a_single_story?language=en

Garcia, A., & O'Donnell-Allen, C. (2015). *Pose, wobble, flow: A culturally proactive approach to literacy instruction*. New York: Teachers College Press.

Glenn, W. J. (2012). Developing understandings of race: Preservice teachers' counternarrative (re)constructions of people of color in young adult literature. *English Education, 44*(4), 326–353.

Justice.education. (n.d.). Fall 2018 dialogue. Retrieved from https://justice.education/fall-2018-dialogue/

Paris, D., & Ball, A. F. (2009). Teacher knowledge in culturally and linguistically complex classrooms: Lessons from the golden age and beyond. In L. M. Morrow, R. Rueda, & D. Lapp (Eds.), *Handbook of research on literacy and diversity* (pp. 379–395). New York: Guilford Press.

Chapter Two

"It's Just Not What I Thought It Would Be"

Teacher Candidates Navigating Tensions in Identity

Katharine Covino

The push-and-pull between theory and practice is not new to the field of secondary education. The middle school or high school English classroom always reveals itself to be different and demanding in ways novice teachers cannot fully understand or predict. Though prevalent and foundational, such tensions are nevertheless keenly felt by those new to the field. Looking at studies of methods courses and field experiences, Newell and Connors (2011) show how frequently novice teachers feel conflicted by the opposing messages they receive from divergent sources, including university instructors, classroom mentor-teachers, and secondary school administrators (p. 254). Their writing echoes earlier work by Borko and Mayfield (1995) who argue that "learning to teach is a complex process determined by [the] expectations, demands, and feedback from key actors in the university and public school settings" (p. 501). Clearly, for novice teachers, negotiating such tensions is perilous and taxing work.

Those interested in exploring these tensions often refer to writing by Feiman-Nemser and Buchmann (1985), specifically through their use of the term *two-world pitfall*. The pair offers two central ideas. First, they observe that "university learning and classroom teaching are worlds apart" (p. 59). Second, they take issue with "the fallacious assumption that making connections between these two worlds is straightforward and can be left to the novice" (p. 63).

In other words, (1) the university classroom is often significantly different from the secondary classroom, and (2) bridging the gap between these settings can be difficult for beginning teachers. In a more recent piece, Zeichner (2010) shares his belief that tensions between university and secondary classrooms represent a perineal problem—"the Achilles' heel of teacher education" (pp. 90–91).

Navigating these tensions can be overwhelming, confusing, and frustrating for novice teachers. More often than not, they simply don't know what to do. Again and again they are forced to decide what should take precedence: the expectations of their education professors or the expectations of their supervising practitioners. Traversing these constant disconnects has real and profound effects on the ways novice teachers envision their own set of pedagogic practices and beliefs. This is particularly true for the evolving ways novice educators come to view themselves as teachers. Exploring and reflecting on these tensions, this chapter will investigate the struggles of novice teachers as they form their identities amid the various *worlds* they inhabit (Gere, Fairbanks, Howes, Roop, & Shaafsma, 1992; Smagorinsky, Cook, Moore, Jackson, & Fry, 2004).

CAPTURING THE VOICES OF NOVICE TEACHERS

Given the emphasis on identity formation at the intersection of theory and practice, the study reported here focuses on the voices of student teachers, teacher candidates, and novice teachers. In their own words, the group of preprofessional and early career educators thoughtfully addressed the extent to which their secondary classroom experiences served to reinforce or challenge what they had read about, discussed, and practiced in university courses. Through reflective writing and candid conversations, they openly shared their experiences navigating the tensions and disconnects they encountered.

Taken together, their responses shed light on the relationship between tension and identity. While studies of teacher identity are not new—West and Williams (2015) report in their review of literature that the intersection of identity and literacy instruction is among the most commonly examined topics of pedagogic research—what *is* new and needful is attention to novice teachers. That is to say, while there is a lot of research about identity and teaching, there is a significant gap when it comes to the changing identities of novice secondary English teachers.

Looking more specifically at research design, the recently conducted qualitative study drew on both identity theory (Gee, 2000; 2002; 2014) and activity theory (Fleer, 2016; Roth & Lee, 2007) in its consideration of identity as a fluid and dynamic individual performance *and* identity as a reaction to and with overlapping activity systems. Newell, Gingrich, and Johnson (2001) explain: "Rather than assuming that learning to teach is a solitary endeavor, activity theory emphasizes the *settings* in which preservice teachers learn to teach. Settings are particularly powerful factors in shaping how beginning teachers learn to envision their own practices and beliefs" (p. 305).

Fusing these interlocking strands is work by Smagorinsky et al. (2004). In "Tensions in Learning to Teach: Accommodation and the Development of a Teaching Identity," he and his coauthors explore how the tensions "between the two worlds, the two activity systems, of the university and school" (p. 22) affect the ongoing identity work of novice English teachers.

DATA COLLECTION AND ANALYSIS

In line with other studies investigating identity formation, the qualitative data collected and analyzed for the research project in this chapter included open-ended questionnaires as well as a lengthy transcribed focus group discussion. In terms of data analysis, the inductive process was an ongoing and iterative collaboration for the primary researcher and the research assistant. Together, the pair engaged in constant comparison analysis, a branch of thematic analysis, in their work to identify patterns and themes within and across the data (Fram, 2013; Glaser & Strauss, 2008; Glesne, 2011; Lincoln & Guba, 1985).

In pursuit of interrater reliability, the pair argued and debated throughout the process of cooperative co-coding until they reached consensus (Herrmann, 2015; Giles, Carrillo, Wang, Stegall, & Bumgarner, 2013). Given the focus on the interplay between tensions and identity, Gee's (2012) identification of tension as a primary means of thematic organization (and as a starting point for deeper analysis) proved helpful. Eventually, codes related to tensions in (1) teaching, (2) reflection, and (3) mentoring solidified. Paying close attention to these areas of tension helped to clarify the process of identity formation for this group of secondary English teachers.

The teacher candidates who served as participants in this investigation were all students who had recently completed Special Methods of Teaching English and prepracticum field experiences. Four of the seven—Elle, Evan, Finn, and Lily (all names of people and places are pseudonyms)—represented part of a cohort that had just finished Special Methods of Teaching English coursework and prepracticum placement. These four students had not yet entered their semester of practicum/student teaching.

Johanna and Abigail were just starting their first and second years of teaching, respectively. They had both completed Special Methods of Teaching English and practicum/student teaching within the past 2 years. Samantha, an early career teacher, proved the most senior of the group. She had completed Special Methods of Teaching English and practicum/student teaching more than 5 years ago. All the participants were known to the researcher from her teaching at various local universities but were not currently her students.

Before moving on, it makes sense to offer a brief look at the program sequence for candidates pursuing degrees and licensure in English secondary education. Formal admittance to the 4-year program occurs midway through sophomore year—following (1) the successful completion of Introduction to Secondary School Teaching in English, (2) the receipt of two positive Candidate Disposition Forms from a university professor and a supervising practitioner, and (3) a passing score on the MTEL 01 Communication and Literacy.

Upon admittance, candidates must successfully complete two aligned concentrations within the English Studies Department—proving their competency both in English content courses and in secondary education courses. During their senior year, candidates proceed through Special Methods of Teaching English and a final prepracticum during the fall semester before proceeding directly into their practicum/student teaching in the spring.

Special Methods of Teaching English is designed to support candidates in their content pedagogy as they gain practice designing and implementing standards-based instruction and assessment for diverse, multicultural student populations. During this final preparatory course, teacher candidates prepare and teach lessons—both to their peers in the Special Methods class and to the secondary students at their prepracticum site. Practicum/student teaching, during the spring of their senior year, offers candidates a chance to gradually take over a full teaching load and to gain experience teaching secondary English students under the guidance and mentorship of both a university supervisor and a supervising practitioner.

TENSIONS AND DISCONNECTS

The analysis of the open-ended questionnaires and the focus group transcription revealed interesting insights into the process by which the teacher candidates formed (and re-formed) their identities amid various tensions and disconnects. Specifically, three major themes emerged: (1) tensions navigating teaching, (2) tensions navigating reflection, and (3) tensions navigating mentoring relationships. The central part of the chapter will closely examine these areas of tension, reconceptualizing them as barriers to praxis and agentic identity formation.

Teaching

Teaching proved to be a pivotal area of tension for all the teacher candidates in the study. They spoke repeatedly about the frustration they felt, forced to jockey back and forth between their university classroom and their secondary classroom. One particular area of struggle proved to be the misalignment between mock teaching (teaching peers) and actual teaching (teaching secondary students). Lily, who had just finished her prepracticum placement, openly shared her views. "I think that [it] is just a fantasy of what you want the kids to respond to, but in real life, they do not respond to most of that." Evan, a senior in the same cohort as Lily, shared similar feelings.

> Time management and classroom management are things that you can only get from real classroom experience. You can plan out how your lesson is going to go in terms of time, but I don't think you're ever going to really accurately get a good idea of how it's going to go until you're in a classroom. I think the same can be said for classroom management. Obviously, when you're in front of your peers, it's going to go differently than if you're in a classroom of 30 eighth graders or something like that. It's going to go differently.

The group seemed frustrated by the inauthenticity and artificiality of teaching their classmates as opposed to teaching teenagers. Finn, an older, career-changing, postbaccalaureate student in the same cohort as Lily and Evan, commented on the contrived nature of mock teaching: "I just [had] to pretend I was teaching to a high school class because I knew that I wasn't really teaching to a high school class."

Johanna, a recent graduate in the early months of her first year of teaching, reflected back on the practice of teaching to peers during her college career. Pinpointing the lack of alignment between mock teaching and actual teaching in a concise and powerful way, she noted that what worked with peers would only work with teenagers "on a perfect day, in a perfect world, with perfect students, when it's sunny out." Able to speak with authority about the differences between mock teaching and actual teaching, Johanna went on:

> Teaching to hypothetical students, you don't . . . you're never aware of those real-world, real-life things that happen. Part of the time, or most of the time, it's not even just the lesson you're teaching; it's all of the other things that are happening, like the IEPs, the adaptations you have to make, the modifications, the kids that are going in and out of the room. How are you going to make sure they're caught up if they go to the bathroom four times during class? So, those are all real-life things that happen that you don't really think about.

Tensions also arose from misalignment related the content and focus of the lessons required in the two settings. Often, the teaching demands posed by university instructors conflicted with the needs of the secondary classrooms. The majority of the novice teachers in the study viewed their mini-lessons as intrusions to the natural flow of the secondary classrooms where they were completing the prepracticum/practicum hours. During the focus group, Lily shared how her teaching seemed interruptive: "They [the mini-lessons] are out of place because you're given a lesson and you just have to plop it into the curriculum that they're already teaching."

Evan agreed. He talked about his experience teaching a literary analysis unit that "didn't mesh at all with what she [the classroom teacher] was doing and was contradictory to why I was there and wouldn't help the students." Finn openly discussed how the disconnect between the two teaching environments proved frustrating for him, his classroom teacher, and the high school students. "It did cause a lot more work for me because, in some cases, I'd done a monstrous lesson for Special Methods, and then I really had to modify it quite a bit to make it work for my supervising practitioner and for that secondary school classroom and those students."

No one had more to say about the tensions arising from the divergent demands of teaching in both *worlds* than Elle. A member of the same cohort as Finn, Lily, and Evan, Elle shared how she felt like a gate-crasher in the high school classroom: "It felt like we were interrupting." She, too, grappled with the lack of alignment between the two settings and felt frustrated that the demands of the university classroom superseded the needs of the secondary classroom. "We have to kinda just mash all of these things together, make this monstrosity of a lesson, and then just plop ourselves down in the middle of whatever the kids are learning, and say like, 'Hope this works! Hope this fits in with what they're doing!' But it's awful."

While Elle's voice proved the loudest, her words conveyed the group's shared struggles with tensions related to teaching. They all felt torn by the divergent demands of the *two worlds* in which they served. The inauthenticity of mock lessons taught to peers and the lack of alignment between the university and secondary classrooms negatively affected the ways the budding educators viewed themselves as teachers. Their words and their tone made clear how deeply these tensions affected their identity formation. Viewed conversely as artificial or intrusive, their teaching did not seem valued or valuable. And they did not feel like teachers.

Reflection

Reflection emerged as another area of tension for the teacher candidates in the study. In their preliminary open-ended questionnaires, they shared their awareness of the importance of recursive planning and reflection (Johnston, 1997; Wiggins & McTighe, 2005). Their initial responses made clear that they generally understood the constructivist benefits of reflective practice from a conceptual point of view (Herrmann, 2015; Smagorinsky & Whiting, 1995). Moving from theory to practice, however, the story changed dramatically. Underlying tensions and disconnects related to inconsistency crept to the fore. Different students had had different instructors for various education classes (including Special Methods of Teaching English). For this reason, they had had very different experiences regarding pedagogic reflection in a university setting.

Evan, a senior about to enter practicum/student teaching, made clear that while he understood the importance of reflection, he had not had consistent opportunities to engage in it in a meaningful way. "I don't think that [reflection] is something that I have been able to participate in. Most of the time, in Special Methods, it's sort of like, okay, so you finished this lesson, you've given the lesson, on to the next one. And I don't think there's much room for reflection."

Elle agreed. She shared Evan's aggravation in not being able to engage in reflection as part of her university coursework. "That is definitely not something that is being advocated for in our college classroom. We write reflections, so, I mean, in that opportunity you could say, 'Oh, maybe I should have done this . . .' but the dialogue between you and your prospective students isn't really there." Like Evan, Elle wanted to review the mini-lessons she offered and then teach them again. Reflection without the ability to reteach the lesson diminished the practice and robbed it of its meaning. Perhaps Abigail, a second-year high school teacher, summed it up the best: "I remember having to reflect in Special Methods, and it was, like, not a real reflection and I didn't feel like it was super helpful." These students viewed reflection in a university setting as a requirement—a box to be checked—rather than an effective practice.

Tensions and inconsistencies existed in field-based reflection as well. Partnered with different mentor teachers in different classrooms, the teacher candidates encountered different sets of expectations for and experiences with recursive planning and reflective practice. Though they understood that reflecting on classroom teaching could help them grow and mature as educators, they shared how their opportunities to engage in meaningful reflection seemed erratic and unpredictable. Though a few from the group found themselves in situations that required reflection, it seemed as though they had stumbled upon them almost by accident. This certainly proved to be the case with Finn, the career-changing, postbaccalaureate student who was forced by necessity into the process of recursive planning.

> I would often have to rework a lesson plan I'd done for class to better suit my supervising practitioner's needs or, at the very least, lift part of it out and customize aspects of it. Having to write a reflection . . . helped crystallize some of the more subtle takeaways. . . . It's very instructive to design a lesson [and] then implement it: you see the things that didn't work so well, as well as what you got right.

Like his classmate, Evan encountered reflection by chance. Guided not by will or intention but rather by his supervising practitioner, Evan related how his opportunity for field-based reflection "was manufactured by my supervising practitioner because she asked me to give the same lesson that I had already given to another class of hers. So, I was able to think about it for, it must have been a week or two, and really think, okay how can I make this better, how do I differentiate this with this particular class, what changes need to be made."

Though both Finn and Evan ultimately chanced upon opportunities for reflection as students in Special Methods of Teaching English during their prepracticum field experiences, their paths were crooked and uneven. Chance, rather than purpose or design, led them. Though professionals in both the university and the classroom settings universally touted the value of reflection, neither environment offered the teacher candidates anything but limited and inconsistent avenues for authentic and constructive recursive planning.

For the majority of teacher candidates in the study, reflection remained a theoretical goal, instead of an enriching practice. Lacking opportunities to reflect, they did not see themselves as reflective. Nor, for the most part, did they see value in reflection. Tensions surrounding reflection adversely affected the process through which this group of educators came to view themselves as teachers.

Mentoring

Mentoring relationships stood out as another source of tension for the teacher candidates. Their experiences with field placements throughout their educational coursework mirrored writing by Smagorinsky and Whiting (1995). In line with that piece, many of the budding educators in the study discovered that "simply putting prospective teachers in the field is no guarantee that they will have good experiences" (p. 104). In the article, the pair raises the specter of truly disastrous relationships between preservice teachers and their mentors in the field. While such extreme encounters were not common to the group, Lily did share one particularly bad experience: "I was just a fly on the wall and I had to stay a fly on the wall. I was there to observe and give the lessons [and] that was it." When pressed for more detail, she opened up about the hostility she encountered from her supervising practitioner.

> I don't think my supervising practitioner liked me as a person and that is why she didn't want me to be speaking to her students, and I didn't really like her as a person because I didn't feel like she liked me as a person, so the entire time that I was there, we were just really awkwardly conflicting with one another.

Her unfortunate mismatch stood out in the small group of teachers in the study. In the larger realm of education research, however, such antagonistic relationships are far from unique. Like Sharon, the student teacher at the heart of a more recent study by Smagorinsky et al. (2004), Lily "felt cheated by being denied the latitude that she saw available to some of her peers in their more flexible and reciprocal relations with their mentor teachers" (p. 21).

Far more common, though no less stressful, were smaller disconnects, daily tensions that required skill and luck to navigate. One of the most frequently discussed areas of struggle had to do with teaching candidates asserting themselves within the classroom: finding their voices, personas, and identities, and presenting themselves as "real teachers" both to the students and to their mentor teachers. As the following segment from the focus group makes clear, all the novice teachers and teacher candidates in the group struggled to find their footing as a colleague and an equal to their mentor teachers.

Excerpt From the Focus Group

Abigail: Sitting in the back observing and taking notes, I felt like I was just in a high school class all over again.

Johanna: I almost feel like there should be some, I don't want to say initiative, but sometimes again we're just sitting in the back. We don't feel like we need to be there, but at the same time, I feel like there should be more connection. I know it's difficult for a bunch of preprac students to ask a teacher, "What can I do?"

Elle: It shouldn't be difficult, you're right, the person should want to be involved.

Johanna: Exactly.

Elle: Especially when it's a preprac where you're transitioning into your practicum, you should want to be more involved.

Nodding and agreement all around

Johanna: Right, and I feel like students should be more proactive because I would always sit back and not want to disturb.

Elle: It's hard.

Johanna: It *is* hard.

Nodding and agreement all around

The nodding and mutual agreement voiced by the novice teachers and teacher candidates during the focus group highlighted their collective struggle with tensions related to mentoring. Their shared obstacle: both to support and to be supported by their mentor teachers. This emergent tension echoed almost exactly findings by Herrmann (2015). Much like the teachers in that study, many of the educators here found themselves in an uncomfortable in between where "they were not the students' 'real' class- room teachers, yet they were not really university students either. They found themselves in a middle ground between student and teacher" (p. 104).

Poised at the boundary of two worlds, they needed guidance and encouragement from their mentors, but they wanted independence and autonomy in their own right. Their tense and tenuous status, stuck halfway between student and teacher, had clear and obvious bearings on the ways they viewed themselves as teachers. Neither wholly one nor the other, they felt disembodied—neither "real" students nor "real" teachers.

NEGOTIATING TENSIONS AND DISCONNECTS: FINDINGS AND IMPLICATIONS

So, how did the teacher candidates in this study negotiate these tensions? And more critically, how did their ability to navigate the disconnects they encountered intersect with their identity building? Looking critically at the experiences of the student teachers, teacher candidates, and early career teachers, this chapter concludes with two key findings.

Both findings demanded that educators undergo foundational shifts in mind-set. In each case, those best able to embrace the fundamental shifts in thinking were the slightly more mature educators in the group. Having lived and taught in both *worlds*, the early career teachers were able to critically reflect on their collection of diverse experiences. Positioned to offer valuable guidance and mentorship, both for the younger cohort within this study and for other teacher candidates engaged in identity work at the intersection of theory and practice, these preservice teachers embodied and spoke from a richer bank of knowledge and practice.

Guided by a deeper understanding, they possessed a more sophisticated view of themselves as teachers and, building on this sense of self, could offer their near peers a more dynamic and empowered means of constructing a teaching identity in which their divergent personas in the two worlds could align and entwine, rather than diverge and conflict. In short, they found a way to learn from tensions and to practice (and model) a different identity paradigm.

Tensions as Tools

Throughout the course of the study, the teacher candidates railed against the disconnects they encountered amid the two worlds they inhabited. A few in the group, however, adopted a mind-set that allowed them to traverse the tensions more successfully. They found ways of embracing tensions as teachable moments. Recast in this light, the tensions became tools: "potentially productive [to] the formation of a satisfying teaching identity" (Smagorinsky et al., 2004, pp. 22–23).

Reflecting with the benefit of retrospection and experience, the slightly more experienced teacher candidates in the group had sage advice for their near peers. A cohort or two ahead of Elle, Evan, Finn, and Lily, the three women in classrooms of their own were able to look back on their days as Special Methods of Teaching English students with the benefit of hindsight. Abigail, at the start of her second year of teaching, offered her practicum/student teaching experience as an example.

> In terms of my identity with the person I was paired with, I think that we had very different teaching philosophies. In the beginning, I was like, "Oh, this is going to be a long experience." But then it ended up being a wonderful experience because we were so different. [I] don't think you necessarily have to be paired with someone who has the same teaching philosophy, but just with someone who respects that you are different.

In this short section of text, Abigail laid out her process for negotiating tension. First, she noticed a disconnect. She and her supervising practitioner had starkly different teaching philosophies. Like many novice teachers, her initial reaction was one of anxiety and dread. But as she came to discover, the tension was not fatal to her growth but rather foundational to it.

Working with her mentor, she came to view two divergent philosophies of teaching English as valid. In this way, she discovered that while it is not possible to eliminate tensions that exist within and between the two worlds, it is possible to learn from them (Newell & Connors, 2011). In sharing her experience, Abigail modeled her ability to use tensions as a productive tool for agentic identity formation, a lesson she offered both to her near peers in this study and to all novice teachers.

Teachers as Learners

No aspect of the two-world pitfall affected the identity of the teacher candidates as deeply as their drive to shed their "student self" and fully evolve into their "teaching self." For the cohort about to leave Special Methods of Teaching English and enter their semester of practicum/student teaching—

Elle, Evan, Finn, and Lily—the progression toward becoming a "real" teacher was a finite, one-way transition. And it was a transition that stymied them.

A couple of teachers in the study, however, found ways of successfully inhabiting a more synergistic identity. Standing at the center of an overlapping Venn diagram, these teachers embraced a constructivist philosophy that conjoined the roles of teacher and learner (Smagorinsky & Whiting, 1995). Again, the slightly more mature candidates had keener insights than their less experienced peers. Just ahead of their colleagues, the teachers in classrooms of their own were able to share moments when their identities shifted from student to teacher and then back again.

During the focus group, Johanna shared how her awareness of her double role had grown over time. She instructed the younger cohort that interweaving both roles "helps us understand who we are, with the whole identity building, as a teacher and a student; that's how you build your identity." Through her experience, Johanna had discovered that part of being a competent and confident secondary English teacher involved recognizing that teachers never stop being learners. Abigail agreed:

> You know, I think the comment that you're always a student, in a sense, rings completely true especially when you're a teacher because you're always learning. And no matter how young you are or how old you are in the profession, how many years, I think you can always learn.

Many in the younger cohort, which had just completed Special Methods of Teaching English, pitted their roles in the two worlds against each other. They sought legitimacy as teachers by abandoning their identities as students. The more experienced educators, however, modeled a different identity paradigm—teachers as lifelong learners (Darling-Hammond, 2010). They knew they were "real" teachers, not because they were infallible experts holding tight to the reins of power and control, but rather because they were novice learners open to and interested in collaborative learning in an environment where knowledge could be built constructively by *all* those within the classroom (Dewey, 1916; Vygotsky, 1978). Accepting a more recursive path of identity formation, one with deep roots in both worlds they inhabited, these early career teachers modeled a more empowered identity for their peers, and for all novice teachers engaged in identity work at the intersection of theory and practice.

REFERENCES

Borko, H., & Mayfield, V. (1995). The roles of the cooperating teacher and university supervisor in learning to teach. *Teaching and Teacher Education, 11*(5), 501–518.

Darling-Hammond, L. (2010). Teacher education and the American future. *Journal of Teacher Education, 61*(1–2), 35–47.

Dewey, J. (1916). *Democracy and education: An introduction to the philosophy of education.* New York: Macmillan.
Feiman-Nemser, S., & Buchmann, M. (1985). Pitfalls of experience in teacher preparation. *Teachers College Record, 87*(1), 53–65.
Fleer, M. (2016). The Vygotsky project in education: The theoretical foundations for analyzing the relations between the personal, institutional and societal conditions for studying development. In D. S. P. Gedera & P. J. Williams (Eds.), *Activity theory in education: Research and practice* (pp. 1–19). Rotterdam, NL: Sense.
Fram, S. M. (2013). The constant comparative analysis method outside of grounded theory. *Qualitative Report, 18*, 1–25.
Gee, J. P. (2000). Identity as an analytic lens for research in education. *Review of Research in Education, 25*, 99–125.
Gee, J. P. (2002). Literacies, identities, and discourses. In M. J. Schleppegrell & M. C. Colombi (Eds.), *Developing advanced literacy in first and second languages: Meaning with power* (pp. 159–177). Mahwah, NJ: Lawrence Erlbaum.
Gee, J. P. (2012). *Social linguistics and literacies: Ideology in discourses.* London: Routledge, Taylor & Francis.
Gee, J. P. (2014). *How to do discourse analysis: A toolkit.* London: Routledge, Taylor & Francis.
Gere, A. R., Fairbanks, C., Howes, A., Roop, L., & Shaafsma, D. (1992). *Language and reflection: An integrated approach to teaching English.* Upper Saddle River, NJ: Prentice Hall.
Giles, C., Carrillo, L. T., Wang, Y., Stegall, J., & Bumgarner, B. (2013). "Working with my mentor is like having a second brain/hands/feet/eyes": Perceptions of novice teachers. *English Journal, 102*(3), 78–86.
Glaser, B. G., & Strauss, A. L. (2008). *The discovery of grounded theory: Strategies for qualitative research.* New Brunswick, NJ: Transaction.
Glesne, C. (2011). *Becoming qualitative researchers: An introduction* (4th ed.). Boston, MA: Pearson.
Herrmann, B. (2015). "All of a sudden I have these real students": Preservice teachers learning to teach English. *Teacher Education and Practice, 28*(1), 90–109.
Johnston, P. H. (1997). *Knowing literacy: Constructive literacy assessment.* York, ME: Stenhouse.
Lincoln, Y. S., & Guba, E. G. (1985). *Naturalistic inquiry.* London: Sage.
Newell, G. E., & Connors, S. P. (2011). "Why do you think that?": A supervisor's meditation of a preservice English teacher's understanding of institutional scaffolding. *English Education, 43*(3), 225–261.
Newell, G. E., Gingrich, R. S., & Johnson, A. B. (2001). Considering the contexts for appropriating theoretical and practical tools for teaching middle and secondary English. *Research in the Teaching of English, 35*(3), 302–343.
Roth, W.-M., & Lee, Y.-T. (2007). "Vygotsky's neglected legacy": Cultural-historical activity theory. *Review of Educational Research, 77*(2), 186–232.
Smagorinsky, P., Cook, L. S., Moore, C., Jackson, A. Y., & Fry, P. G. (2004). Tensions in learning to teach: Accommodation and the development of a teaching identity. *Journal of Teacher Education, 55*(1), 8–24.
Smagorinsky, P., & Whiting, M. E. (1995). *How English teachers get taught: Methods of teaching the methods class.* Urbana, IL: National Councils of Teachers of English.
West, J. A., & Williams, C. (2015). Grounding our teaching in research: Implications from Research in the Teaching of English, 2009–12. *English Journal, 104*(6), 17–24.
Wiggins, G., & McTighe, J. (2005). *Understanding by design* (Expanded 2nd ed.). Upper Saddle River, NJ: Pearson.
Vygotsky, L. S. (1978). *Mind in society: The development of higher psychological processes.* Cambridge, MA: Harvard University Press.
Zeichner, K. (2010). Rethinking the connections between campus courses and field experiences in college-and-university-based teacher education. *Journal of Teacher Education, 61*(1–2), 89–99.

A Response to Chapter 2

Amber Warrington and Michelle Fowler-Amato

In her chapter "'It's Just Not What I Thought It Would Be': Teacher Candidates Navigating Tensions in Identity," Katharine Covino highlights the voices of early career English language arts (ELA) teachers in order to better understand the challenges these teacher candidates faced as they transitioned from the university to the classroom. Though eager to draw on what they had learned across their coursework, the participants saw themselves as guests in these spaces and, therefore, tended to wait for permission to draw upon their knowledge in classroom spaces.

While most came to understand their supervising teachers' expectations over time, sharing a space was often stressful, and teacher candidates described that they felt cheated when their relationship with their supervising practitioners was strained. When the participants in Covino's study took on the role of teacher in these spaces, they saw themselves as interrupting learning, recognizing that the lessons they had carefully crafted in their university courses seemed out of place in the secondary ELA classes in which they were working. Though they seemed to understand that it was the job of ELA teachers to support students in their growth as readers and writers, the teacher candidates simultaneously recognized their methods instructors and supervising practitioners as audiences for their work and often struggled to figure out who they were truly planning for throughout their teacher education programs and related fieldwork.

Similarly, as teacher candidates, these teacher candidates grappled with the role that reflection can and should play in better meeting the needs of their students as well as in continuing to grow as practitioners. In their methods courses, reflection typically took the form of written responses that teacher candidates were invited to compose after planning lessons that might be taught in the future. Though the participants had opportunities to design lessons with real students in mind during student teaching, reflection seemed inconsistent throughout their teacher education programs.

The teacher candidates who engaged in this practice in the field often did so because their supervising practitioners required them to rethink a lesson prior to teaching it to a new group of students. Rather than viewing reflection as an opportunity to consider their teacher identities, the students with whom they worked, and that the contexts in which these students learned affected their decision-making in the classroom (Zeichner & Liston, 2014), many of the teacher candidates continued to see reflection as an assignment, similar to what they had experienced in their university methods courses.

While the participants in Covino's study described the tensions they experienced as frustrating, a few of the teacher candidates simultaneously positioned these tensions as tools, supporting them in developing new understandings about teaching, reflection, and mentorship. For example, though the lessons designed in their methods classes felt out of place when taught in the secondary ELA classroom, this recognition led the participants to understand that teaching is responsive. Planning without considering the teacher identities they hoped to take on, the students who would be experiencing the lessons, and the contexts in which these students were learning proved to be significantly less effective (Zeichner & Liston, 2014).

Describing "tensions as teachable moments," Covino encourages teacher educators to work with teacher candidates to name the tensions they experience as they move across the worlds of university methods courses and secondary classrooms. In ELA methods courses, teacher educators and teacher candidates can inquire into those tensions, asking why they exist and what they reveal about different, and sometimes conflicting, approaches to ELA instruction. Teacher educators can provide opportunities for teacher candidates to recognize ways they are invited to replicate or transform traditional ELA curriculum, instruction, and assessment in their field placements. This space of dialogue might assist teacher candidates in crystallizing their own visions and philosophies related to teaching students in ELA classrooms.

Covino's work presents a call to ELA methods instructors to work alongside supervising practitioners to build greater alignment between coursework and field experiences, particularly related to teacher candidates' lesson design and implementation. Instructors might explore possibilities for inviting supervising practitioners to methods classes, working with supervising practitioners to design methods courses, and educating supervising practitioners on the coaching roles they inhabit. In these ways, methods instructors can position supervising practitioners as teacher educators and partner with them to create more coherent preparation experiences for teacher candidates (Mosley Wetzel, Hoffman, & Maloch, 2017).

Some methods courses have implemented field-based models (Assaf, Garza, & Battle, 2010; Bales & Saffold, 2011; Singer, Catapano, & Huisman, 2010) to work toward a smoother transition from university to fieldwork for teacher candidates. When the methods course is fully integrated into the school context, teacher candidates can immediately apply course learning to classroom settings. This partnership building, however, is often institutionally invisible work for methods instructors, work that certainly strengthens preparation programs yet takes time away from other faculty responsibilities.

As teacher educators think with Covino about building stronger connections between teacher candidates' university and field experiences, they also consider the role that teacher education plays in teachers' early career learning and growth. The early career teachers in Covino's study had the professional maturity to position themselves as learners, taking up an inquiry stance (Cochran-Smith & Lytle, 2009) toward their developing teacher identities and classroom practices. ELA methods instructors might partner with early career teachers to build upon that productive stance toward learning and growth by creating collaborative groups of preservice, early career, and experienced teachers, fostering mentoring relationships among early career and experienced teachers, and providing professional learning experiences that early career teachers find meaningful and aligned with their interests (Skerrett, Warrington, & Williamson, 2018). Because teacher candidates are between worlds—in the space between students and teachers—teacher educators have opportunities to extend teacher education into teachers' early careers when teachers are more fully able to take up the identities and roles of classroom teachers.

REFERENCES

Assaf, L. C., Garza, R., & Battle, J. (2010). Multicultural teacher education: Examining the perceptions, practices, and coherence in one teacher preparation program. *Teacher Education Quarterly, 37*(2), 115–135.

Bales, B. L., & Saffold, F. (2011). A new era in the preparation of teachers for urban schools: Linking multiculturalism, disciplinary-based content, and pedagogy. *Urban Education, 46*(5), 953–974.

Cochran-Smith, M., & Lytle, S. L. (2009). *Inquiry as stance: Practitioner research for the next generation.* New York: Teachers College Press.

Mosley Wetzel, M., Hoffman, J. V., & Maloch, B. (2017). *Coaching with CARE: A model of reflective teacher development.* New York: Routledge.

Singer, N. R., Catapano, S., & Huisman, S. (2010). The university's role in preparing teachers for urban schools. *Teaching Education, 21*(2), 119–130.

Skerrett, A., Warrington, A., & Williamson, T. (2018). Generative principles for professional learning for equity-oriented urban English teachers. *English Education, 50*, 116–146.

Zeichner, K., & Liston, D. (2014). *Reflective teaching: An introduction.* New York: Routledge.

Chapter Three

The Potential of Problematic Practice

Educating Teachers for the Secondary ELA Classroom

Melanie Shoffner

"Well, sure, this sounds great, but what about the students who didn't get it? The article doesn't mention them!" A version of this sentiment echoes through methods classes every semester. Preservice teachers eagerly dig into readings that focus on real teaching practices in real secondary English language arts (ELA) classrooms—such as the articles found in *English Journal* and *Voices From the Middle*—but eventually someone will point out that it all sounds too good to be true. How can it be that the assignment is always effective, the students are always engaged, and the teacher is always successful?

Preservice teachers aren't wrong when they question the emphasis on effective teaching practices: Methods classes do focus on success. Teacher educators emphasize successful strategies and positive approaches in order to develop successful, reflective, student-centered teachers (Darling-Hammond & Bransford, 2005). Teacher educators may not emphasize failure, however, other than to exemplify poor pedagogy or highlight mistaken assumptions. Although teaching is inherently a problematic practice, Cochran-Smith (2004) purports another viewpoint:

> Teaching has technical aspects to be sure, and teachers can be trained to perform these. But teaching is also, and more importantly, an intellectual, cultural, and contextual activity that requires skillful decisions about how to convey subject matter knowledge, apply pedagogical skills, develop human relationships, and both generate and utilize local knowledge. (p. 298)

Teachers develop facility in these areas throughout their careers, and they become more skillful in their decision-making, in part, because they encounter problems, make mistakes, and question decisions. Knowing this, teacher educators should address failure directly in the methods classroom to better support preservice teachers when they enter the ELA classroom.

Rather than a simple warning of what not to do, examples of mistakes and missteps allow preservice teachers to examine how and why teachers address issues as they do. By bringing actual ELA classroom problems and concerns into methods classes, teacher education can better reflect the realities of teaching while supporting the development of preservice teachers' understandings of and abilities within those complex realities.

This chapter considers the potential of addressing failure in the methods classroom through work with practitioner problems, scenarios gleaned from student teachers' and practicing teachers' experiences in the ELA classroom that engage preservice teachers in problematizing real classroom issues. After an explanation of practitioner problems, the chapter explores how teacher educators can engage preservice teachers with complex issues of practice before they enter the ELA classroom through discussions of real teachers' mistakes, difficulties, and concerns.

THE CASE FOR PRACTITIONER PROBLEMS

Teacher educators are well aware of the seeming disconnects between theory and practice that "permeate the work of English teacher education" (Whitney, Olan, & Fredricksen, 2013, p. 184). Preservice teachers often see "the world of the university in which educators (re)imagine practice and interrogate teaching practices and assumptions [as distinct from] the world of the classroom, where educators must practice and act" (Meyer & Sawyer, 2006, pp. 48–49).

To connect these worlds, teacher educators engage preservice teachers in various activities that require meaningful consideration of ELA teaching and learning: collaboration with preservice librarians (Gross & Witte, 2016) and school counselors (Shoffner & Morris, 2010); facilitated discussions (Williamson, 2013) and English language learner (ELL)–focused instruction (de Oliveira & Shoffner, 2009); multimedia case studies (Hewitt, Pedretti, Bencze, Vaillancourt, & Yoon, 2003), social memoirs (Braun & Crumpler, 2004), and Teaching Inquiry assignments (Meyer & Sawyer, 2006).

Practitioner problems are also a way to connect these worlds before preservice teachers enter the classroom as practitioners themselves. As defined here, practitioner problems are real scenarios taken from actual classroom teaching that address challenging issues without definitive solutions. Practitioner problems are, by design, brief; while they outline the situation under consideration, they avoid excessive context or detailed explanation. Because there is no one right answer, preservice teachers must consider different perspectives and multiple factors to make sense of the problems and identify potential responses.

Teacher educators can purposefully collect problems from past and present students that will provoke discussion of authentic issues in the secondary ELA classroom, such as those presented in this chapter. The benefit of collecting personal stories from personally known teachers, rather than using generic case studies (Carter, 1992), is that teacher educators are privy to the teachers' contexts as well as their responses. By selectively sharing additional details about the scenario or revealing the teacher's response to the problem, teacher educators can encourage preservice teachers to consider different perspectives or challenge their taken-for-granted understandings.

Practitioner problems, then, serve as prompts for reflective discussion (Dewey, 1960; Zeichner & Liston, 2013), asking preservice teachers to consider how they would respond to the given situations and what would guide their responses. Offering scenarios with few details requires preservice teachers to fill in specifics, drawing from their own experiences and understandings and, by extension, accessing their personal beliefs.

In this way, preservice teachers activate their personal practical theory (Handal & Lauvas, 1987) as they engage in reflective practice. By drawing on personal and professional dispositions (Schussler, Stooksberry, & Bercaw, 2010; Shoffner, Sedberry, Alsup, & Johnson, 2014) to make sense of the scenarios, they are also taking into account the role of the affective domain (Isenbarger & Zembylas, 2006; Shoffner, 2009) that further complicates the difficult nature of teaching (Labaree, 2000).

Reflective discussion of practitioner problems can also support preservice teachers' understandings of the intersections of research, theory, and practice that ground ELA teaching (Shoffner et al., 2017; Zeichner & Liston, 2013). By drawing on course readings, in addition to their experiences and dispositions, preservice teachers have opportunities to consider issues from multiple perspectives, which may help to mediate the tensions often found between theory and practice in the methods classroom (Whitney, Olan, & Fredricksen, 2013).

While a teacher educator at a university located in the midwestern United States, I collected the practitioner problems included in this chapter from current and former preservice teachers: predominantly white, middle-class, midwestern women who returned to teach in midwestern classrooms. Over several years, I integrated these practitioner problems, as written here, into my methods courses, typically using them as whole-class or small group discussion prompts at the beginning of class. The discussion that follows draws from this experience.

PROBLEMATIZING INTERACTIONS WITH STUDENTS

As preservice teachers develop their pedagogical understandings, they are also making sense of the personal, integrating what Cochran-Smith (2003) considers "matters of both head and heart, both reason and passion" (p. 374). The affective domain offers numerous important elements for preservice teachers to explore, encompassing as it does aspects of emotion, care, dispositions, cultural responsiveness, and relational teaching (Gay, 2000; Isenbarger & Zembylas, 2006; Kitchen, 2005; Smith, Skarbek, & Hurst, 2005).

Practitioner problems that address interactions between teachers and students encourage preservice teachers to examine their personal understandings of affective elements as well as applications of that understanding in their future teaching. Course readings that offer different perspectives on student-teacher interactions—addressing factors such as classroom management (e.g., Weinstein, Curran, & Tomlinson-Clarke, 2003), motivation (e.g., Wentzel, 2003), and diversity (e.g., Dodge & Crutcher, 2015)—add to preservice teachers' discussion of such practitioner problems.

For example, this scenario, focused on a student's behavior in the classroom, might lead to a discussion of issues beyond classroom management:

> Our intrepid teacher is having difficulty with a student. Chris is disruptive through small actions: drumming on the desk, making "funny" comments, talking to neighbors, forgetting books and papers, seldom doing the reading yet volunteering answers to discussion. Chris responds positively and politely when reprimanded during class, but the actions continue.

Initial consideration of the practitioner problem is likely to focus on the managerial details of the situation (Mills & Satterthwait, 2000) to determine what steps are necessary to maintain classroom control. What can the teacher do to stop the disruption? How can the teacher minimize the student's behavior? As the discussion continues, however, preservice teachers are likely to problematize a seemingly straightforward issue of classroom management.

For example, preservice teachers often ask for clarification of the student's grade level. The teacher educator might offer the truthful response of 11th grade but also question how their responses might change if the student were in 8th grade. Discussing differences in grade level and, by extension, age requires preservice teachers to draw on their understandings of adolescents' intellectual, social, and emotional development as well as their beliefs about personal responsibility and individual maturity.

Preservice teachers also question the interventions available to the teacher, understanding that there are varying degrees of teacher autonomy when it comes to addressing student behavior. Some preservice teachers point out that schools may not allow students to be sent out into the hallway, while others observe that specific procedures may require the teacher to assign a detention. When preservice teachers suggest contacting parents, discussion ranges from positive interactions with parents to awareness of different home situations.

All of the aforementioned issues can arise for discussion when preservice teachers consider other practitioner problems, such as the one outlined below:

> Although Ms. K has tried to keep a positive attitude, she is struggling. Of the ten boys in school who are considered troublemakers, eight are in her second-period class. Most look as if they are 18 although they are only in the eighth grade. They have tough home lives; parental support seems nonexistent. They are disruptive in class: throwing things, extremely loud, and disrespectful. Grades are no motivation since the school does not hold students back. When other teachers see the class list, they respond with, "How did that happen? Who the hell put all of those kids together?" Since there is little administrative support, Ms. K's mentor tells her to ignore them and teach the others. Ms. K doesn't know what else to do.

The managerial elements of classroom management and instruction are obviously important, but as the preservice teachers quickly surmise, there are many other elements at play in this scenario as well. They often ask where the teacher is located, what ELA content she is teaching, whether she interacts with the boys outside the classroom or if she has spoken to them one-on-one. Answers to their questions often lead to discussions of student-teacher relationships, authentic engagement, and racial stereotypes (Shoffner, 2011; Shoffner & Brown, 2010; Weinstein, Curran & Tomlinson-Clarke, 2003).

While sometimes requiring prompting, preservice teachers also consider what role gender plays in these particular situations. How might the teacher's reaction differ if Chris identifies as male instead of female? What, if anything, changes, knowing that the teachers identify as female rather than male? Discussions of heteronormativity and gender stereotypes (Ressler & Chase, 2009) become part of the discussion as preservice teachers think more critically about how the teacher may choose to interact with misbehaving students.

PROBLEMATIZING INTERACTIONS WITH COLLEAGUES

Preservice teachers frequently think about potential issues with future students, but they are perhaps less likely to consider the same of future colleagues. Teachers may spend the majority of their day as the sole adult in the classroom, but interactions with administrators and colleagues are an equally important aspect of teaching.

Course readings that address both positive and negative interactions with colleagues (e.g., Mr. H., 2012; Wells & Mitchell, 2016) allow preservice teachers to consider future interactions. Practitioner problems extend that consideration by offering a relatively straightforward situation that opens discussion to more complicated issues, such as those found in this scenario:

> Mr. D is the first-year writing teacher on a middle-grades team of five teachers who cover the subjects of writing, reading, science, math, and social studies. For the current unit, students are completing a packet of activities covering all five subjects. When Mr. D reaches his assigned section, he finds that half of his students do not have their packets because the veteran science teacher has not yet returned them.

Preservice teachers frequently start discussion with the obvious issue of pedagogical adaptability; regardless of the lesson plan for the day, the teacher must now create a new lesson in the moment. Possible responses to the question of what happens next encourage preservice teachers to consider in-the-moment instructional decisions, creating stand-alone lessons for emergency situations and developing flexibility as a teacher.

Preservice teachers also focus on working with colleagues, however. Many share past personal experiences with group work—usually negative in nature—before moving on to question issues of collaboration, collegiality, and seniority. What elements are necessary to create a collegial environment? How does one navigate being "the new guy" on a team of veteran colleagues? Where can one turn for help as a beginning teacher?

Issues of collegiality are also under consideration when preservice teachers discuss the following practitioner problem:

> While Ms. P is taking tickets at the school wrestling meet, one of the youngish science teachers introduces himself. Two days later, he sends her a Facebook request, which she accepts without much thought. She receives the following message a few minutes later: "I've been thinking about you all weekend. I am so sorry we didn't get to talk more at the meet. I have been trying to think of excuses to come see you all day. If you aren't in a serious relationship, I'd love to take you out for drinks; let me know." Ms. P responds that she is taking her student teaching very seriously and doesn't want to cross any lines or create any distractions. He responds with, "Fine," but now she is worried about running into him at school.

As with the previous practitioner problem, this one asks preservice teachers to consider how one interacts with colleagues in potentially negative situations. Preservice teachers are quick to point out issues of expectation, power, and gender in the scenario. While discussion is likely to cover what the student teacher should do next, from defriending the science teacher on Facebook to mentioning the situation to her cooperating teacher, preservice teachers also consider the power imbalance between the two, the stigma of acknowledging discomfort with unwanted attention, and societal expectations of both men and women.

Both practitioner problems offer the opportunity to think more critically if the teacher educator initially omits certain facts. Obscuring the gender identity of the teachers, for example, asks preservice teachers to fill in details. Mr. D and Ms. P can be identified only as a first-year teacher and a student teacher, respectively, and the gender-neutral pronoun "they" is used to describe them. What assumptions do preservice teachers make without gender markers? How does the discussion change if gender is assigned?

The same questions apply to obscuring the status of the teachers in both scenarios. Words such as *first year*, *veteran*, *student teaching*, and *youngish* can be omitted when the practitioner problem is first presented. How do preservice teachers make sense of the situations? How do their perspectives change if the descriptions are added back to the scenario? In this way, preservice teachers activate their personal practical theory (Handal & Lauvas, 1987) to solve potential problems and, by extension, have the opportunity to consider potential biases and taken-for-granted perspectives that will influence their future teaching.

PROBLEMATIZING BIG ISSUES

Taking up typical teaching issues, such as classroom discipline and peer collaboration, is an important aspect of practitioner problems since the resulting discussion allows preservice teachers to preemptively reflect on matters they will face on a daily basis. Preservice teachers may start a discussion by brainstorming different approaches to classroom management, however, and finish with an examination of student-teacher relationships. They may first discuss the need for collegial interactions and then question possible power differentials among teachers.

Practitioner problems need not lead to in-depth discussions, of course, but asking preservice teachers to reflect on complex and difficult issues is part of the praxis of teacher education, especially when equity, diversity, and justice are involved (Howard, 2010; Shoffner et al., 2017). Course readings in methods classes offer entry into these issues from a pedagogical perspective (e.g., Berg, 2013; Dunn, 2010; Nieto, 1999; Shoffner & Brown, 2010) that provide a foundation for preservice teachers' discussions of practitioner problems that address similar issues.

Some of the practitioner problems teacher educators collect will address these difficult issues in any context, but changing times can also change the discussions arising from the given scenarios, as this particular practitioner problem exemplifies:

> Ms. Z is the junior varsity volleyball coach at a high school with a 99% white student population. Yesterday, her team played an inner-city school's team with one white player. Today, she overheard a boy in her study hall who had been at the game use several racial slurs. While she reprimanded the boy, she questions the best way to handle racial stereotyping in a small, rural, predominantly white school.

Unfortunately, issues of racism, privilege, discrimination, and hate speech have always been concerns for preservice teachers to consider before they enter the classroom (NCTE, 2017). Current events can direct discussion of those issues in different ways, however. While addressing racism with students remains the subject under discussion, for example, how to do so may change if preservice teachers reference #BlackLivesMatter or address the removal of Confederate monuments. Rather than discussing the practitioner problem as an issue of student responsibility, conversation can expand to consider the contemporary societal and cultural influences that shape students' understandings and expressions of racism.

Issues of gender and power (Bender-Slack, 2010) are applicable to practitioner problems that address hatred as well. Preservice teachers have questioned how their response would differ if other factors were considered. Would they say the same thing speaking to a student they know versus to a student they overheard in the hallway? Would they respond differently to a female student versus a male student or to a 6th grader versus an 11th grader? They have also considered whether to involve other teachers or administrators. Is this a matter to manage on their own as beginning teachers, or is it wiser to bring in a more experienced educator?

Preservice teachers have asked similar questions when discussing the following practitioner problem:

> After studying Wiesel's *Night*, Ms. L assigns a portfolio project that requires students to gather artifacts and write responses to extend their understanding of the unit's themes. A formerly disengaged student asks to write on how Nazis remain functional in society today. When Ms. L agrees, the student shows Ms. L a swastika tattoo on their upper chest. Ms. L makes no comment but stresses the need to evaluate beliefs, make connections, and draw conclusions for a strong response. The student turns in an informative, well-reasoned paper, but Ms. L wonders if she did the right thing.

By deliberately withholding the gender identity and grade level of the student, the scenario forces preservice teachers to make assumptions as they engage in discussion; obscuring similar identifiers about the teacher also problematizes the situation. Knowing upfront that the student was a 17-year-old female or that the teacher was a white woman in her late 20s would still require preservice teachers to consider complex issues. Waiting to provide that information, however, encourages preservice teachers to ask questions and engage perspectives as they discuss.

As in the previous practitioner problem, this one requires preservice teachers to address current events as they discuss the issues of equity, diversity, and justice attached to the scenario: the rise of white supremacy, the events in Charlottesville (Virginia), the espoused views of the killers in the Emanuel African Methodist Episcopal Church (South Carolina), and the Marjory Stoneman Douglas High School (Florida) shootings.

The same cultural relevancy applies to the practitioner problem above that referenced a student teacher's discomfort when another teacher expressed his interest in her. In discussing potential responses and possible implications, preservice teachers also consider how the #MeToo movement and society's response to sexual assault shape their understandings of and beliefs about the interaction in general.

CONCLUSION

Teacher educators know that ELA teaching is a complicated endeavor (Labaree, 2000; Shoffner et al., 2017, 1st para.); they also know that "teachers need more than a set of activities, ideas, and techniques to help them become deliberate, thoughtful teachers who understand the relationship between their teaching and the quality of their students' learning" (Crowe & Berry, 2007, p. 31). In methods classes, teacher educators can work to educate preservice teachers to manage the complexities that shape ELA teaching before they enter the classroom.

Working with practitioner problems is one way for preservice teachers to engage in meaningful reflective practice. As they examine real teachers' failures, struggles, and concerns, preservice teachers are pushed to think like teachers, where they "think creatively about complex situations, consider multiple options, make decisions about best courses of action, and understand why they do what they do" (Crowe & Berry, 2007, p. 31). In this way, practitioner problems add support to what teacher educators know: "Intellectual experiences count when it comes to learning to teach" (Whitney, Olan, & Fredricksen, 2013, p. 199).

REFERENCES

Bender-Slack, D. (2010). Texts, talk . . . and fear? English language arts teachers negotiate social justice teaching. *English Education, 42*(2), 181–203.

Berg, M. (2013). Tolerance to alliance: Deconstructing dichotomies to advocate for all students. *Voices From the Middle, 20*(3), 32–36.

Braun, J. A., Jr., & Crumpler, T. P. (2004). The social memoir: An analysis of developing reflective ability in a preservice methods course. *Teaching and Teacher Education, 20*, 59–75.

Carter, K. (1992). Creating cases for the development of teacher knowledge. In H. Munby & T. Russell (Eds.), *Teachers and teaching: From classroom to reflection* (pp. 109–123). New York: Falmer.

Cochran-Smith, M. (2003). Sometimes it's not the money: Teaching and heart. *Journal of Teacher Education, 54*(5), 371–375.

Cochran-Smith, M. (2004). The problem of teacher education. *Journal of Teacher Education, 55*(4), 295–299.

Crowe, A. R., & Berry, A. (2007). Teaching prospective teachers about learning to think like a teacher: Articulating our principles of practice. In T. Russell & J. Loughran (Eds.), *Enacting a pedagogy of teacher education: Values, relationships and practices* (pp. 31–44). New York: Routledge.

Darling-Hammond, L., & Bransford, J. (Eds.). (2005). *Preparing teachers for a changing world: What teachers should learn and be able to do*. San Francisco: Jossey-Bass.

de Oliveira, L., & Shoffner, M. (2009). Addressing the needs of English language learners in an English education methods course. *English Education, 42*(1), 91–111.

Dewey, J. (1960). *How we think: A restatement of the relation of reflective thinking to the educative process*. Chicago: D. C. Heath. (Original work published 1933).

Dodge, A. M., & Crutcher, P. A. (2015). Inclusive classrooms for LBGTQ students: Using linked text sets to challenge the hegemonic "single story." *Journal of Adolescent and Adult Literacy, 59*(1), 95–105.

Dunn, P. A. (2010). Re-seeing (dis)ability: Ten suggestions. *English Journal, 100*(2), 14–26.

Gay, G. (2000). *Culturally responsive teaching: Theory, research, and practice*. New York: Teachers College Press.

Gross, M., & Witte, S. (2016). An exploration of teacher and librarian collaboration in the context of professional preparation. *New Review of Children's Literature and Librarianship, 22*(2), 159–185.

Handal, G., & Lauvas, P. (1987). *Promoting reflective teaching: Supervision in action*. Philadelphia: Open University Press.

Hewitt, J., Pedretti, E., Bencze, L., Vaillancourt, B. D., & Yoon, S. (2003). New applications for multimedia cases: Promoting reflective practice in preservice teacher education. *Journal of Technology and Teacher Education, 11*(4), 483–500.

Howard, T. C. (2010). Culturally relevant pedagogy: Ingredients for critical teacher reflection. *Theory Into Practice, 42*(3), 195–202.

Isenbarger, L., & Zembylas, M. (2006). The emotional labour of caring in teaching. *Teaching and Teacher Education, 22*(1), 120–134.

Kitchen, J. (2005). Conveying respect and empathy: Becoming a relational teacher educator. *Studying Teaching Education, 1*(2), 195–207.

Labaree, D. F. (2000). On the nature of teaching and teacher education: Difficult practices that look easy. *Journal of Teacher Education, 51*(3), 228–233.

Meyer, T., & Sawyer, M. (2006). Cultivating an inquiry stance in English education: Rethinking the student teaching seminar. *English Education, 39*(1), 46–71.

Mills, M., & Satterthwait, D. (2000). The disciplining of preservice teachers: Reflections on the teaching of reflective teaching. *Asia-Pacific Journal of Teacher Education, 28*(1), 29–38.

Mr. H. (2012). Call it what it is: Confronting the teacher-on-teacher bully down the hall. *English Journal, 101*(6), 64–69.

NCTE Standing Committee Against Racism and Bias. (2017, August 15). There is no apolitical classroom: Resources for teaching in these times. Retrieved from http://blogs.ncte.org/index.php/2017/08/there-is-no-apolitical-classroom-resources-for-teaching-in-these-times/

Nieto, S. (1999). Culture and learning. In *The light in their eyes: Creating multicultural learning communities* (pp. 47–71). New York: Teachers College Press.

Ressler, P., & Chase, B. (2009). Sexual identity and gender variance: Meeting the educational challenges. *English Journal, 98*(4), 15–22.

Schussler, D. L., Stooksberry, L. M., & Bercaw, L. A. (2010). Understanding teacher candidate dispositions: Reflecting to build self-awareness. *Journal of Teacher Education, 61*(4), 350–363.

Shoffner, M. (2009). The place of the personal: Exploring the affective domain through reflection in teacher preparation. *Teaching and Teacher Education, 25*(6), 783–789.

Shoffner, M. (2011). Considering the first year: Reflection as a means to address beginning teachers' concerns. *Teachers and Teaching: Theory and Practice, 17*(4), 417–433.

Shoffner, M., Alsup, J., Garcia, A., Haddix, M., Moore, M., Morrell, E., Schaafsma, D., & Zuidema, L. A. (2017, November 30). What is English language arts teacher education? National Council of Teachers of English. CEE position statement. Retrieved from http://www2.ncte.org/statement/whatiselateachereducation/

Shoffner, M., & Brown, M. (2010). From understanding to application: The difficulty of culturally responsive teaching as a beginning English teacher. In L. Scherff & K. Spector (Eds.), *Culturally relevant pedagogy: Clashes and confrontations* (pp. 89–112). Lanham, MD: Rowman & Littlefield.

Shoffner, M., & Morris, C. W. (2010). Preparing preservice English teachers and school counselor interns for future collaboration. *Teaching Education, 21*(2), 185–197.

Shoffner, M., Sedberry, T., Alsup, J., & Johnson, T. S. (2014). The difficulty of teacher dispositions: Considering professional dispositions for preservice English teachers. *Teacher Educator, 49*(3), 175–192.

Smith, R. L., Skarbek, D., & Hurst, J. (2005). *The passion of teaching: Dispositions in the schools*. Lanham, MD: Rowman & Littlefield Education.

Weinstein, C., Curran, M. E., & Tomlinson-Clarke, S. (2003). Culturally responsive classroom management: Awareness into action. *Theory Into Practice, 42*(4), 269–276.

Wells, M. S., & Mitchell, D. J. (2016). Dialogism in teacher professional development: Talking our way to open-door teaching. *English Journal, 106*(2), 35–40.

Wentzel, K. R. (2003). Motivating students to behave in socially competent ways. *Theory Into Practice, 42*(4), 319–326.

Whitney, A. E., Olan, E. L., & Fredricksen, J. E. (2013). Experience over all: Preservice teachers and the prizing of the "practical." *English Education, 45*(2), 184–200.

Williamson, P. (2013). Enacting high leverage practices in English methods: The case of discussion. *English Education, 46*(1), 34–67.

Zeichner, K. M., & Liston, D. P. (2013). *Reflective teaching: An introduction* (2nd ed.). New York: Routledge.

A Response to Chapter 3

Brandon Sams and Mike Cook

In her chapter, "The Potential of Problematic Practice: Educating Teachers for the Secondary ELA Classroom," Melanie Shoffner reminds us that the methods course, and the ways we have traditionally conceptualized and used it for the purposes of educating future teachers, has tended to focus almost solely on success and not on failure. She articulates a call to address failure explicitly in the methods class, and she suggests using "practitioner problems," scenarios designed to help preservice teachers (PTs) problematize and reflect on classroom issues to approach this goal.

Shoffner provides teacher educators a clear and useful discussion of how we can bring in relevant and contextualized problems, issues, and situations from our previous students, who have completed clinicals in the same schools and districts to facilitate the problematization discussions, and suggests collecting personal stories from students in the field. These stories, or practitioner problems as she identifies them, include important context and geographic specificity, unlike the generic teacher situations many teacher educators have used. Shoffner explains that personal stories will allow PTs to more fully consider the problems and situations from varying perspectives.

There is much to appreciate about Shoffner's use of authentic and relevant practitioner problems. First, her approach acknowledges the affective domain of teaching and learning and its complex processes. By using practitioner problems, she encourages PTs to put aside their rose-colored glasses when looking at and considering English teaching and the process of learning to teach and asks PTs to address the theory-practice disconnect all too often present in methods courses and helps PTs see the overlap between the secondary and postsecondary worlds—they can begin connecting these spaces, both theoretically and practically, before entering the secondary classroom. Perhaps even more importantly, practitioner problems help PTs use mistakes and missteps to consider how teachers instruct, think about, and position students. On a more macro level that encompasses the previously mentioned benefits, engaging PTs in grappling with problems, issues, and struggles promotes reflective practice, a vital component of teaching and developing as teachers (see Shoffner, p. 40).

In reflecting on our own work with PTs, we noted how our English methods courses may, all too often, focus solely on "what works." Reading Shoffner's work has helped us question when and how we marginalize conversation about failure, complexity, and difficulty (see Shoffner, p. 41). In centering "what works" in our courses, we may be framing learning to teach as a seamless narrative of success and growth even when we know from experience and common sense that learning to teach is fraught with difficulty, disappointment, and joy in equal measure. We should ask, "How can it be that the assignment is always effective, the students are always engaged, and the teacher is always successful?" These are well-posed questions and ones that challenge us as teacher educators to provide space for and learn from practitioner problems.

As we read Shoffner's work, we noted that using *practitioner problems* in our methods courses could be one way to address the issues with emotion work we identified in our chapter. We describe two different students who discontinued their internships and our programs and query how we could have better prepared them for the emotion work of the profession. We speculate that these students didn't feel they had permission—in the cultures of learning we had created—to voice and process the frustrations and confusions that accompany learning to teach. From this examination, we argue that the "feeling rules" (see Sams and Cook, p. 151) of teacher education and of learning to teach need to be rewritten in our own classes and, more generally, in the profession.

Exploring practitioner problems with our students as Shoffner does with hers might give our students permission to more freely voice frustration, explore disappointment, and examine classroom conflict. The students we wrote about in our chapter struggled during internship because the ideal and real were in conflict. They had constructed ideals about teaching, learning to teach, and themselves as teachers that were in various ways shattered during the internship experience. We speculate that exploring practitioner problems in our future methods courses will better prepare PTs for the emotion work of teaching during internship and beyond.

The methods course will continue to pose challenges to teacher educators and PTs alike. Shoffner's strategy of exploring practitioner problems is a big step in the right direction to mitigate some of the challenges. Her approach to practitioner problems prompts teacher educators to ask difficult and useful questions about the practice of teaching, including those problems and scenarios that remain invisible in the "what works" framework. Infusing practitioner problems scenarios in the methods courses can help us move from "what works" to a more capacious and realistic understanding of classrooms and students as multifaceted and contextual systems that require attunement to emotion, improvisation, and complexity. We thank Shoffner for guiding our attention in these needed directions.

Part II

External Pressures on Teachers' Professionalization

Chapter Four

Writing Problems and Promises in Standardized Teacher Performance Assessment

Sarah Hochstetler and Melinda J. McBee Orzulak

The national emphasis on accountability in education has prompted a magnified focus on teacher quality throughout primary and secondary teachers' professional development (U.S. Congress, 2001; Noddings, 2013). This growing focus requires assessments at multiple points in a teacher's career and has expanded to include a preservice teacher's candidacy. Many states, in response to questions about teacher professional readiness, mandate that emerging educators pass a teacher performance assessment (TPA) during the student teaching component of their preparation programs.

There are various versions of this kind of assessment, ranging from PACT (Performance Assessment for California Teachers) to MoPTA (Missouri Pre-Service Teacher Assessment), but the assessment gaining traction nationally is edTPA (Educative Teacher Performance Assessment). At the time of this writing, edTPA is being implemented in some capacity in "766 Educator Preparation Programs" across 40 states and the District of Columbia, though only 12 states have a distinct statewide policy pertaining to the assessment (edTPA, n.d.b).

The increasing reliance on TPAs as a measure of teacher candidates' effectiveness, in some states the sole arbiter, demands that we critique these high-stakes testing instruments' impact on methods coursework. We answer the call from the National Council of Teachers of English's (NCTE) recent position statement opposing high-stakes performance assessments for teacher candidates (NCTE, 2017), and we join the larger professional conversation of how responses to these performance assessments require critical scholarship and an examination of our teaching in reply.

In this chapter we will draw on our experiences as writing methods instructors in a state mandating a high-stakes TPA to explore how this assessment has forced us to carefully analyze the rhetoric of and professional discourses for how we engage with TPAs and to what effect.

We investigate the tensions in preparing preservice teachers for TPAs with three goals: to historicize the emergence of national standardized performance assessments; to highlight how discourses related to these assessments and professional knowledge for the teaching of writing intersect with our practice as writing teacher educators (WTEs); and to explore options with our teacher candidates for responding to high-stakes standardized assessments. Specifically, we will use edTPA, the TPA required in our home state of Illinois, in conversation with NCTE's position statement, "Professional Knowledge for the Teaching of Writing" (2016), as an illustrative case to inform teacher educators' responses to and preparation of candidates for TPAs.

EMERGENCE OF TPAS FOR PRESERVICE TEACHERS

As noted above, we have witnessed the popularization of TPAs in the wake of national calls for improved teaching and teacher education. Specifically, the rhetoric of "improvement" is often attributed to the 1983 publication of *A Nation at Risk* (ANAR), a document that catalyzed public fear of educational failure (National Commission on Excellence in Education, 1983). An obvious response to the "crisis" in education is the rise of the reform movement, the most visible wide-scale example being the No Child Left Behind Act (NCLB) of 2001, which set the stage of the Common Core State Standards (CCSS). The goals for both included clearer standardization and accountability through data-driven instruction that supported the calls for "highly qualified" teachers.

Teacher performance assessments emerged in relation to these broader standardized assessment trends. Early teacher candidate performance assessments drew from Education Testing Service's (ETS) development of the National Board for Professional Teaching Standards exam developed in the late 1990s. Currently, competing "national" standardized performance assessments are housed with the Pearson-operationalized edTPA and ETS's 2015 rollout of PPAT (Praxis Performance Assessment for Teachers) for teacher candidates.

From California to a Multistate Model

The first widespread employment of standardized preservice teacher performance assessment can be traced back to California. PACT grew from legislation mandating students enrolled in teacher credentialing programs successfully complete a performance assessment of their readiness to enter the profession for initial licensure, starting in 2008 (Chung, 2008). Programs could meet compliance by either requiring student participation in a state-sponsored teacher performance assessment, created in collaboration with ETS, or developing their own assessments that were carefully aligned with California's standards for quality (Chung, 2008). PACT was developed as an alternative performance assessment by a consortium of programs motivated by the desire for a performance assessment that both reflected their individual contexts and sought to evaluate teaching from an authentic stance, including the context, grade level, and content area (Chung, 2008; Chung & Pecheone, 2006).

The Stanford Center for Assessment, Learning and Equity (SCALE) developed, field-tested, and validated the PACT and then later developed the edTPA (operationalized in 2013) as a *national* version of a subject-specific, portfolio-based teacher performance assessment in partnership with American Association of Colleges for Teacher Education (AACTE). On the website's "Welcome" page, edTPA is described as born of a desire to "create a nationally available assessment for new entrants to teaching—designed by teachers and teacher educators to reflect the real work of teaching, to support the learning of candidates, and to give useful feedback to programs that prepare teachers" (edTPA, n.d.c).

The developers sought to build a "valid, reliable measure that would respect the complexity of teaching, [and] reflect the academic knowledge and intellectual abilities required to advance student learning" (edTPA, n.d.c). The result is an online portfolio-style assessment requiring candidates to demonstrate skill in "planning around student learning standards, adapting plans for students based on their specific needs, implementing and assessing instruction, developing academic language, evaluating student learning, and reflecting on how to improve student outcomes by continuing to refine teaching plans and strategies" (edTPA, n.d.c).

In short, the assessment focuses on the three pillars of planning, instruction, and assessment with specific guidelines for varied subject areas. Other TPAs offer similar foci but do not necessarily include discipline-specific handbooks, guidelines, and rubrics.

Tensions of Local Versus National Assessments

Hébert (2017) has noted key differences in transparency and the ways PACT validity research cited by SCALE as justification for edTPA has glossed over key differences among the two TPAs:

> PACT—a regional assessment that is localized with respect to teacher education in that it is connected to the California Teaching Performance Expecta-

tions and locally scored—differs too drastically from the edTPA to be used as its basis of research. Hence, much more transparency is needed on behalf of SCALE and AACTE with respect to highlighting these differences and limitations and offering additional research that focuses explicitly on the edTPA. (p. 77)

While PACT offers all materials online for teacher educators and candidates to access, for instance, edTPA materials remain a mystery for programs that have not adopted them, with password-protected sites and nondisclosure agreements for scorers.

Most TPAs are scored through external raters, with some possible exceptions. SCALE's site notes that edTPA can be scored "locally for formative purposes" (SCALE, n.d.), but official scoring is evaluated externally through Evaluation Systems of Pearson, SCALE's operational partner, which contrasts to the local/internal scoring of the PACT. ETS's Praxis Performance Assessment for Teachers (PPAT) and the MoPTA (also developed by ETS) include a "formative" first task that is locally rated but never scored as part of the assessment. In edTPA, teacher preparation programs are provided with strict guidelines of how to provide limited "support" for candidates; ultimately, Pearson recruits and trains "qualified" individuals (e.g., teacher educators and National Board Certified Teachers) to score portfolios. Currently, they offer national and regional scoring training pools; a regional scoring option is a more recent phenomenon, which our most recent research uncovered has been available to states starting in 2016 (edTPA, n.d.a). Different TPAs offer different levels of revision after initial scoring, but all have fees for resubmission.

AN ILLUSTRATIVE CASE STUDY

Our Context

Over the last 7 years in the state of Illinois, where we work as WTEs at neighboring universities, we have watched our state become a major proponent of and leader in the implementation of edTPA. In accordance with Illinois law, as of fall 2015, the licensure of all teacher candidates was determined not by internal measures like evaluations from clinical experiences or methods courses but by candidates' scores on an online structured portfolio assessment to be assembled and submitted to Pearson ePortfolio and their national scoring pool during the student teaching internship. Some universities have linked a passing score on edTPA to university program completion, positioning the test as the determiner of candidate readiness and—alarmingly—eligibility for graduation.

Each content area's edTPA handbook highlights one or two teaching strategies or foci that are deemed essential by experts in that particular area. The content area experts consulted in creating the English language arts (ELA) edTPA chose a textual focus. They might argue that this focus does not mean there aren't many other essential skills in ELA teaching; it just happens that text-based teaching was highlighted for this particular "subject-specific" edTPA. However, the pedagogical skill and focus in the English-language arts handbook is interpretation of texts; this focus means that it is less likely that candidates will choose a writing focus for edTPA learning segments (three to five consecutive lessons).

Our Response

The use of edTPA and other high-stakes, standardized TPAs as a measure of teacher candidates' effectiveness requires us to critique this testing instrument. We do recognize the benefits of a practice-based approach requiring a reflective stance and portfolio format, which mirrors some of what we include in our methods courses as a more reliable assessment than a high-stakes multiple-choice assessment. Conversely, we see need for using edTPA as a case study to showcase how programmatic or individual interpretation of a high-stakes TPA may marginalize aspects of ELA teaching.

We focus on the effects of writing instruction (and writing teacher education) through what the edTPA labels as the "subject-specific pedagogy" assessment for English language arts, due to its focus on "complex texts." In response to this focus on teaching texts (likely interpreted as literary texts due to the examples provided in edTPA handbooks and by some universities), the impulse of some departments might be to significantly modify current methods course curriculum or shift sequencing of methods courses to prioritize literature over writing.

In these rearranged spaces, writing may be conceptualized as only a tool for demonstrating learning, and not a rich location for self-exploration or learning about rhetorical appeal or audience awareness (Fecho, 2011; Gere, 1994; Yagelski, 2011). In teacher preparation programs, learning to write may be permanently switched to writing to learn. This concerns us in many ways, the most pressing of which is the potential deformation of how writing and writing instruction are understood, employed, and valued by future teachers of English as a result of a singular but powerful assessment.

HISTORY OF MARGINALIZATION OF WRITING

The example given above—of programs resequencing classes to prioritize reading and literature-based coursework to the detriment of writing teacher education—may be extreme, but it draws attention to the need for critical responses to TPAs and analysis of the content prioritized in those assessments. In our case, we note that edTPA may marginalize writing teacher education, as performance assessments may shape our discourses in teacher education. As our colleagues in higher education are well aware, composition (as a field of study) has struggled to gain equal footing with literature in university English departments (Hairston, 1982; Russell, 2002). This pattern of marginalization was reflected, to an extent, in some English education programs where the teaching of writing was often an afterthought in teacher preparation (Neill, 1982; Tremmel, 2002). Writing pedagogy, when included, was offered through a generalized, all-encompassing "English methods" course where it was typically second tier to literature methods and framed as an assessment tool or skill set in service of a text.

However, in the decades after the rise of composition in the university, there was a push against the domination of literature and literary study in English teacher education. More specifically, the single English methods course model was sometimes replaced in licensure programs by two distinct courses, with the intention of equal attention to literature methods *as well as* writing pedagogy (Tremmel, 2002).

The historical conflicts between writing and literature in university English departments and English education programs are also present in the secondary English classroom: Research has shown that while English teachers may teach literature collaboratively and creatively, they may associate grammar and writing with traditional approaches and as something they "hate" or dread teaching in comparison to literature (Brosnahan & Neulieb, 1995). This power dynamic influences the preparation of English majors who become teachers, meaning that subject matter preparation for English teachers most often involves literary study, with limited emphasis on composition or language study. To compound this problem, the edTPA is likely to be interpreted as solely a literature-based teaching exercise, to the potential exclusion of meaningful writing and language study.

The potential for the edTPA to perpetuate the historically marginalized status of writing in the context of the middle or high school English classroom is a concern we share. Our analysis of the edTPA documents showed the edTPA may further marginalize writing instruction in teacher education if English educators don't unpack assigned tasks for their intersections with effective writing instruction. Already some "models" being developed by individual programs offer examples of lessons based exclusively on canonical short stories and literary vocabulary.

Additionally, conversations with candidates and colleagues imply that baseline interpretations of handbook prompts support our initial predictions: Many of the edTPA portfolios for teacher candidates in our English education programs feature some sort of literature or other text as the centerpiece of the learning segment. However, we also hear of ways writing/language-based lesson sequences can be successful in meeting the requirements—if candidates are introduced to this possibility in their methods course.

Opportunities to Respond to and Critique Performance Assessments

Initially, we worked together across institutional contexts to consider how writing teacher educators could avoid having our contribution to edTPA pigeonholed as a student "work sample" or "product" to demonstrate knowledge of literary vocabulary. We wanted to resist casting the "subject specific pedagogy" in ELA as solely literature based, and a first step was to analyze how the assessment referred to writing and writing instruction. In doing so, we realized the need to shape definitions of "academic language" for the teaching of writing, and to highlight that academic language in ELA is not just about vocabulary and text complexity. This began a discussion of considering common language in writing teacher education and acknowledging what already exists. Even as we sought to support candidates with producing a text-based edTPA learning segment with robust engagement with writing and language pedagogy, the assessment itself provided an opportunity for continued discussion about writing and the discourses related to performance assessment.

As we grappled with the challenges of analyzing aspects of a TPA in relation to existing professional discourses related to the teaching of writing, we realized that similarly, our candidates will need to apply critical lenses to high-stakes "national" assessments as they encounter assessment conversations as teachers. How can we, as teacher educators, model critical, thoughtful engagement?

Helping candidates understand multiple "national" discourses related to their preparation remains critical: our state's policy for edTPA completion (as 1 of only 12 states in all 50 that have a similar requirement) as well as NCTE's critical response to this type of assessment, particularly to using a high-stakes TPA as a requirement for licensure as it is in our state (NCTE, 2017). As writing teacher educators, we advocate for using NCTE's "Professional Knowledge for the Teaching of Writing" (2016) as another national discourse about ELA instruction for a starting place rather than edTPA documents. We can use this professional knowledge, for example, to help candidates use a research base for their arguments about teaching writing and to grapple with tensions related to these national conversations.

To do so, we offer examples of how to use the professional principles from the "Professional Knowledge for the Teaching of Writing" to reshape discourse in a writing methods course where edTPA is also a thread shaping the conversation. In this process, we considered relevant questions for discussions of standardized assessments: How does the TPA affirm (or contradict) what the professional organization defines as equitable, effective learning? For instance, how does the assessment gauge success within the "subject-specific" learning? Does this metric have potential to marginalize aspects of subject-specific learning?

Purposes for Writing

One key NCTE (2016) principle focuses on the ways "writing grows out of many purposes." As candidates consider this principle in relation to supporting writing in their classrooms, teacher educators can raise questions of how standardized forces have highlighted some purposes over others (as the framing statement of the NCTE document describes in relation to CCSS). We can support candidate growth understanding this principle as we help them name different purposes for their writing as teachers:

1. *Writing as an argument for teaching.* Many writing methods courses ask candidates to think of themselves as writers and reflective practitioners—understandings that will be put into practice as they write lessons as an argument for an audience like edTPA scorers or future principals. This writing task brings up questions of audience, assessment, and validity that candidates will need to grapple with in response to the assessments their students will encounter. Dawson and Case (2016) reframe edTPA as a "written argument for competency" and an opportunity to ask teacher candidates to "use elements of rhetorical argumentation to develop written arguments" about teaching practice.
2. *Writing to reflect.* Good planning means knowing about one's students, as we know, and is required in edTPA planning tasks; writing as reflection is one way to generate this knowledge. Teacher candidates will need to articulate their students' personal, cultural, and community assets; we argue that writing and writing instruction can lead to these understandings. The edTPA also asks candidates for reflective writing in the "instruction" and "assessment" sections that is supported by evidence. To begin this task, candidates can draw on concepts from composition-based coursework as well as writing methods to carefully craft responses for this specific genre of writing.
3. *Writing to advocate.* In "Writing as Praxis," Robert Yagelski (2012) challenges educators to reshape education reform conversations to "emphasize the humanness of schooling and the capacity of writing to help us live our lives more fully and mindfully" (p. 202). In concert with supporting candidates as writers and future teachers is viewing TPAs as an opportunity for writing as advocacy. Given the alignment of many writing methods courses with the general understanding of

writing as a tool to effect change, we can encourage our candidates to respond to TPAs by communicating their feedback to state boards of education and other decision-makers, and voice their experiences and insights to these powerful bodies for the purpose of helping shape the TPA or push back against specific elements of the assessment that may or may not reflect their concepts of "best practices" in teaching the ELA.

Methods courses can provide opportunities for candidates to generate questions related to tensions among national discourses. For instance, as candidates consider varied purposes for writing, and which purposes are promoted in their experiences with TPA, they might ask, What purposes for writing are marginalized in this process? What are implications for me as a writing teacher as I design lessons? As they grapple with these questions, they may consider further the role of teacher as advocate and writing as one way to push back in relation to the tensions they observe.

Analysis of Complex Social Relationships, Language, and Conventions

Other key principles related to professional knowledge for teaching writing explore the complex relationships among social relationships and "appropriate" language use, including how conventions are approached in the teaching of writing processes. For us, these principles offer ways to help candidates grapple with questions such as, What rhetoric related to the TPA needs to be unpacked, critiqued, or resisted? How does the professional knowledge for teaching writing offer ways to understand and critique terms such as *error* or *academic language* as used in the edTPA? In relation to NCTE principles, we briefly discuss areas that intersect with our work in writing methods courses:

1. *Analyze published discourses.* Teacher candidates can consider published critiques of how edTPA narrowly defines terms such as *academic language*, documented by NCTE (NCTE, 2017). Candidates can make connections to their professional knowledge from writing teacher education, as we argue that this knowledge remains crucial in candidates' successful understandings of edTPA's use of "academic language" in ways that add depth to their understanding of the complexities of language in teaching (see Hochstetler & McBee Orzulak, 2015). For instance, candidates explore how academic language can encompass knowledge of writing instruction (not just literary vocabulary and literary analysis). WTEs can help candidates connect to what they have learned about writing in unfamiliar genres and how to teach

genre and audience analysis, including understanding of varied syntax in different genres (e.g., Fleischer and Andrew-Vaughn's *Writing Outside Your Comfort Zone*).

2. *Analyze instructional discourse.* Another opportunity for supporting our teacher candidates in these key understandings from writing teacher education is to discuss instructional discourse as part of lesson design and planning. We can help them consider how their language use (both talk and writing) as teachers positions different kinds of students in ELA classrooms. By calling attention to interactional awareness, we can help them understand that they shape discourse in every ELA lesson. For example, this could entail analyzing writing mini-lessons with discussion of teacher discourse and issues of accommodation for the moment of teaching and with varied students (McBee Orzulak, Lillge, Engel, & Haviland, 2014).

3. *Analyze TPA rhetoric.* Principles related to conventions also enable us to help candidates consider practices for examining patterns in students' work and unpacking convention-related terminology. In the analysis component of the edTPA, candidates are asked to examine student learning related to language demands, including their patterns of "error." In the analyses of student work, however, the terminology of student "error" used by edTPA requires unpacking in relation to the teaching of writing. How do we conceive of "error" differently than in other fields? How do we prevent perpetuation of ineffective correction feedback that has plagued traditional prescriptivist grammar instruction? An emphasis on pattern-based analysis may be needed to help candidates move beyond a simplistic "error"-hunting approach in their responses to writing. In particular, candidates may need practice looking for class patterns—of both students' needs and strengths—and identifying specific areas for focal students.

Across the NCTE (2016) principles, we see opportunities for candidates to deepen their understanding of the nuances with engaging with language as teachers while also applying their understanding of writing principles to push back against narrow definitions as they make their arguments about competency in teaching for the edTPA.

Highlighting Writing as a Process and Assessment as Complex

As a performance assessment, the edTPA provides a useful case study in our discussions of methods for evaluation, in writing methods courses and beyond. For example, the multiple rubrics used in TPAs lend themselves for analysis, inviting a conversation about the pros and cons of rubric use (Popham, 1997; Wilson, 2007). Further, we can encourage a rhetorical analysis of the assessment and ponder *what is being valued and evaluated* by a TPA portfolio, to borrow language from Nancie Atwell (1987).

Using the language surrounding and within the assessment provides rich data for our teacher candidates to mine when thinking about discourse in education, broadly, and the ways such discourse affects writing and writing instruction—for example, how we consider writing products and processes both in planning and evaluation. As Gorlewski (2013) unpacks, questions about "standards" versus "standardized" assessment are important for consideration by ELA teachers; we have an opportunity to model these conversations in methods courses.

As candidates design prompts, attention to process approaches and other language supports could help them justify the purposes behind instructional moves. For example, they will need to plan both informal and formal assessments of learning in the learning segment. Descriptions of student language they plan to hear (oral) and see (written) is important to this planning; their understandings of the complex ways that written and oral language intersect will be vital.

WRITING AND REWRITING TPA RESPONSES AS METHODS INSTRUCTORS

We have found that the NCTE principle of *writing as a tool for thinking* further applies to us as we seek to respond in scholarly writing to the pedagogical changes driven by the TPA trend. Our own writing advocacy can serve as a model for our students as we write alongside them in response to these changes. Even in writing this chapter, areas have been highlighted for us based on our latest research into TPAs:

- Need to help candidates understand differences between localized, university-/school-based assessment versus high-stakes "national" assessment as they learn about analyzing assessment tools
- Need to analyze circulating discourses about assessments (e.g., All states are using high-stakes TPAs, and this process is inevitable.)

As we researched TPAs for this article, we are reminded that the overall story is more complicated than what appears on testing websites. Currently, some states are considering when/how to re-up their commitments when contracts expire with ETS or Pearson. Some states that appear on testing companies' adoption maps only represent some institutions in those states. Not all states and institutions are using TPAs as high-stakes, nationally scored assessments; not all are using it for licensure.

These assessments are powerful moments in our candidates' teaching internships. In fact, for many, a TPA is the capstone teaching encounter that concludes candidate experiences in our programs. We encourage stakeholders to look closely at the ways TPAs have potential to shape ELA and, specifically, writing teacher education:

- What are the current assumptions about TPA adoption and scoring in my state?
- How is preparing for the TPA shaping administration decisions regarding methods courses and sequencing?
- Does the TPA limit writing to an assessment role, or as a "writing task" and "written product" in response to a text?
- What are the effects of the TPA on our candidates' understandings of teaching ELA?

Teacher performance assessments have only emerged in the last two decades. As states reject and adopt these assessments, we can encourage dialogue among colleagues, professional organizations, state and national educational leaders, and the testing companies themselves, for the purpose of questioning how such assessments affect the way we conceptualize, value, and employ writing, as well as other ELA pedagogical understandings.

REFERENCES

Atwell, N. (1987). *In the middle: Writing, reading, and learning with adolescents*. Montclair, NJ: Boynton/Cook.

Brosnahan, I., & Neulieb, J. (1995). Teaching grammar affectively: Learning to like grammar. In S. Hunter & R. Wallace (Eds.), *The place of grammar in writing instruction* (pp. 204–212). Portsmouth, NH: Boyton/Cook.

Chung, R. R. (2008). Beyond assessment: Performance assessments in teacher education. *Teacher Education Quarterly, 35*(1), 7–28.

Chung, R. R., & Pecheone, R. L. (2006). Evidence in teacher education: The performance assessment for California teachers (PACT). *Journal of Teacher Education, 57*(1), 22–36.

Dawson, C., & Case, A. F. (2016, November). *Argumentation as advocacy: Preparing teachers to strategically argue for their practice and students*. National Council of Teachers of English Annual Convention, Atlanta, GA.

edTPA. (n.d.a). FAQ. Retrieved from http://edtpa.aacte.org/faq#51

edTPA. (n.d.b). Participation map. Retrieved from http://edtpa.aacte.org/state-policy

edTPA. (n.d.c). Welcome to the official edTPA website. Retrieved from http://edtpa.aacte.org/welcome

Fecho, B. (2011). *Writing in the dialogical classroom: Students and teachers responding to the texts of their lives*. Urbana, IL: National Council of Teachers of English.

Fleischer, C., & Andrew-Vaughn, S. (2009). *Writing outside your comfort zone: Helping students navigate unfamiliar genres*. Portsmouth, NH: Heinemann.

Gere, A. R. (1994). Kitchen tables and rented rooms: The extracurriculum of composition. *College Composition and Communication, 45*(1), 75–92. doi:10.2307/358588

Gorlewski, J. (2013). Research for the classroom: Standards, standardization, and student learning. *English Journal, 102*(5), 84–88.

Hairston, M. (1982). The winds of change: Thomas Kuhn and the revolution in the teaching of writing. *College Composition and Communication, 33*(1) 76–88.

Hébert, C. (2017). What do we really know about the edTPA? Research, PACT, and packaging a local teacher performance assessment for national use. *Educational Forum, 81*(1), 68–82. doi:10.1080/00131725.2016.1242680

Hochstetler, S., & McBee Orzulak, M. J. (2015). Moving writing out of the margins in edTPA: "Academic language" in writing teacher education. *Teaching/Writing: The Journal of Writing Teacher Education, 4*(2), 73–89.

McBee Orzulak, M. J., Lillge, D. M., Engel, S., & Haviland, V. (2014). Contemplating trust in times of uncertainty: Uniting practice and interactional awareness to address ethical dilemmas in English teacher education. *English Education, 46*(5), 80–102.

National Commission on Excellence in Education. (1983). *A nation at risk: The imperative for educational reform*. Washington, DC: U.S. Government Printing Office.

National Council of Teachers of English. (NCTE). (2016). Professional knowledge for the teaching of writing. NCTE position statement. Retrieved from http://www2.ncte.org/statement/teaching-writing/

National Council of Teachers of English. (NCTE). (2017). Resolution opposing high-stakes teacher performance assessment. NCTE Resolution. Retrieved from http://www2.ncte.org/statement/teacher-cand-perf-assess/

Neill, S. B. (Ed.). (1982). Teaching writing: Problems and solutions. Sacramento, CA: Education News Service.

Noddings, N. (2013). *Education and democracy in the 21st century*. New York: Teachers College Press.

Popham, W. J. (1997). What's wrong—and what's right—with rubrics. *Educational Leadership, 55*(2), 72–75.

Russell, D. (2002). *Writing in the academic disciplines: A curricular history* (pp. 271–307). Carbondale: Southern Illinois University Press.

Stanford Center for Assessment, Learning and Equity (SCALE). (n.d.). About edTPA. Retrieved from https://scale.stanford.edu/teaching/edtpa

Tremmel, R. (2002). Striking a balance: Seeking a discipline. In R. Tremmel & W. Broz (Eds.), *Teaching writing teachers of high school and first year composition* (pp. 1–16). Portsmouth, NH: Boynton/Cook.

U.S. Congress. (2001). *Elementary and secondary education act: No child left behind act of 2001*. Washington, DC: U.S. Department of Education.

Wilson, M. (2007). Why I won't be using rubrics to respond to students' writing. *English Journal, 96*(4), 62–66.

Yagelski, R. P. (2011). *Writing as a way of being: Writing instruction, nonduality, and the crisis of sustainability*. New York: Hampton Press.

Yagelski, R. P. (2012). Writing as praxis. *English Education, 44*(2), 188–204.

A Response to Chapter 4

Connor K. Warner

Few topics in teacher education today provoke such strong emotions as high-stakes teacher performance assessments (TPAs). While mandated TPAs are a national phenomenon, one of the most important points that Sarah Hochstetler and Melinda McBee Orzulak raise is that the reality of TPA policy and implementation is developing and morphing, and we as teacher educators need to develop a critical awareness of that reality. Most treatments of TPAs, whether from scholarly or popular presses, focus on the most widespread of these instruments, the edTPA (SCALE, 2017). However, the edTPA is not the only TPA affecting teacher education in the United States, a reality that Hochstetler and McBee Orzulak acknowledge early in their chapter. I argue that the context of varied and competing TPAs is more important and more complex than the field often acknowledges, and that a deeper understanding of this issue will reinforce the gravity of the concerns the authors of Chapter 4 raise.

Several state-specific TPAs, such as the California Teaching Performance Assessment (CalTPA) and the Kansas Performance Teaching Portfolio (KPTP) have been operational far longer than the edTPA or even the Performance Assessment for California Teachers (PACT) upon which the edTPA was based. In fact, CalTPA was the first TPA to form a consequential component of teacher licensure anywhere in the United States, and many subsequent TPAs were created either to emulate perceived positive attributes of CalTPA or to address its observed flaws.

Additionally, the Educational Testing Service (ETS), in partnership with the Missouri Department of Elementary and Secondary Education, has developed an exam to rival the edTPA; the exam was mandated for initial teacher licensure in Missouri from 2015 to 2018 as the Missouri Pre-Service Teacher Assessment, and rolled out nationally as the Praxis Performance Assessment for Teachers (ETS, 2017). Despite this breadth and relative depth of TPA implementation, national understanding of TPAs remains limited primarily to understanding of the edTPA.

Understanding TPAs primarily through the lens of the edTPA is problematic, because the edTPA differs from most other high-stakes TPAs in a key way: it is subject specific (Pecheone, Whittaker, & Darling-Hammond, 2013). While the PPAT and KPTP exist only in a single form that all teacher candidates from early childhood education to secondary mathematics take, and the CalTPA includes one subject-specific task and then three tasks common to all candidates, the edTPA offers 27 subject-specific assessments. According to Pecheone et al. (2017), though the 27 different assessments share a common architecture, each of the subjects requires different rubrics, different scorers, and different handbooks.

This difference leads to a significant disparity in logistical complexity between the edTPA and other high-stakes TPAs. For example, the handbook providing teacher educators and candidates from all grade levels and disciplines with technical and logistical instructions for the most recent version of the PPAT assessment is 58 pages long (ETS, 2018). Comparable information for the edTPA is contained in more than 27 handbooks with multiple rubrics and rubric levels, encompassing hundreds of pages of text (Dover & Schultz, 2016; Meuwissen & Choppin, 2015; Pecheone et al., 2013). Candidates and teacher educators have struggled with inconsistencies in language across handbooks and rubrics (Au, 2013), and some researchers have posited that discussing 27 different edTPAs might be more accurate than arguing that a unified construct called *the* edTPA exists (Reagan, Schram, McCurdy, Chang, & Evans, 2016).

Given the unique, subject-specific nature of the edTPA, it is worth considering to what degree the tensions explored by Hochstetler and McBee Orzulak are likely to occur in contexts affected by any high-stakes TPA as opposed to contexts specifically shaped by the edTPA. Certainly the tension between local responsivity and external control will be inherent in any assessment scaled up to the national level.

At the moment, only the edTPA and the PPAT are in that category, but even the state-level high-stakes TPAs (e.g., CalTPA, KPTP, MoPTA, and PACT) have and will generate conflict as local teacher education programs shift resources, adapt curriculum, and change practice in ways they would likely not have done absent the mandate of a high-stakes assessment (Liu & Milman, 2013; Luster, 2010; Warner, 2015). This tension, and the associated struggle of teacher education instructional staff between compliance with mandates and authentic program improvement, is well documented in the scholarly literature across multiple TPAs (Bjork & Epstein, 2017; Cronenberg et al., 2016; Peck, Gallucci, & Sloan, 2010; Warner, Bell, McHatton, & Atiles, in press).

The second tension that Hochstetler and McBee Orzulak explored was tension created by the dual nature of high-stakes TPAs as formative experiences and summative assessments. This issue runs as far back as the initial literature on portfolio assessment in teacher education, which eventually formed the basis of the portfolio component of the assessment for the National Board of Professional Teaching Standards (NBPTS) and, through it, the foundation of modern high-stakes TPAs (Darling-Hammond, Hammerness, Grossman, Rust, & Shulman, 2005; Shulman, 1988).

Teaching portfolios (and the TPAs that evolved from them) were designed to be formative learning experience via the selection of artifacts of practice and reflections upon those artifacts and summative assessments of teacher practice and thinking via expert scoring of the portfolios (Shulman, 1998). However, a number of scholars have recognized that differing, and sometimes competing, purposes of teaching portfolios have created significant tensions for both candidates completing the portfolios and teacher preparation programs attempting to incorporate them (Borko, Michalec, Timmons, & Siddle, 1997; Darling-Hammond et al., 2005; Zeichner & Wray, 2001). These tensions have only been exacerbated as teaching portfolios have morphed into high-stakes TPAs, regardless of the particular form of that TPA (Margolis & Doring, 2013; Meuwissen & Choppin, 2015; Warner, 2015).

The last tension, which forms the centerpiece of Hochstetler and McBee Orzulak's argument, is the tension stemming from discontinuity between the representation of the discipline of English language arts (ELA) and the broader understanding of ELA held by themselves, their teacher education programs, and the disciplinary community at large. Previous scholars have argued that TPAs serve as powerful reifications of particular definitions of good teaching and that those definitions have the potential to create significant tensions if those definitions differ from those initially held by candidates or espoused by teacher education programs and cooperating preK–12 faculty (Dover & Schultz, 2016; Sato, 2014; Warner, 2015). However, concern over disciplinary conceptualizations seems to be confined to literature analyzing the edTPA. This makes sense given the edTPA's subject-specific nature and its emphasis on candidate use of discipline-specific academic language as defined by the edTPA handbooks.

Ressler, King, and Nelson (2017) argue that disciplinary understandings of ELA within the edTPA frequently differed from those held by experts in the field of English and literacy, and that candidates could, and likely would, score poorly on their edTPA submissions if they did not adopt the understanding of the discipline enshrined in the handbooks. Hochstetler and McBee Orzulak take this argument a step further, postulating that, given the power of high-stakes assessments, the pressure exerted by the edTPA on candidate conceptualization of the discipline of ELA may eventually morph the discipline itself, shaping both understanding and practice of ELA in preK–12 schools and universities. If this is true and if, as Hochstetler and McBee Orzulak argue, the conceptualization of ELA inherent in the edTPA is a severely limited one, then the subject-specific nature of the edTPA, touted by its promoters as the unique feature making it superior to other TPAs (SCALE, 2017), may also be the feature most likely to generate far-reaching and perhaps unintended consequences.

REFERENCES

Au, W. (2013). What's a nice test like you doing in a place like this? The edTPA and corporate education "reform." *Rethinking Schools, 27*(4), 22–27. Retrieved from http://www.rethinkingschools.org/archive/27_04/27_04_au.shtml

Bjork, C., & Epstein, I. (2017). The unintended consequences of the edTPA. *Phi Delta Kappan.* Retrieved from http://www.kappanonline.org/the-unintended-consequences-of-edtpa/

Borko, H., Michalec, P., Timmons, M., & Siddle, J. (1997). Student teaching portfolios: A tool for promoting reflective practice. *Journal of Teacher Education, 48*(5), 345.

Campbell, C., Ayala, C. C., Railsback, G., Freking, F. W., Mckenna, C., & Lausch, D. (2016). Beginning teachers' perceptions of the California Teaching Performance Assessment (TPA). *Teacher Education Quarterly, 43*(2), 51–72.

Cronenberg, S., Harrison, D., Korson, S., Jones, A., Murray-Everett, N. C., Parrish, M., & Johnston-Parsons, M. (2016). Trouble with the edTPA: Lessons learned from a narrative self-study. *Journal of Inquiry and Action in Education, 8*(1), 109–134.

Darling-Hammond, L., Hammerness, K., Grossman, P., Rust, F., & Shulman, L. (2005). The design of teacher education programs. In L. Darling-Hammond & J. Bransford (Eds.), *Preparing teachers for a changing world: What teachers should learn and be able to do* (pp. 390–441). San Francisco: Jossey-Bass.

Dover, A. G., & Schultz, B. D. (2016). Troubling the edTPA: Illusions of objectivity and rigor. *Educational Forum, 80*(1), 95–106.

Educational Testing Service (ETS). (2017). The PPAT assessment task requirements. Retrieved from https://www.ets.org/ppa/test-takers/teachers/build-submit/requirements/

Educational Testing Services (ETS). (2018). *PPAT assessment candidate and educator handbook, version 3.1.* Retrieved from https://www.ets.org/s/ppa/pdf/ppat-candidate-educator-handbook.pdf

Liu, L. B., & Milman, N. B. (2013). Year one implications of a teacher performance assessment's impact on multicultural education across a secondary education teacher preparation program. *Action in Teacher Education, 35*, 125–142.

Luster, J. (2010). Why states should require a teaching performance assessment and a subject matter assessment for a preliminary teaching credential. *Research in Higher Education Journal, 8*(1), 1–16.

Madeloni, B., & Gorlewski, J. (2013). Wrong answer to the wrong question: Why we need critical teacher education, not standardization. *Rethinking Schools, 27*(4). Retrieved from http://www.rethinkingschools.org/archive/27_04/27_04_madeloni-gorlewski.shtml

Margolis, J., & Doring, A. (2013). National assessments for student teachers: Documenting teaching readiness to the tipping point. *Action in Teacher Education, 35*(4), 272–285.

Meuwissen, K. W., & Choppin, J. M. (2015). Preservice teachers' adaptations to tensions associated with the edTPA during its early implementation in New York and Washington states. *Education Policy Analysis Archives, 23*(103), 1–29.

Pecheone, R., Whittaker, A., & Darling-Hammond, L. (2013). *2013 edTPA field test: Summary report.* Stanford, CA: Stanford Center for Assessment, Learning and Equity. Retrieved from https://scale.stanford.edu/sites/default/files/2013-edtpa-field-test--summary-report-11.pdf

Pecheone, R., Whittaker, A., & Klesch, H. (2017). *Educative assessment and meaningful support: 2016 edTPA administrative support.* Stanford, CA: SCALE. Retrieved from https://secure.aacte.org/apps/rl/res_get.php?fid=3621&ref=rl.

Peck, C. A., Gallucci, C., & Sloan, T. (2010). Negotiating implementation of high-stakes performance assessment policies in teacher education: From compliance to inquiry. *Journal of Teacher Education, 61*(5), 451–463.

Reagan, E. M., Schram, T., McCurdy, K., Chang, T.-H., & Evans, C. M. (2016). Politics of policy: Assessing the implementation, impact, and evolution of the Performance Assessment for California Teachers (PACT) and the edTPA. *Education Policy Analysis Archives, 24*(9), 1–27.

Ressler, M. B., King, K. B., & Nelson, H. (2017). Ensuring quality teacher candidates: Does the edTPA answer the call? In J. H. Carter & H. A. Lochte (Eds.), *Teacher performance assessment and accountability reforms: The impacts of the edTPA on teaching and schools* (pp. 119–140). New York: Palgrave Macmillan.

Sato, M. (2014). What is the underlying conception of teaching of the edTPA? *Journal of Teacher Education, 65*(5), 421–434.

Shulman, L. (1988, November). A union of insufficiencies: Strategies for teacher assessment in a period of educational reform. *Educational Leadership, 46*(3), 36–41.

Shulman, L. (1998). Teacher portfolios: A theoretical activity. In N. Lyons (Ed.), *With portfolio in hand: Validating the new teacher professionalism* (pp. 23–37). New York: Teachers College Press.

Stanford Center for Assessment, Learning and Equity (SCALE). (2017). Why edTPA? Retrieved from https://secure.aacte.org/apps/rl/res_get.php?fid=2748&ref=rl

Warner, C. K. (2015). *Formative impacts of high-stakes portfolio assessment on preservice English teachers: A qualitative study of belief, attitude, and identity* (doctoral dissertation). Retrieved from KU Scholarworks database (http://hdl.handle.net/1808/19523).

Warner, C. K., Bell, C., McHatton, P., & Atiles, J. (in press). Navigating mandates and working toward coherence: Our journey with a high-stakes teacher performance assessment. *Educational Forum.*

Zeichner, K., & Wray, S. (2001). The teaching portfolio in US teacher education programs: What we know and what we need to know. *Teaching and Teacher Education, 17*, 613–621.

Chapter Five

Changing English

Technology and Its Impact on the Teaching of English Education

Donna L. Pasternak

English teacher educators feel pressure to incorporate technology into teaching English for reasons that range from struggles with assessment moving to web-based platforms to the need to now address the impact of new literacies on communication practices or requirements to align thinking with opinions that value technology as a panacea for learning (Pasternak, Caughlan, Hallman, Renzi, & Rush, 2018). Since most K–16 students will use some type of technology to communicate with instructors, navigate a school's infrastructure, participate in instruction and school communities, and learn a discipline's content knowledge and technology's impact on transforming that knowledge (Gorgina & Hosford, 2008), the pressures listed above ask teacher candidates and the educators who instruct them in their methods classes to effectively integrate technology into their disciplines.

Moreover, adding to these external pressures, internal to the profession, the National Council of Teachers of English (NCTE) and its affiliate organization, English Language Arts Teacher Educators (ELATE), have published position statements and policy briefs that address technology-based literacies and instructional practices (NCTE, n.d.b; n.d.c) and instructional standards for English teachers to integrate technology into teaching English (NCTE, n.d.a).

For technology to be effectively integrated into a discipline, teacher educators need to address conceptual, procedural, and attitudinal or value-based knowledge specific to their disciplines (Guzman & Nussbaum, 2009). Thus, technology should be a tool for learning (Gorder, 2008; Harris, Mishra, &

Koehler, 2009) that supports instructional practices (Ertmer, 2005) and is integral to the learning process (Pierson, 2001). Meeting these conditions has been difficult to enact across English teacher education programs and has resulted in uneven implementation of technology into the disciple, because English teacher educators are not always confident or competent in their technology expertise (Doerr-Stevens & Woywod, 2018; Hawthorne, Goodwyn, George, Reid, & Shoffner, 2012; Pasternak, Hallman, Caughlan, Renzi, Rush & Meineke, 2016; Pasternak et al., 2018).

However, English teachers are expected to actively engage with technology and integrate it into teaching English with a sense of commitment that alienates some (Pasternak et al., 2018) and confirms for others that the future of English teaching is "predicated on a model of English operating in a multimodal, digital environment in which students are fully engaged in a creative relationship with reading and writing all kinds of texts" (Goodwyn, as cited in Hawthorne et al., 2012, p. 299). This disparity of attitudes toward technology and its effect on teaching and learning English has caused challenges and successes across the field as future English teachers are educated for 21st-century classrooms (Nelson, Voithofer, & Cheng, 2019).

TECHNOLOGY AND TEACHING ENGLISH IN THE 20TH AND 21ST CENTURIES

Until the late 20th century, English coursework meant the study of literature, language, composition, and oratory. Being literate meant being proficient at reading a print text, understanding and using its information, and handwriting a response to it. Now, being literate in English requires proficiency with reading and writing digital texts, media objects, codes, images, sounds, social practices, and critical perspectives and producing responses to them, which are as equally diverse (Bruce & Levin, 2003; Conference on English Education [CEE until 2018; thereafter English Language Arts Teacher Educators, or ELATE], 2008; Kinzer & Leander, 2003; Swenson, Young, McGrail, Rozema, & Whitin, 2006; Yagelski, 2005), creating new literacies that now fall under the domain of *teaching English*. Therefore, today's teachers teach English with an understanding that multimodal literacies and technology integration are essential aspects of the discipline (CEE, 2008; Hamilton, Heydon, Hibbert, & Stooke, 2015; Pasternak et al., 2018).

These changes to English content pressure English teacher educators to develop critical approaches toward technology's impact on the field, pushing them to come to terms with the internal and external tensions that change provokes. As English educators come to terms with an internal understanding of how technology has changed literacy practices, they must also consider the externally imposed suppositions that technology is a panacea for learning

(U.S. Department of Education, Office of Educational Technology, 2016) and critically decide on its value to their students' learning of English.

Since the 1990s, changes in English content have been reflected in the standards under which teacher candidates are educated. English teachers use technology to understand the content of the English language arts (ELA) but must "develop proficiency and fluency with the tools of [it]" (NCTE, 2013, para. 2) as well. According to George, Pope, and Reid (2015), recent revisions of the ELA teacher education standards "saw the integration of contemporary literacies and contemporary technologies on such a regular basis that it seems safe to say that technology has been part of the ELA discipline itself, not just a tool for teaching and learning" (p. 9).

Scholars assert that the ability to read and compose multimedia texts may become as foundational to the ELA as the study of literature, composition, language, and oratory (George et al., 2015). Thus, it appears that technology not only supports learning the traditional content of English but also becomes content when the software or hardware must be learned, a condition that produces tension for English teacher educators because they are now obligated to educate English teachers to "integrate, infuse, and implement [technology] in [their] classes" (George et al., 2015, p. 9).

Indeed, integrating technology effectively into English teacher education programs has challenged many teacher educators (Ertmer, 1999; Hawthorne et al., 2012; Pasternak et al., 2016; Pasternak et al., 2018), despite research on implementing technology into teaching and learning the ELA being significant (Pasternak, Caughlan, Hallman Renzi, & Rush, 2014). Much of the research conducted in technology implementation examines the efficacy of employing technology in K–16 classroom practices rather than its application in the ELA methods classroom, although there are a notable number of studies that explore this work with preservice teachers (e.g., Carlson & Archambault, 2013; Cherner & Curry, 2017; Lee & Young, 2010; Ortega, 2013; Pasternak, 2007; Pasternak et al., 2016; Thieman, 2008).

TECHNOLOGY RESEARCH: OPENING SPACES FOR COLLABORATION/CLOSING SPACES FOR ASSESSMENT

Much of the research that examines technology's impact on teaching English can be divided into two groups: (1) technology that *opens* spaces for collaborative learning, such as wikis, blogs, discussion boards, video composing, and online tutoring (e.g., Dymoke & Hughes, 2009; Garcia & Seglem, 2013; Houge & Geier, 2009; Lee & Young, 2010; Matthew, Felvegi, & Callaway, 2009; Rust, 2017; Ryan & Scott, 2008; and Zoch, Myers, & Belcher, 2016); and (2) technology that *closes* spaces to support individualized learning or assess that learning, such as desktop applications, e-portfolios, and multimodal and multimedia software (e.g., Carlson & Archambault, 2013; Chung & van Es, 2014; Figg & McCartney, 2010; Johnson, 2016; Lai & Calandra, 2010; McVee, Bailey, & Shanahan, 2008; Ortega, 2013; Schieble, Vetter, & Meacham, 2015; and Seo, Templeton, & Pellegrino, 2008).

Tensions have arisen in integrating technology into the discipline, because literacy practices supported through technology do not always align well with assessment systems, a situation that complicates evaluating students' proficiency with digital texts (Hawthorne et al., 2012). Hamilton et al. (2015) observe that new literacy practices created through multimodality are marginalized across educational settings due to assessment misalignment in countries such as Canada, the United Kingdom, Australia, and Sweden. In particular, the chapters in Hamilton et al. (2015) explore the vibrancy of literacy practices common to daily communication practices and their misalignment with English language arts standards tested to evaluate literacy competency.

Pasternak et al. (2018) recently studied how methods are taught in ELA programs, confirming that integrating technology into teaching and learning English is essential *other* content that needs to be taught to teachers. That larger, national study of English teacher education included a nationally distributed questionnaire (the Conference on English Education [CEE] Methods Commission National Survey), analyses of collected syllabi, and focus group interviews.

The questionnaire gathered responses to 90 questions that were a mixture of fixed (multiple-choice), partially structured, and open-ended items, some of which were randomly distributed to respondents. The questionnaire was designed to collect general data on English education programs, methods courses, and programmatic responses to change. At the questionnaire's conclusion, respondents were asked to voluntarily upload their methods course syllabi for analysis. Analysis of the survey data led to focus group interviews. This chapter specifically explores tensions and resolutions in integrating technology into the ELA methods course or across a program expressed by respondents in the survey's open-ended questions and in the focus group interviews.

TECHNOLOGY: (DIS)COMFORT IN THE ELA METHODS CLASSROOM

Despite an awareness across the field that technology, multiple literacies, multimodal texts, and digital learning are essential other content in ELA instruction, English teacher educators are unequally challenged to integrate it meaningfully into their courses or across their programs (Pasternak et al., 2018). When asked about how they approached their students' knowledge base concerning technology, some respondents assumed their teacher candidates were already heavily using technology in their subject area courses or presumed that, since technology was pervasive in teacher assessment and certification practices, it was out of their purview to augment that learning in their methods courses.

With e-portfolio assessment seemingly now standard to the field for teacher licensure purposes, other respondents expressed a strong commitment to 21st-century technologies as part of the ELA curriculum (see Hochstetler and McBee Orzulak's chapter and Warner's response). Joseph Shain (all names are pseudonyms) warned about the complexity of integrating technology effectively into the ELA: "You need to combine your technology with your pedagogy with your content knowledge to create these meaningful moments of instruction for your students [teacher candidates and grade school students]."

Other respondents echoed Shain's observations about what is needed to master technology integration while others acknowledged its value to the field. English teacher educators expressed a critical awareness of which technologies were integrated into the methods class, recognizing that technology choices were often driven by individual teacher candidates–specific or instructor-specific expertise with an isolated application, observations that have been reinforced in other scholarship (Rust & Cantwell, 2018; Shelton, 2018).

When technology integration was looked at across programs, teacher educators felt its usage was rarely on a critical, actively engaged level. Charles Bates observed that his ELA program engages in technology teaching and learning, "but it still primarily means Prezi and PowerPoint. It depends on the rare student, maybe 10%, that are doing something really creative or engaging with literacy or a multimodal text. I think that's still very, very slow and something we define as cutting edge or dynamic."

In contrast, Caroline Stewart felt that technology was appropriately integrated throughout the teacher education program in which she worked, a program that was jointly structured across both the Department of English and the School of Education, where technology was infused across coursework but was "not technology for the sake of technology." In Stewart's teacher education program, she felt that technology integration was not high stakes. Rather, it involved modeled practices that fit into a teacher candidate's practice:

> We try to demonstrate [a] kind of seamless incorporation of technology, so not to call attention to using Skype, for example, but to use it for what it—what we want it to be used for, like interviews with authors in adolescent literature and that kind of thing. So that we're not making it seem difficult to use by calling attention to it. We use, I just have to say, a variety of technologies. Students

create weekly websites for their unit plans, for example ... we try to incorporate technology seamlessly as a tool for greater goals.

Correspondingly, Dave Sommer observed that the essentialness of technology integration into ELA generated valuable discussions about how the study of multimodal texts supports teacher candidates to think through a text and not just teach it by having them explore "videos, songs, websites, blogs—a variety of stuff, and really think ... about how all of these different modes of textuality speak to one another," underscoring technology's impact on changing literacy practices. Contrastively, other respondents felt that their teacher candidates were pushing them for more technology integration, but the content they wanted was for finding teaching ideas that were current practices. Bill Warner explained,

> Our recent graduates tell us they'd really like to have more resources, more websites where they could draw teaching activities, more programs for—that they could become familiar with so that they could use them in the classroom. It's just a never-ending growth area. Our students at least feel like they're not keeping up with that. It's hard. They're going to college all the time and they're using the things they have to use that are right in front of them; there's a wide variety out there that they're not aware of.

In contrast to these acknowledged needs for technology integration in the ELA methods class, many universities and teacher education programs have policies that ban the use of technology in their classrooms, despite many ELA methods classes requiring teacher candidates to integrate technology into the curriculum and lessons they create, submit materials through course management systems, watch videos on YouTube, collaborate with K–12 students virtually, and assess their students through e-portfolios (Pasternak et al., 2018). Technology usage policies warn of its disruptive nature to the traditional college classroom and send the message that technology is beyond classroom management approaches. Policies may discredit the opportunities available to teachers and their students regarding differentiation in teaching ELA. Dave Sommer observed,

> Every classroom, every high school classroom I go into, cell phones are just—they have to be dealt with one way or another. Whether it's getting kids to put them away or getting kids to integrate them into the class—every kid pretty much is carrying around this really powerful pocket computer that's got the answers to information questions all the time.
> One of the things I think we have talked about both in terms of classroom management but also in terms of integrating that powerful little computer that kids have—how do we use that in productive ways in a classroom? Even if it's sort of an informal learning tool, how do we allow kids to use that? How do we make sure that there's an equitable distribution when that—the phones are not

equitably distributed? All those are questions I think that we do grapple with as well.

Policies that prohibited technology in the methods class may restrict how to manage it for learning, adapt it for equitable distribution, support it as a powerful learning tool, and critically evaluate it for who is supplying it and promoting it as a panacea to learning.

TECHNOLOGY: ACROSS, IN, OR OUTSIDE A PROGRAM'S COURSEWORK

In the focus group discussions, the question was asked, "How can teacher candidates effectively integrate technology into their practices in a meaningful way after taking a course that does not apply it to ELA content?" Some respondents explained that the teacher candidates either took a specific technology course or had an educational technologist guest lecture in the ELA methods class for a onetime workshop. Dave Sommer acknowledged, "although we're not directly providing [instruction] within our methods course . . . we're certainly making space for it in our classes."

Alex Terrell confirmed that his teacher candidates take a separate technology class but are then required to *infuse* the technology they learned in that class into the curriculum and lessons they create for a methods class they take in another semester. According to Terrell, infusion tends to manifest in creating platforms for presentations or information gathering, placing responsibility on the teacher candidates to find opportunities to apply their learning from the technology class. In this situation, Terrell noted, "I don't get the feeling that they're having an opportunity to really fully utilize the technology to the degree that they could."

Despite the unevenness of teacher education programs engaging in technology integration in many ELA methods courses, Anita Vogel mentioned that teacher candidates are taking more and more digital literacy and media credits in hers. She said that they ask teacher candidates to explore literacy by examining its relationship to technology and the choices made in its application, such as in Schoology and in voice-over PowerPoints.

> We use it—I think we need to be more thoughtful and consistent about how we do it, but right now we're using a lot of modeling. While we do our normal thing, we're integrating in the technology as a means of expression and response and then reflecting on how that technology changed that activity. That happens in methods, it happens in the general methods course, and it happens in other places throughout the program.

Vogel observes that her program tends to model technology by asking teacher candidates to reflect on its usage but without applying it in their own ELA lessons.

TECHNOLOGY: INSIDE AND OUTSIDE A PROGRAM

Respondents reported that the availability and use of technology was often differentially distributed between the university and K–12 settings. Amanda Reiter expressed concern with a university that is technology rich but a local school district that is not:

> I really make sure to have that conversation with students, and also to talk about how you use technology in the classrooms when you have limited resources. Most of my students teach in schools that are very underresourced and don't even have very good Internet access. We talk about ways to still use technology when you don't have a lot to work with. That can be really challenging, and I've never really had a very good answer for that. Sometimes it's encouraging students to use their own devices or to use their own resources when your school may not have those resources.

Similarly, underresourcing can be problematic when technology is used to collaborate with high school students. Collaborative applications can be haphazard and cause tension between the program and the field experience that may arise if the technology's use is not mutually beneficial to both the teacher education program and the K–12 school or it is just a convenient tool to connect a teacher candidate with a high school student. Sean Prinsen noticed,

> As I'm sure you guys know, any time you try to do this kind of inter-institutional thing, it's just like a logistical nightmare, right? For my students to be able to work with their high school partners, and they [high school students] just throw everything up on Google Docs. They're [high school students] like, "I'll send it to her [teacher candidate] and she can edit it tonight," or whatever.

In the response above, scheduling the collaboration and having meaningful contact between the high school student and the teacher candidate can be problematic at best. At worst, high school students might only have access to technology at their high school, while the teacher candidate might only have access while on campus, which could be one or two days a week. This limited window makes it difficult to maintain sufficient contact. Both scenarios leave many unanswered questions as to why a collaboration might not work under these inequitable circumstances.

In contrast, questions arose throughout the focus groups as to which educational entities drive technology trends in ELA. Anita Vogel expressed concern that technology knowledge was driven by the school districts: "The school systems are actually driving the increase in digital learning because they're supplying student teachers, for example, with sets of tablets or iPads and saying, 'You have to use these. Get going with them. We're going paperless.' That's really encouraged us to integrate more and more technology knowledge throughout our program."

Dave Sommer expressed similar concerns about how high school placements are driving technology usage, causing tensions between the program and the field experience as to what to focus on:

> A lot of the schools that our students go into have Google Drive accounts. Students are using Chromebooks, and they're doing a lot of their writing; the high school students are doing a lot of their writing on Google Docs and sharing those with teachers and getting feedback from teachers that way and doing peer feedback that way. We do some modeling of that just through using Google Docs and Google Drive in our class. That's a technology that when I was teaching I didn't have, so I'm learning that along with them.

Joseph Shain agreed with Sommer in feeling a little behind the times when out-resourced by a field placement. As Shain noted earlier in this chapter, for technology to be meaningful content in an ELA methods class, "You need to combine your technology with your pedagogy with your content knowledge to create these meaningful moments of instruction for your students [teacher candidates and grade school students]." Knowing which technology applications to address in the methods classes can be specific to one field placement but not another. When the technology becomes content to teach content, Shain warned,

> I'm very frustrated because I'm losing class time because I'm teaching technology while I'm teaching a subject area. . . . Because as [Anita Vogel] said, I really feel the school district is driving the teacher education program. They put their policies in place, they spend a bajillion dollars on this technology, and now I have to teach that technology. Don't get me wrong; we have a very close school district that's referred to as the "corridor of shame" because of the poverty levels down there, and they have—they might have pencils in the classroom.

A tension between programs and school districts manifests in the inequity of the technology available across school districts. If the methods class integrates technology appropriate to the best-funded school district, respondents felt this time may be ill spent when teacher candidates are placed in school districts with limited technology. Respondents questioned which technology purchases a program can even require of its teacher candidates. Some programs were able to purchase laptops, or require their teacher candidates to do so; others presume that their teacher candidates have technology or can borrow it from the university or public library, as in the presumption about the extent to which a teacher educator feels responsibility for integrating it into a methods course mentioned earlier.

Joseph Shain was very explicit in addressing the tension caused by the unequal resourcing of technology among the university, the program, and the school districts. Shain observed that English and technology are merged more fluidly in the secondary school classroom and high school students seem to accept its presence more casually:

> They [teacher candidates] walk into the classroom, and they're looking around and all the kids have technology. It quickly hits them that the way they were taught in their college education is not . . . the way they need to teach as a future high school teacher. This really makes them angry. Literally, it makes them angry. I have to put out fires because their expectations don't match the reality, and the technology and the infusing of technology into the curriculum is one of these issues. My students either stay angry through their entire internship and they make it through, or they embrace it. I've seen some very great ways that they've done that. . . . You get these cool moments of collaboration, but your question is technology . . . used to teach content, but also be content? Yeah, I agree with that, because you have to teach them how to use technology. They have to actually study technology. A standalone course won't work. Teacher educators who are unsure of how to actually do it then rely on that standalone course, and every time there's technology they might get a couple extra credit points on a rubric, but that's not really reinforcing it. How . . . do I make all that come together?

With the rapid change in technology and the inequity evident in funding it across institutions of higher education as well as K–12 schools, the onus seems to be on teacher candidates to apply technology to their teaching situations because their field experiences will vary and the methods course cannot account for those variances and inequities in placements. English teacher educators need to decide how to prioritize the integration of technology into teaching and learning English. As evident from this discussion, easy answers are not forthcoming to a profession struggling to define its essential content.

TECHNOLOGY: FUNDING AND CURES FOR TEACHING

Looking at technology integration critically, teacher educators want to know who provides funding for it or owns it, who promotes it, how it enhances or detracts from the ELA learning experience, and how it changes the role of the teacher. Sean Prinsen explains,

> We had a teacher from a local high school. Her graduate degree is in educational technology. She's super smart and she put together just a wonderful

presentation for our student teachers on the use of technology and how she uses it in a . . . public high school. I really loved the presentation, and yet this kind of just enthusiasm for technology—I wanted to have a conversation after that about the assumptions that are underwriting this kind of endorsement of technology. I mean, it's tied to certain, a certain tradition. It's tied to a certain epistemology. It's tied to a certain economic paradigm. I worry about that sometimes.

Observations about the funding of technology in schools and universities—from the purchase of required standardized assessment platforms that are domain specific (see Hochstetler and McBee Orzulak's chapter and Warner's response) to the dependency on teacher-proof computerized lesson modules or reading programs—challenge what is known about the ELA and technology integration. Sean Prinsen worries "about the uncritical use of technology" because "there seems to be so much general enthusiasm for the use of technology in classroom[s]. . . . Who's supplying this technology? What does this technology imply about the role of the teacher? What costs—both literal and kind of figurative—are associated with this technology?" These questions must surely be answered by the field as its standardized assessments are taken over by large, for-profit publishing houses and measurement firms (see Hochstetler and McBee Orzulak's chapter and Warner's response).

TECHNOLOGY: CHANGING ENGLISH ADVANTAGE, DISADVANTAGE, OR BOTH?

Over the past 30 years, national ELA teacher standards expect ELA teachers to show increased proficiency in technology's application to the ELA content, but teacher educators are understandably at odds with the outside forces that seem to define what it means to be proficient and effective in its use and promotes it as a panacea to effective teaching and K–12 student engagement.

Technology is unevenly employed to learn ELA instructional practices in the methods course. Expertise is a two-step process that requires English educators to be proficient in their field but also in software applications and the devices on which they run. Technology integration is considered essential to other content, and attempts are ongoing to provide space in the methods class to explore its use. However, teacher candidates use technology even less frequently in their field and student teaching placements than in their methods courses (Pasternak et al., 2018). There is a belief that resources are inconsistently distributed between the K–12 schools and the universities educating future teachers; therefore, dedicating time in the methods class to technology integration can often be time ill spent. The availability of technology in higher education, as well as in school districts, continues to be problematic and dependent upon a community's commitment to it.

In light of a recent U.S. Department of Education report (2016) promoting technology as a panacea for education, English teacher educators are faced with numerous challenges when integrating it to meet teacher education standards (NCTE, 2013). As technology integration becomes more expected, English teacher educators will have to determine where they have expertise and resources, the needs of the communities in which they place teacher candidates, and the value of changing English.

NOTE

Acknowledgments: This research was supported by the University of Wisconsin–Milwaukee (UWM) School of Education, the UWM Graduate School, and the UWM Research Growth Initiative.

REFERENCES

Bruce, B., & Levin, J. (2003). Roles for new technologies in language arts: Inquiry, communication, construction, and expression. In J. Flood, D. Lapp, J. R. Squire, and J. M. Jensen (Eds.), *Handbook of research on teaching the English language arts* (pp. 649–657). Mahwah, NJ: Lawrence Erlbaum.

Carlson, D. L., & Archambault, L. (2013). Technological pedagogical content knowledge and teaching poetry: Preparing preservice teachers to integrate content with VoiceThread Technology. *Teacher Education and Practice, 26*(1), 117–142.

Cherner, T., & Curry, K. (2017). Enhancement or transformation? A case study of preservice teachers' use of instructional technology. *Contemporary Issues in Technology and Teacher Education, 17*(2), 268–290.

Chung, H. Q., & van Es, E. (2014). Pre-service teacher's use of tools to systemically analyze teaching and learning. *Teachers and Teaching, 20*(2). https://doi.org/10.1080/13540602.2013.848567

Conference on English Education (CEE). (2008). What do we know and believe about the roles of methods courses and field experiences in English education? CEE position statements. Retrieved from http://www.ncte.org/cee/positions/roleofmethodsinee

Doerr-Stevens, C., & Woywod, C. (2018). Stepping onto fertile ground: Urban teachers' preparation for interdisciplinary inquiry. *Pedagogies: An International Journal, 13*(2), 169–180. doi:10.1080/1554480X.2018.1463851

Dymoke, S., & Hughes, J. (2009). Using a poetry wiki: How can the medium support preservice teachers of English in their professional learning about writing poetry and teaching poetry writing in a digital age? *English Teaching: Practice and Critique, 8*(3), 91–106.

Ertmer, P. A. (1999). Addressing first- and second-order barriers to change: Strategies for technology integration. *Educational Technology Research and Development, 47*(4), 47–61. doi:10.1007/BF02299597

Ertmer, P. A. (2005). Teacher pedagogical beliefs: The final frontier in our quest for technology integration? *Educational technology research and development, 53*(4), 25–39.

Figg, C., & McCartney, R. (2010). Impacting academic achievement with student learners teaching digital storytelling to others: The ATTTCSE digital video project. *Contemporary Issues in Technology and Teacher Education, 10*(1). Retrieved from http://www.citejournal.org/vol10/iss1/languagearts/article3.cfm

Garcia, A., & Seglem, R. (2013). "That is dope no lie": Supporting adolescent literacy practices through digital partnerships. In P. J. Dunston, S. K. Fullerton, C. C. Bates, P. M. Stecker, M.

W. Cole, A. H. Hall, D. Herro, & K. H. Headley (Eds.), *62nd yearbook of the literacy research association* (pp. 186–198). Altamonte Springs, FL: Literacy Research Association.

George, M., Pope, C., & Reid, L. (2015). Contemporary literacies and technologies in English language arts teacher education: Shift happens! *Contemporary Issues in Technology and Teacher Education, 15*(1), 1–13. Retrieved from http://www.citejournal.org/vol15/iss1/languagearts/article1.cfm

Gorder, L. M. (2008). A study of teacher perceptions of instructional technology integration in the classroom. *Delta Pi Epsilon Journal, 50*(2), 63–76.

Gorgina, D., & Hosford, C. (2008). Higher education faculty perceptions on technology integration and training. *Teaching and Teacher Education,* 25(5), 690–696.

Guzman, A., & Nussbaum, M. (2009). Teaching competencies for technology integration in the classroom. *Journal of Computer Assisted Learning, 25*(5), 453–469.

Hamilton, M., Heydon, R., Hibbert, K., & Stooke, R. (2015). *Negotiating spaces for literacy learning: Multimodality and governmentality*. London: Bloomsbury.

Harris, J., Mishra, P., & Koehler, M. (2009). Teachers' technological pedagogical content knowledge and learning activity types: Curriculum-based technology integration reframed. *Journal of Research on Technology in Education (International Society for Technology in Education), 41*(4), 393–416.

Hawthorne, S., Goodwyn, A., George, M., Reid, L., & Shoffner, M. (2012). The state of English education: Considering possibilities in troubled times. *English Education, 44*(3), 288–311.

Houge, T. T., & Geier, C. (2009). Delivering one-to-one tutoring in literacy via videoconferencing. *Journal of Adolescent and Adult Literacy, 53*, 154–163.

Johnson, L. (2016). Writing 2.0: How English teachers conceptualize writing with digital technologies. *English Education, 49*(2), 28–62.

Kinzer, C. K., & Leander, K. (2003). Technology and the language arts: Implications of an expanded definition of literacy. In J. Flood, D. Lapp, J. R. Squire, and J. M. Jensen (Eds.), *Handbook of research on teaching the English language arts* (pp. 546–565). Mahwah, NJ: Lawrence Erlbaum.

Lai, G., & Calandra, B. (2010). Examining the effects of computer-based scaffolds on novice teachers' reflective journal writing. *Educational Technology Research and Development, 58*, 421–437.

Lee, J., & Young, C. (2010). Building wikis and blogs: Pre-service teacher experiences with web-based collaborative technologies in an interdisciplinary method course. *Then Journal, 287*. Retrieved from http://thenjournal.org/index.php/then/article/view/47

Matthew, K. I., Felvegi, E., & Callaway, R. A. (2009). Wiki as a collaborative learning tool in a language arts methods class. *Journal of Research on Technology in Education, 42*(1), 51–72.

McVee, M. B., Bailey, N. M., & Shanahan, L. E. (2008). Teachers and teacher educators learning from new literacies and new technologies. *Teaching Education, 19*(3), 197–210.

National Council of Teachers of English. (2013). The NCTE definition of 21st century literacies. NCTE position statements. Retrieved from http://www2.ncte.org/statement/21stcent-definition/

National Council of Teachers of English (n.d.a). NCTE/CAEP connection. Retrieved from http://www2.ncte.org/groups/elate/ncte-caep-connection/

National Council of Teachers of English (n.d.b). NCTE policy briefs. Retrieved from http://www2.ncte.org/resources/policy-briefs/

National Council of Teachers of English (n.d.c). NCTE position statements. Retrieved from http://www2.ncte.org/resources/position-statements/all/

Nelson, M. J., Voithofer, R., & Cheng, S. (2019). Mediating factors that influence the technology integration practices of teacher educators. *Computers and Education, 128*, 330–344.

Ortega, L. (2013). Digital practices and literacy identities: Preservice teachers negotiating contradictory discourses of innovation. *Contemporary Issues in Technology and Teacher Education, 13*(4). Retrieved from http://www.citejournal.org/vol13/iss4/languagearts/article1.cfm

Pasternak, D. L. (2007). Is technology used as practice? A survey analysis of preservice English teachers' perceptions and classroom practices. *Contemporary Issues in Technology and Teacher Education, 7*(3). Retrieved from http://www.citejournal.org/volume-7/issue-3-07/english-language-arts/is-technology-used-as-practice-a-survey-analysis-of-preservice-english-teachers-perceptions-and-classroom-practices

Pasternak, D. L., Caughlan, S., Hallman, H., Renzi, L., & Rush, L. (2014). Teaching English language arts methods in the United States: A review of the research. *Review of Education, 2*(2), 146–185.

Pasternak, D. L., Caughlan, S., Hallman, H., Renzi, L., & Rush, L. (2018). *Secondary English teacher education in the United States*. Reinventing Teacher Education. London: Bloomsbury.

Pasternak, D. L., Hallman, H. L., Caughlan, S., Renzi, L., Rush, L. S., & Meineke, H. (2016). Learning and teaching technology in English teacher education: Findings from a national study. *Contemporary Issues in Technology and Teacher Education, 16*(4). Retrieved from http://www.citejournal.org/volume-16/issue-4-16/english-language-arts/learning-and-teaching-technology-in-english-teacher-education-findings-from-a-national-study

Pierson, M. E. (2001). Technology integration practice as a function of pedagogical expertise. *Journal of Research on Computing in Education, 33*(4), 413.

Rust, J. (2017). Pedagogy meets digital media: A tangle of teachers, strategies, and tactics. *Contemporary Issues in Technology and Teacher Education, 17*(2). Retrieved from http://www.citejournal.org/volume-17/issue-2-17/english-language-arts/pedagogy-meets-digital-media-a-tangle-of-teachers-strategies-and-tactics

Rust, J., & Cantwell, D. (2018). No one fits in a box: Preservice teachers' evolving perceptions of self and others. *Contemporary Issues in Technology and Teacher Education, 18*(2), 313–342.

Ryan, J., & Scott, A. (2008). Integrating technology into teacher education: How online discussion can be used to develop informed and critical literacy teachers. *Teaching and Teacher Education, 24*(6), 1635–1644.

Schieble, M., Vetter, A., & Meacham, M. (2015). A discourse analytic approach to video analysis of teaching: Aligning desired identities with practice. *Journal of Teacher Education, 66*, 245–260.

Seo, K. K., Templeton, R., & Pellegrino, D. (2008). Creating a ripple effect: Incorporating multimedia-assisted project-based learning in teacher education. *Theory Into Practice, 47*, 259–265. doi:10.1080/00405840802154062

Shelton, C. (2018). "You have to teach to your personality": Caring, sharing and teaching with technology. *Australasian Journal of Educational Technology, 34*(4), 92–106.

Swenson, J., Young, C. A., McGrail, E., Rozema, R., & Whitin, P. (2006). Extending the conversation: New technologies, new literacies, and English education. *English Education, 38*, 351–369.

Thieman, G. Y. (2008). Using technology as a tool for learning and developing 21st century citizenship skills: An examination of the NETS and technology use by preservice teachers with their K–12 students. *Contemporary Issues in Technology and Teacher Education, 8*(4), 342–366. Retrieved from http://www.citejournal.org/volume-8/issue-4-08/social-studies/using-technology-as-a-tool-for-learning-and-developing-21st-century-citizenship-skills-an-examination-of-the-nets-and-technology-use-by-preservice-teachers-with-their-k-12-students/

U.S. Department of Education, Office of Educational Technology. (2016). Future ready learning: Reimagining the role of technology in education. In *2016 National Technology Plan*. Retrieved from http://tech.ed.gov

Yagelski, R. (2005). Computers, literacy and being: Teaching with technology for a sustainable future. Retrieved from http://www.albany.edu/faculty/rpy95/webtext/

Zoch, M., Myers, J., & Belcher, J. (2016). Teachers' engagement with new literacies: Support for implementing technology in the English/language arts classroom. *Contemporary Issues in Technology and Teacher Education, 17*(1), 25–52.

A Response to Chapter 5

Julie Bell

In reading and discussing Donna L. Pasternak's chapter about technology with her, I discovered three key takeaway points:

1. The way teacher educators integrate technology into English methods courses is uneven across the field.
2. One of the major barriers to incorporating technology in methods courses is teacher educators' (dis)comfort levels in using technology and teaching technology use.
3. One of the major barriers to English teacher candidates implementing technology in practicum field placements is uneven access to technology across schools and districts.

UNEVEN TECHNOLOGY INTEGRATION IN ENGLISH METHODS COURSES

Donna L. Pasternak writes, "[A] disparity of attitudes toward technology and its effect on teaching and learning English has caused *challenges and successes* across the field as future English teachers are educated for 21st-century classrooms" (p. 78, emphasis added). When I asked Pasternak if there have been mostly challenges or successes in English methods technology implementation, she replied, "I think the response has been uneven across teaching and learning." She cited Nelson, Voithofer, and Cheng (2019) as support, whose study revealed uneven technology integration and standards alignment across all disciplines in teacher education.

Pasternak further argued technology must be woven throughout teacher candidates' programs of study, rather than being included in only one (English methods) course. She compared this weaving to other major concepts in teacher education: social justice, literacy learning, and content standards. If candidates encounter any of these concepts in only one course, they are less likely to consider how to implement them in their own teaching.

I suggest another possible barrier to implementation may be that teacher educators model what technology integration could look like, but they do not explicitly call attention to their modeling. Caroline Stewart, a teacher educator and participant in Pasternak's study, said, "We try to demonstrate [a] kind of seamless incorporation of technology, so not to call attention to using Skype, for example, but to use it for . . . interviews with authors in adolescent literature and that kind of thing" (p. 81). While I appreciate Stewart's authentic use of technology, I wonder how likely teacher candidates are to implement based solely on modeling.

INDIVIDUAL TEACHER EDUCATORS' (DIS)COMFORT WITH TECHNOLOGY

For me, one of the most interesting assertions in Pasternak's chapter was about technology *as* content: "It appears that technology not only supports learning the traditional content of English but also *becomes content* when the software or hardware must be learned" (p. 79, emphasis added). Pasternak went on to tell me she thinks this is one of the "most tension producing of the barriers to implementation." Based on Pasternak's (2007) study, she commented that teacher educators must "have the confidence to stumble and 'not know' in front of students." Like any other content (e.g., writing, poetry, and contemporary young adult literature), teacher educators often avoid teaching the unfamiliar.

Pasternak pointed me in the direction of Shelton (2018), who also found technology implementation in higher education was deeply connected to academics' identities. Perhaps not surprisingly, Shelton (2018) concluded academics were less likely to use technology in their teaching if they thought it hindered their "personality" and teaching identity (p. 103). Similar to Pasternak, Shelton also found technology in the classroom could be "associated with feelings of loss of control or authority" by academics (p. 95).

Relinquishing control in the classroom frequently induces discomfort in educators, which may help explain why some teacher educators "ban" technology in their own classrooms but expect candidates to incorporate it into their teaching. Pasternak addressed this irony both in her chapter and in our conversation. We agreed that banning technology likely does a disservice to students who need assistive technology, and it is the teacher's responsibility (preK–12 or higher education) to engage students in the lesson.

UNEVEN ACCESS TO TECHNOLOGY ACROSS SCHOOLS AND DISTRICTS

In our conversation, Pasternak and I acknowledged an assumption some teacher educators and candidates make about urban and rural school districts: They are not investing in technology due to budget constraints. However, as Pasternak asserted, access to technology often has more to do with the climate of the district (and administrators and teachers therein) than it does with the budget. For example, my university partners with a district where nearly 71% of the students are eligible for free or reduced-price lunch (Iowa Department of Education, 2017). At the same time, they are a 1:1 district; every student has a Google Chromebook, and teachers deliver content and interact with students via Google Classroom.

The priority in partnering with local districts must always be the preK–12 students. Consequently, teacher educators have a responsibility to be aware of the technology to which mentor teachers and students in partner districts have access. Beyond awareness, teacher educators may be able to advocate for increasing technology in a district, but only if they and their candidates can articulate specific benefits for students. Also, as with teacher educators, access to technology means nothing if preK–12 teachers do not have professional development to feel comfortable with technology.

FUTURE DIRECTIONS

After my reading of Pasternak's chapter and our conversation, I argue the first step in more even technology implementation in English methods courses must be teacher educators' awareness of the following:

1. How technology is incorporated not only in our own courses but also across teacher candidates' programs of study;
2. Our own (dis)comfort in using technology and teaching technology as content; and
3. Our partner districts' (lack of) access to technology.

Once teacher educators know this information, we may take action to remedy problem areas.

Action may include talking to other teacher educators—those who teach methods and those who do not—and collaborating in ways similar to preK–12 teachers. Action may also include seeking out professional development, consulting with technology experts in Colleges of Education or across campus, or positioning our teacher candidates as experts in technology as content. Finally, action may include following a partner district's lead by teaching candidates about technology available at a particular school, or even finding grants to assist in implementing technology in ways beneficial to teacher candidates, teachers, and preK–12 students alike.

REFERENCES

Iowa Department of Education. (2017). 2016–17 Iowa Public School K–12 students eligible for free and reduced-price lunch by district. Retrieved from https://educateiowa.gov/documents/district-frl/2018/08/2016-17-iowa-public-school-k-12-students-eligible-free-and-reduced

Nelson, M. J., Voithofer, R., & Cheng, S. (2019). Mediating factors that influence the technology integration practices of teacher educators. *Computers and Education, 128*, 330–344.

Pasternak, D. L. (2007). Is technology used as practice? A survey analysis of preservice English teachers' perceptions and classroom practices. *Contemporary Issues in Technology and Teacher Education, 7*(3). Retrieved from http://www.citejournal.org/volume-7/issue-3-07/english-language-arts/is-technology-used-as-practice-a-survey-analysis-of-preservice-english-teachers-perceptions-and-classroom-practices

Shelton, C. (2018). "You have to teach to your personality": Caring, sharing and teaching with technology. *Australasian Journal of Educational Technology, 34*(4), 92–106.

Chapter Six

"We Need to Go Next Door and Talk About Our Lessons"

One State's Context and Collaboration Around Standards-Based Reform

Lara Searcy and Christian Z. Goering

Imagine the following scenario: teacher educators are educated at various places around the country—such as the University of Georgia, Michigan State University, and the University of Wisconsin—to get faculty jobs, to teach courses including the methods course, and to conduct research. These instructors who teach teacher educators have attracted doctoral candidates from around the country and, to a lesser extent, around the world. These doctoral candidates are inculcated with a national and international view of the education of teachers and scholars, go out on the job market, and get plopped down in the middle of states around the country, many times with no previous experience in that state, to teach that state's future English teachers.

What if, for instance, a teacher educator educated outside of the borders of the state of Oklahoma was plopped down to begin a career in the Sooner State—a unique situation considering its state-specific preK–12 academic standards and teacher licensure exams? Where would this person find the support to understand teaching in their new home?

This chapter problematizes just this situation: how a new teacher educator from one state learns to understand what state-dependent teacher preparation looks like. While this chapter focuses on the challenges of teaching the methods course in the state of Oklahoma, commentary deeply examines how important contextual factors are in educating teachers and future teacher educators.

RESEARCH BACKGROUND

Students in today's public school classrooms have been under the influence of educational reform their entire school career—from *A Nation at Risk* (1983) to Goals 2000, No Child Left Behind (2001), and the Common Core State Standards (2010). As Taubman (2010) states, the effects of these top-down educational policies not only affect students but also greatly affect educators: they inform our teaching practices, constrict our daily life in schools, and influence how and what we think and do in the classroom, how we spend our professional time, how we are evaluated, and ultimately the meaning of our work.

Therefore, it is important to understand how government policies, such as standards-based reform, are enacted in practice (Brennan, Ellis, Maguire, & Smagorinsky, 2018), and why getting context specific—in this chapter's case, the state of Oklahoma—provides a more narrow focus of how the discipline of English education is taught. English teacher educators, according to Smagorinsky and Whiting's (1995) seminal work, *How English Teachers Get Taught*, need to examine, identify, and reflect on the qualities of their content methods course that are context dependent.

Using a collective case study with six Oklahoma secondary English language arts methods course instructors (four instructors from public institutes and two instructors from private, not-for-profit institutes), the findings described here answer the call put forth by the Reinventing Teacher Education series editors (Brennan et al., 2018) that there is "value in replicating the design of the [CEE Methods Commission National Study *Secondary English Teacher Education in the United States* (2018)] in other domains of teacher education, by providing important baseline studies and opportunities for comparative teacher education research" (p. vii).

The following descriptions examine how (if at all) six English teacher educators in Oklahoma are reshaping their methods course in response to curricular and political challenges. These curricular and political challenges, however, are emblematic of what teacher educators in general contend with as they design methods courses to best support teacher candidates and can be applied to states "next door."

CONTENT: SECONDARY ENGLISH METHODS COURSE

It is in the secondary English methods course where teacher candidates should practice, reflect, and grow in their instructional practices as well as discuss the realities and constraints teachers will face in schools, or in a state (Pasternak, Caughlan, Hallman, Renzi, & Rush, 2018). This content and pedagogical knowledge about what English teacher candidates should know and be able to do informs the discussion of how teacher candidates engage in meaningful, theoretically motivated, and important learning (Smagorinsky & Whiting, 1995). However, when content is affected by context—for example, state-specific content standards—there is a considerable amount of time, energy, and effort spent adhering to educational policies that promote preparing teachers for a single state.

In today's 21st-century classroom, standards and assessment are influential areas, so the focus on the inclusion and alignment of state standards and state licensure in English methods courses recognizes the importance of how policy documents affect English teacher education, for better or worse (Pasternak et al., 2014; Pasternak et al., 2018). Therefore, knowing state context can provide insight into the tensions that often influence the content taught in a course.

CONTEXT: OKLAHOMA

Tensions, such as Oklahoma's "claim that the federal government was using the *Common Core State Standards* to undermine local school control" (Feemster, 2015), provided the reason for Oklahoma's repeal of the Common Core State Standards (CCSS) in June 2014. Oklahoma first adopted the CCSS in June 2010, supported them with a 4-year transition plan, and was prepared for full implementation in fall 2014. However, "propelled by a national wave of local-control school politics and accusations that the Obama administration was guilty of federal overreach in education," Oklahoma sought to ensure that their state values were represented in the standards process (Feemster, 2015). In addition, Oklahoma has a unique political context since it is ranked 49th in the nation in teacher pay and has the highest budget cuts in the nation for public education.

The six instructors of the research study were aware of these challenges, and they seemed to be proactively engaged in creating action plans to address the changing dynamic of teacher education in the state. As one instructor stated, "The severe reduction in pay and inequality of pay between Oklahoma and other states have been enough [for some candidates] to rethink education as a major because they don't think they can make a livable wage from it." Therefore, it is becoming common that there is a pipeline of Oklahoma-educated teachers going to different states once they graduate college (Hardiman, 2017). If this is true, then there needs to be collaboration with teacher education programs within the state and with states "next door" since the domain of English education needs to learn how to address emerging challenges of preparing teachers for classrooms in a national context (Smagorinsky, 2018, p. xii).

THE ROLE OF STANDARDS

Those who prepare English teacher candidates need to understand how to design a methods course that prepares English teacher candidates for a changing world that includes curricular and political challenges (Caughlan et al., 2017). Curricular changes include states' development of their own K–12 standards and assessments, and political changes include accountability measures that challenge the efficacy of traditional programs of teacher certification (Caughlan et al., 2017).

Political changes ultimately affect curricular decisions since "top-down educational policies" seek to reform teacher preparation as a means of strengthening our educational system (Brass & Webb, 2015, p. vii; NCTQ, 2014). One such reform involves standards, and according to *The State of State English Standards* report (2005), standards are "the most powerful engine for education improvement currently operating in the United States, and all part of that undertaking—including teacher preparation—is supposed to be aligned with a state's standards" (Stotsky, 2005, p. 6).

The CEE Methods Commission National Study *Secondary English Teacher Education in the United States* (2018) conducted by Pasternak, Caughlan, Hallman, Renzi, and Rush, with data collection from 2011 to 2015, examines how teacher candidates are prepared in K–12 content standards, especially when most teacher candidates today have gone through their school experiences under such mandates (p. 68). Ninety-nine percent of respondents reported addressing K–12 content standards in their program (with 45.50% reporting they are addressed "in the English methods course" and 44.83% reporting "throughout coursework"), yet despite a seemingly "universal inclusion of standards as a topic in methods course, it's even more interesting that so little has been said about the place of standards in teacher preparation in the English teacher education research literature" (Caughlan et al., 2017, p. 287). Therefore, the role standards play—both in one state's secondary English methods courses and nationally—is pertinent to the field of English education because "employers want to know how [candidates] can teach to standards [and] the state regulators want to know how [candidates] can create standards-based assignments, and so on" (Pasternak et al., 2018, p. 68).

Most of the six instructors of secondary English methods course in Oklahoma, when asked, "What is your understanding of how the English language arts methods course should prepare teacher candidates to address the content standards in their teaching?" noted that candidates needed an initial awareness to the standards, "to be able to speak the language," because they "are a significant statement" that is "appropriate for early career teachers and are a guideline for teacher candidates." As one instructor replied, "I can say, 'these are our expectations,' and this is what you need to know. And then eventually, I can share with them that theoretical piece."

For other instructors, the timing of when to introduce the standards affects the role they place on them in the course. "I [the instructor] have internalized standards, and maybe it informs the instructional choices, sequence, and material selections, but in that class, I don't make it specific. For many of the students it's their first class just wrapping their minds around teaching students who don't like to read and write. What does that look like? What are you going to do?" Therefore, for most of the instructors in the research study, the standards get an introduction and are required for creating lesson plans, but after that, they may implicitly guide the course with intentional focus but are not an explicit element.

This echoes results from the CEE Methods National Study (Pasternak et al., 2018) where standards may be seen as a part of curricular and political aspects in the methods course, but they run parallel to the knowledge about English language arts and do not need to be explicitly referenced in such discussions (Pasternak et al., 2018, p. 69).

For Oklahoma in particular, critical orientation and discussions about the Oklahoma Academic Standards for English Language Arts (OAS-ELA) may be more prevalent than in other states because of its unique standards adoption timeline from 2010 to 2016 that involved adopting the Common Core State Standards (CCSS) in 2010, planning for full implementation in August 2014, but repealing it in June 2014. Because of this adoption timeline, it was important to ask the six methods course instructors, "What challenges, if any, has your course faced due to the standards/expectations constantly changing (particularly during the 2010–2016 timeline)?" Five instructors responded that it had not really affected their course, and two instructors started their position of teaching the secondary English methods course right when the new standards were implemented. In general, many echoed the approach "that we should be doing our jobs in how to write good lesson plans that will meet any set of academic standards."

This understanding of the critical orientation and role standards play in the content course exceeds the statistics from the most recent CEE Methods National Study (Pasternak et al., 2018) where only a small number of English methods instructors approach the standards critically by providing a critical orientation of the sociohistorical or political context of standards (Pasternak et al., 2018; Caughlan et al., 2017). When asked, "How do you include a critical orientation to the standards? And if you don't, why?" five of the six instructors stated that they do include a critical orientation discussing the standards—with the one that does not stating, "I don't think we really do and I'm not sure why." One instructor who does provide critical orientation stated that "discussion is both practical (how) but also critical (why? why these standards?)," and another stated, "We discuss the strengths and weaknesses of the standards." However, some mentioned that the discussion may only cover a class period early in the semester.

Similarly, when asked the question posed by the CEE Methods National Study (Pasternak et al., 2018), "How do you have candidates compare different standards (e.g., their state standards with those of other states or with the NCTE or INTASC standards)?" only two instructors have candidates consider which assignments from this course and previous courses align with specific standards, or they have informal discussions about the standards. However, the other instructors address that this may be happening in other education coursework.

Similarly, as one instructor addresses, "we're asking [candidates] to do the alignment. So on their lesson plan, they say here is my focus OAS standard. They could easily say here is my focus CCSS. And then after, they could include other standards tangentially. Then their student outcomes have to be aligned to those standards, and then the assessments and activities have to be aligned to [Depth of Knowledge]." By discussing the role policy documents, such as standards, play in a course's design, candidates gain their own expectations about what they "should know and be able to do." Candidates need "opportunities to disrupt their 'acceptance' of state standards," and they can do so by providing a critical orientation—comparing state and national standards and discussing the origin of standards and the somewhat ambivalent attitude many English educators in the United States have about standards-based teaching (Pasternak et al., 2018, pp. 68–69).

Three of the instructors who are familiar with both the CCSS and OAS-ELA standards specifically discussed the organization of the standards and admitted that "the [OAS-ELA] are organized in a more helpful way [than the CCSS], which makes it easier to discuss how to implement them. They are certainly easier to teach, in my opinion, from CCSS and how it was organized based on experience in teaching in [another state]." For example, the OAS-ELA standards are organized by eight overarching standards, and each standard reflects both reading and writing applications: (1) Speaking and Listening, (2) Reading and Writing Process, (3) Critical Reading and Writing, (4) Vocabulary, (5) Language, (6) Research, (7) Multimodal Literacies, and (8) Independent Reading and Writing.

According to the Oklahoma State Department of Education, the new standards are organized in a way that promotes independent, critical readers and writers where skills easily transfer to civic engagement and citizen participation (OSDE, 2015b). As noted by the instructors, understanding "the purpose of standards and how to use them flexibly and with purpose, and reflection on their own experiences with standards-based schooling" provides additional questions about the teaching of English language arts (Pasternak et al., 2018, p. 84).

Regarding the newly created OAS-ELA, many of the instructors stated that they were involved in creating or adopting the new standards, so they were able to provide anecdotal background about the process during standards discussions. This is a unique difference for the state compared to the national CCSS since the OAS have been branded "for Oklahoma by Oklahomans" and included a more democratic process in their creation and adoption. Therefore, when asked, "How does your English methods course, if at all, address and incorporate STATE (OAS-ELA) standards?" all instructors answered with some type of activity, such as developing lessons and a unit, scaffolding instruction, studying a grade level, and using them to create rubrics.

One instructor, in particular, addressed that "now that the new OAS standards are being consistently used in the state for—what is this—year two of full implementation—that is definitely helping methods classes have an anchor text." This shows that most Oklahoma English teacher educators are aware of the new standards and are emphasizing one of the five new influential areas in English methods classes: K–12 content standards and assessments, according to the CEE Methods National Study (Pasternak et al., 2018).

However, Oklahoma's state-specific standards do create potential for being excluded from more nationally created resources and conversations. As one instructor mentioned, "We often have to discuss Common Core because our course text only references those standards," and as another instructor shared, "I think [having our own set of standards] is a challenge because it makes Oklahoma feel 'special' and 'different,' which makes it difficult to find a methods book—so I end up talking to them about CCSS, and I say, 'Even if you go to Texas, you're not going to have Common Core.'" Overall, many of the instructors agreed that not being in a Common Core state may be "bothersome but not a huge deal" because "standards are standards—a verb changes here, a clause changes here . . . , but they are embedded and implied in the practices we've been using for years."

Collectively, then, an understanding of how the six English language arts methods course instructors are preparing teacher candidates to address the content standards in Oklahoma is by "teaching them how to write a lesson in a unit plan and how to organize the information they want to teach their students—which in turn means they are going to be meeting the standards." This understanding shows alignment to the National Council of Teachers of English's (NCTE) position statement "What Do We Know and Believe About the Roles of Methods Courses and Field Experiences in English Education?" which states that the methods course needs to "incorporate state and locally established standards and guidelines for the English language arts into units and lessons that reflect such interconnectedness because a knowledge of broad national and state standards should inform—but not limit—the content, processes, and skills addressed in both unit and daily instructional plans" (NCTE, 2005b).

Curricular and Political Challenges

To better understand how English teacher educators are navigating curricular and political changes, it is important to examine "how the secondary English methods course, if at all, has changed due to curricular and political challenges (educational policies)." Because Oklahoma is ranked 49th in the nation in teacher pay and has the highest budget cuts in the nation for public education, there are many challenges teacher education programs currently face due to an overall decreased enrollment in teacher preparation programs (OSSBA, 2016).

Oklahoma is also facing a dire teacher shortage with recent surveys showing many qualified teachers (approximately 383 teachers per month) either leaving the state or the profession (OEA, 2017). This creates a state problem because when "teachers resign, institutional memory is lost, and ties to the community, [or state,] weaken" (Goldstein, 2014, p. 251). In a survey of more than 250 former Oklahoma teachers, "about 133 teachers [53%] reported moving to Texas, and 52 more [21%] went to another neighboring state" (Hardiman, 2017).

When asked why they left and how much the pay difference was, the respondents were "collectively making $4.5 million more in their new state than they did in Oklahoma" (Cullen, 2017; Hardiman, 2017). This creates tensions because "about 48 percent of those leaving have a master's degree which makes them among the most educated, and potentially highest earning Oklahoma teachers, and we're replacing them with people who are emergency certified and have no training in education" (Cullen, 2017; Hardiman, 2017).

So poor compensation, combined with budget cuts and other challenges, have caused many qualified Oklahoma teachers to look for teaching work elsewhere, and "as these well-prepared teachers leave, our state is forced to fill many of their jobs with emergency certified personnel without specific training or experience in education" (Cullen, 2017). For example, "50,000 Oklahoma kids are in classrooms with emergency teachers, with 90 emergency teaching certificates issued every month" (OEA, 2017). This means that "in 2016, 1,500 Oklahoma classrooms were led by either a long-term substitute teacher or a teacher without proper training and qualifications" (OEA, 2017). In 2017, the number of emergency certifications continued to increase with 1,429 approved by the Oklahoma State Department of Education, whereas 5 years ago, the state issued only 32 emergency teaching certificates in a year (Eger, 2017). The effect of these numbers forces many schools to be "reliant on filling vacancies with teachers who are not yet qualified because they have not yet completed the state's requirements for either a traditional or alternative certification" (Eger, 2017).

As the research participants echoed, this is a pertinent concern not only for their English teacher candidates but also for the future of education in the state, and many are proactively seeking ways to recruit and retain qualified teachers and train those who are alternatively qualified. This provides additional opportunities for research because "there is little, if any, research about the subject-specific content and pedagogical preparation candidates receive in the plethora of alternative certification/licensure programs that operate in various contexts across the country" (NCTE, 2005a).Therefore, the need for qualified teachers is a pertinent issue in Oklahoma, and it provides a critical context to examine how one state's English teacher candidates are prepared when many leave to teach "next door."

POTENTIAL DRAWBACKS OF SINGLE-STATE PREPARATION

When asked, "What are the potential benefits and drawbacks of an Oklahoma-only education system for candidates who may or may not plan to teach in Oklahoma?" many instructors saw this to be a relevant question to their teacher candidates because they are indeed looking to other states upon graduation, even for their clinical field experience internships. Due to this, collaborations with states "next door" can provide easier reciprocity if they do use "national" standards where "assumptions and expectations are clear across the states," as the CCSS sought to accomplish (Pasternak et al., 2018, p. 73). Unfortunately, for Oklahoma, who adopted their own state-specific K–12 content standards and teacher licensure exams, reciprocity isn't as easy and has presented many drawbacks.

Drawbacks in the form of having state-specific teacher licensure exams include the potential of having to take additional teacher licensure exams based on state requirements, pending a review of out-of-state test(s) for comparability. For example, Texas also uses a different state-specific state licensure exam, and two bordering states, Missouri and Arkansas, use the Praxis Subject and Content Knowledge for Teaching Assessments. However, Oklahoma uses the Oklahoma Subject Area Test (OSAT), which is similar to the Praxis in that they both assess content and content pedagogical knowledge. As one instructor lamented, "The Praxis is a perfectly fine thing, and we don't have to spend taxpayers' money developing our own [assessment], like the English OSAT. . . . We have been fairly exclusive by limiting the tests and the standards in that way." Therefore, in having state-specific licensure, Oklahoma may be creating additional challenges in already low teacher retention, recruitment, and attrition by using a different system of requirements.

When asked about the benefits of having an "Oklahoma-only education system," the responses were clear: "Benefits? I don't know. I don't see any evident benefits"; "It makes no sense to me that we think we are so different"; and "Um, well, no." Upon elaboration on the topic, one instructor reflected that one benefit might be "if they [Oklahoma teacher education graduates] are staying in state, it builds in them a strong understanding of who their learners are."

NEXT STEPS: COLLABORATE AND "GO NEXT DOOR"

So how are English teacher educators in Oklahoma working together to provide opportunities for meaningful change to occur in how English teacher candidates are prepared, especially in response to its unique political challenges? A few Oklahoma English education educators have begun the development of a community to positively respond to change, such as addressing teacher recruitment and retention through the "Open Your Arms and Teach in Oklahoma" campaign, started in summer 2017: "We tried to get the English educators together. I think we could communicate better. The problem is that when everyone is just in their own institutions, we don't know what the others are doing. We could be gaining so many ideas. Learn from each other's experiences and adjust our different focuses and our different strengths."

Similarly, "we don't know what the others [states] are doing. Just like practicing teachers, we need to go next door and talk about our lessons," so going "next door" to other states is also important to the continued exploration of "challenges posed by standards" (Searcy, 2018, p. vii). Hence, next steps should include sharing evidence from one's own institution with others (among the state and nation) to create teacher educator partnerships in order for English teacher educators to expand the description of English teacher education to meaningful, theoretically motivated, and critical conversations about program development, especially in response to educational reforms. Research that is shared with other professionals through scholarship or through collaborative arrangements "contributes to a deeper understanding of curricula and processes in English education programs and supports the profession's ability to meet broader goals" (NCTE, 2005a).

Creating a collective network promotes advocacy because educators need to be at the forefront of conversations about change, curriculum, and instruction work—especially about how students meet the standards and accomplish what they should know and be able to do (Applebee, 2013). To be part of the conversation, educators need background about the history of curricular and political reforms, and they need to present specific examples and narrative from their classrooms describing the impact of such decisions.

Though standards-based reform has not yet ended any debates on how to best support students' learning, especially in the field of English language arts, they have provided urgency and focus, especially in Oklahoma, on the topic of "what students should know and be able to do" (Pasternak et al., 2014). This urgency and focus, then, must spur continued collaboration because cultivating collaborative cultures is key to any transformation or change. People are motivated to change if meaningful work can be done in collaboration with others (Fullan, 2016). This is why the field of English education, which is positioned between theory and practice, must open the dialogue between educators and other stakeholders in order to enact meaningful change in education reform (Alsup, Emig, Pradl, Tremmel, & Yagelski, 2006).

Teachers must be at the center of the conversation and collaborate during any reform process, as many Oklahomans were asked to do during the drafting of the Oklahoma Academic Standards. English teacher educators, in particular, must assume leadership roles and heighten their own political awareness and activity in educational policy in order to model and encourage preservice teachers and in-service teachers to understand those roles as part of their professional responsibility (Alsup et al., 2006). Returning to the concept that English educators are mostly prepared in contexts that aren't the same as where they teach, focusing preparation on the skills necessary to gain understanding—by looking all around any given state or context—is as important of a skill set as one can gain.

REFERENCES

Alsup, J., Emig, J., Pradl, G., Tremmel, R., & Yagelski, R. (2006). The state of English education and a vision for its future: A call to arms. *English Education, 38*(4), 278–294.

Applebee, A. N. (2013). Common Core State Standards: The promise and peril in a national palimpsest. *English Journal, 103*(1), 25–33.

Brass, J., & Webb, A. (2015). *Reclaiming English language arts methods courses: Critical issues and challenges for teacher educators in top-down times.* New York: Routledge.

Brennan, M., Ellis, V., Maguire, M., & Smagorinsky, P. (2018). Series editors' preface. In D. L. Pasternak, S. Caughlan, H. Hallman, L. Renzi, & L. Rush, *Secondary English teacher education in the United States* (Reinventing Teacher Education, pp. vi–vii). London: Bloomsbury.

Caughlan, S., Pasternak, D. L., Hallman, H. L., Renzi, L., Rush, L. S., & Frisby, M. (2017, April). How English language arts teachers are prepared for twenty-first century classrooms: Results of a national study. *English Education, 49*, 265–297. Retrieved from http://www.ncte.org/library/NCTEFiles/Resources/Journals/EE/0493-apr2017/EE0493How.pdf

Common Core State Standards Initiative. (2016). About the standards. Retrieved from http://www.corestandards.org/about-the-standards/

Cullen, T. A. (2017, August 19). Theresa A. Cullen: Teachers are leaving Oklahoma, and we must act now. *Tulsa World.* Retrieved from https://www.tulsaworld.com/opinion/opinion-featured/theresa-a-cullen-teachers-are-leaving-oklahoma-and-we-must/article_b0c2a94a-38a9-5223-82bf-75f1654954a7.html

Eger, A. (2017, August 24). Teacher shortage: Oklahoma hits record for emergency certifications after just 3 months. *Tulsa World.* Retrieved from http://www.tulsaworld.com/news/

education/teacher-shortage-oklahoma-hits-record-for-emergency-certifications-after-just/article_63d0250f-1530-56d6-937e-d45ef4410eb5.html

Feemster, R. (2015, April 13). Gone but not forgotten? Common Core lingers after Oklahoma's repeal. Retrieved from http://hechingerreport.org/gone-but-not-forgotten-common-core-lingers-after-oklahomas-repeal/

Fullan, M. (2016). *The meaning of educational change (5th ed.)*. New York: Teachers College Press.

Goldstein, D. (2014). *The teacher wars: A history of America's most embattled profession*. New York: Anchor Books.

Hardiman, S. (2017, October 7). Teachers who leave Oklahoma make $19,000 more on average, OU researcher finds. Retrieved from http://www.tulsaworld.com/news/education/teachers-who-leave-oklahoma-make-more-on-average-ou-researcher/article_922ac5ac-842a-5cbd-b313-dfacfb77c4c0.html

National Council of Teachers of English (NCTE). (2005a). Program assessment in English education: Belief statements and recommendations. Retrieved from http://www.ncte.org/cee/positions/programassessment

National Council of Teachers of English (NCTE). (2005b, July 31). What do we know and believe about the roles of methods courses and field experiences in English education? Retrieved from http://www2.ncte.org/statement/roleofmethodsinee/

National Council of Teachers of English (NCTE). (2006). Guidelines for the preparation of teachers of English language arts. Retrieved from http://www.ncte.org/library/NCTEFiles/Groups/CEE/NCATE/Guidelines_for_Teacher_Prep_2006.pdf

National Council on Teacher Quality (NCTQ). (2014). *2014 Teacher Prep Review: A review of the nation's teacher preparation programs*. Retrieved from http://www.nctq.org/dmsView/Teacher_Prep_Review_2014_Report

Oklahoma Education Association (OEA). (2017). Join the fight for funding in Oklahoma. Retrieved from http://fightforfunding.org/learn-more

Oklahoma State Department of Education (OSDE). (2015a). Drafting Oklahoma standards. Retrieved from http://ok.gov/sde/newstandards

Oklahoma State Department of Education (OSDE). (2015b). *Eight overarching English language arts standards in reading and writing*. Retrieved from http://ok.gov/sde/sites/ok.gov.sde/files/documents/files/2.Eight_.is_.great_.overview.pdf

Oklahoma State Department of Education (OSDE). (2015c). Writing of new Oklahoma academic standards English language arts: 2015 frequently asked questions and answers guide. Retrieved from http://ok.gov/sde/sites/ok.gov.sde/files/6-30-15%20ELAOAS%20FAQs.pdf

Oklahoma State School Boards Association (OSSBA). (2016). 2016 OSSBA teacher shortage survey. Retrieved from http://www.ossba.org/wp-content/uploads/2016/08/2016-OSSBA-Teacher-Shortage-Report.pdf

Pasternak, D. L., Caughlan, S., Hallman, H., Renzi, L., & Rush, L. (2014). Teaching English language arts methods in the United States: A review of the research. *Review of Education, 2*(2), 146–185. doi:10.1002/rev3.3031

Pasternak, D. L., Caughlan, S., Hallman, H., Renzi, L., & Rush, L. (2018). *Secondary English teacher education in the United States*. Reinventing Teacher Education. London: Bloomsbury.

Searcy, L. E. (2018). How do English teacher educators in Oklahoma utilize the secondary English methods course to prepare English teacher candidates for today's classroom? *Theses and Dissertations, 2697*. Retrieved from http://scholarworks.uark.edu/etd/2697

Smagorinsky, P. (2018). Foreword. In D. L. Pasternak, S. Caughlan, H. Hallman, L. Renzi, & L. Rush, *Secondary English teacher education in the United States* (Reinventing Teacher Education, pp. viii–xii). London: Bloomsbury.

Smagorinsky, P., & Whiting, M. E. (1995). *How English teachers get taught: Methods of teaching the methods class*. Urbana, IL: National Councils of Teachers of English.

Stotsky, S. (2005, January). *The state of state English standards*. Retrieved from http://files.eric.ed.gov/fulltext/ED485523.pdf

Taubman, P. M. (2010). *Teaching by numbers: Deconstructing the discourse of standards and accountability in education*. Florence, KY: Taylor and Francis.

A Response to Chapter 6

Jessica Gallo

As an English educator, I have noticed a common thread that runs through my students' responses when it comes to thinking about the role of standards in their teaching. Despite my work to instill in them the conviction that they are (or will be) powerful, agentic, and knowledgeable experts in how best to teach English, the teacher candidates in my methods classes often feel they are at the mercy of external forces when it comes to the curriculum they will teach in their classrooms. They know the power of standards to guide and shape their curriculum, yet they feel powerless to change those standards in any way. I feel this sense of resignation acutely; I want them to deeply understand the standards so they can implement them with ease and confidence. At the same time, I want them to be critical consumers of this and all education mandates so they can be (and choose to be) part of the conversation about educational reform rather than passive recipients of it.

I know that English teacher educators across the country feel this ambivalence too. Lara Searcy and Christian Z. Goering's chapter, "'We Need to Go Next Door and Talk About Our Lessons': One State's Context and Collaboration Around Standards-Based Reform," shines a bright light on these tensions that English educators experience in preparing teacher candidates to understand and implement state standards. In focusing on Oklahoma, a state that adopted and then repealed implementation of the Common Core State Standards in favor of creating a set of standards unique to Oklahoma, the authors highlight the challenge of creating methods courses that are at once responsive to state-specific ideals and to the possibility that the teacher candidates will choose another state in which to teach. Additionally, Searcy and Goering's work demonstrates that English educators must be cognizant and strategic in teaching standards because of the real possibility that those standards will change with the next round of education reform.

More than just a call for increased networking among English educators, Searcy and Goering's work demonstrates how English educators are enacting the important recommendations of the 2005 Conference on English Education (CEE, now ELATE) Leadership and Policy Summit (Alsup, Emig, Pradl, Tremmel, & Yagelski, 2006). The Oklahoma English educators in Chapter 6 are doing work that is powerful in two ways.

First, collaboration among English teacher educators stimulates an environment in which we can better understand the diversity of our field. As Alsup et al. (2006) point out, "The very richness of content, context, and process in the discipline of English Education certainly poses a challenge for us to stay abreast of the knowledge proliferating in all quarters, but this in turn often leaves us split among competing identities" (p. 279). Following Searcy and Goering's work then, English educators who collaborate across state lines about how we teach standards in methods classes can share innovative practices for helping teacher candidates develop the capacity to critique the standards as well as to use them with facility regardless of their state context.

Second, Searcy and Goering urge English educators to connect with colleagues in other contexts as a way to move toward a critical advocacy stance. Cathy Fleischer (2016), in "Everyday Advocacy: The New Professionalism for Teachers," encourages teachers to be "everyday advocates," those "teachers who integrate an advocacy stance into their very busy daily routines and who, by doing so, play an important role in changing the narrative about teachers and teaching" (p. 19). While Fleischer's work focuses on classroom teachers, English educators have an important role to play in everyday advocacy too. As Searcy and Goering suggest, "English teacher educators, in particular, must assume leadership roles and heighten their own political awareness and activity in educational policy in order to model and encourage preservice teachers and in-service teachers to understand those roles as part of their professional responsibility" (p. 105).

Taking this recommendation a step further, English educators can unite to amplify the voices of English teachers in conversations about education reform. Because we are in the particular position of working closely with classroom teachers while also studying and creating theory and research, we can provide cover for English teachers who are doing the work in their classrooms while also advocating for change for those teachers.

There are teacher educators who are already doing this work through organizations like ELATE. ELATE (English Language Arts Teacher Educators, formerly CEE) provides opportunities for advocacy and action through collaboration. A core value of ELATE's 2017 position statement provides guidance: "As English language arts teacher educators, we serve as leaders in and advocates for the field in order to address educational issues, heighten political awareness, and contribute to educational policy at the local, state, and national levels" (Shoffner et al., 2017). ELATE is not just about networking. ELATE is charged with transforming productive, collaborative conversations into action and advocacy beyond the organization.

The English educators in Searcy and Goering's study know we can't continue to go it alone when it comes to preparing English teachers to use standards in their teaching. Instead, they argue for cross-state collaboration and advocacy in order to better understand the many roles of standards in teachers' practice and to become more powerful advocates in conversations about educational reform. To do this, English educators can work back and forth between helping future English teachers become everyday advocates and being advocates ourselves. This means explicitly teaching our English education students about how to advocate for their work (see Fleischer's Everyday Advocacy site at https://everydayadvocacy.org/forteachereducators).

At the same time, English educators must collaborate, as Searcy and Goering suggest, with the explicit, stated purpose of developing advocacy projects. For some English educators, this might take the form of active participation in state-level service, such as the Oklahoma English educators' work to develop new standards. For others, this advocacy work might take the form of writing opinion pieces or editorials for local, state, or national newspapers to increase public awareness about what English teachers know and do. For all of us, becoming English educator advocates requires more connection, collaboration, and targeted action. Together, English educators have a vast and varied understanding of English as a field in classrooms and universities, and it is well past time to transform that understanding to public- and policy-level action.

REFERENCES

Alsup, J., Emig, J., Pradl, G., Tremmel, R., & Yagelski, R. P. (2006). The state of English education and a vision for its future: A call to arms. *English Education, 38*(4), 278–294.

Fleischer, C. (2016). Everyday advocacy: The new professionalism for teachers. *Voices From the Middle, 24*(1), 19–23.

Fleischer, C. (2018). For teacher educators. Everyday Advocacy: Changing the Narrative About Literacy Education. Retrieved from https://everydayadvocacy.org/forteachereducators/

Shoffner, M., Alsup, J., Garcia, A., Haddix, M., Moore, M., Morrell, E., Schaafsma, D., & Zuidema, L. A. (2017, November 30). What is English language arts teacher education? National Council of Teachers of English. CEE position statement. Retrieved from http://www2.ncte.org/statement/whatiselateachereducation/

Chapter Seven

Making Video Recording and Reflection Meaningful for English Teacher Candidates

Julie Bell

One source of tension for teacher educators is making university assignments meaningful for teacher candidates (TCs), while also meeting accreditation requirements and teaching standards. Included in this tension is TCs' desire to engage in the "practical" (i.e., field experiences), as opposed to "theoretical" (i.e., methods courses; Whitney, Olan, & Fredricksen, 2013). Providing TCs opportunities to try practices in the field and reflect on these practices is crucial to candidates operationalizing such practices in the future (Grossman et al., 2009).

Teacher educators requiring TCs to videotape and analyze their teaching has increased over the past 40 years (Erickson, 2007) in an attempt to link theory and practice and gather data related to teacher preparation program outcomes. Video is used to combat the fallibility of TCs' memories of teaching (Gelfuso & Dennis, 2017) and to easily share their teaching. The ubiquity of mobile devices has made capturing teaching easier than ever, but such facility also necessitates careful thought about the purposes and intended outcomes of TCs recording teaching.

For candidates to find meaning in videotaping and reflecting, I recommend the following: (a) Time must be spent on logistical aspects of recording; (b) TCs need a common definition of *reflection*; (c) TCs should select their own focus for videotaping with guidance to focus on English-specific content and practices; (d) TCs need multiple opportunities to record within English education contexts; and (e) TCs should share their videos and reflections with audiences beyond English teacher educators.

In this chapter, I elaborate on how the aforementioned tension manifested itself at both a previous and a current university. I describe a theory-research practice cycle I undertook to address this tension and close with considerations about using video for English teacher educators.

ITERATIONS OF THE VIDEO ASSIGNMENT AT A PREVIOUS UNIVERSITY

Prior to teaching the English methods course at my previous university, TCs were required to videotape themselves to reflect on teaching dialogically (Juzwik, Sherry, Caughlan, Heintz, & Borsheim-Black, 2012). Through a process teacher educators called video-based response and revision, TCs recorded themselves teaching four lessons (20 minutes or longer) during their yearlong teaching internships. They transcribed and shared 5-minute video clips with a small group of peers via VoiceThread. As a culminating assignment, TCs individually created digital reflections on the growth of their abilities in dialogic instruction (Juzwik et al., 2012).

Within a few years, a secondary purpose of the video assignment was to introduce TCs to teacher inquiry, using video as data. While TCs conducted inquiries in previous iterations of the course, their inquiries did not include video. This shift was made to streamline course assignments and make them more meaningful for TCs. The other three video recordings remained the same, with TCs uploading their clips to Vimeo, a video-sharing platform similar to YouTube where TCs also commented on each other's videos.

At that time, requirements of the inquiry project included TCs developing research questions about their teaching with their instructor's assistance, reading journal articles or books about their topics, and revising their teaching based on their reading. TCs also used their fourth video recordings to gather inquiry data. Finally, they reported their findings to colleagues, mentors, and teacher educators in a conference-style presentation.

SUMMARY OF AN EXPLORATORY CASE STUDY AT A PREVIOUS UNIVERSITY

I conducted an exploratory case study (Streb, 2010) on using video in an English methods course. See Textbox 7.1 for an explanation of the impetus of the study.

TEXTBOX 7.1. IMPETUS FOR STUDY

When I undertook this study, I was a novice researcher and was interested in exploring a topic that meant something to my practice as a teacher educator. The use of video recording and dialogic instruction had been cornerstones of my previous university's English education courses for several years, and I wanted to consider how these practices affected TCs and teacher educators.

The two main research questions were as follows: (1) In what ways do the reflections of a secondary English intern (student teacher) differ when the teaching practice for reflection is predetermined by the instructor versus self-determined by the intern? And (2) what factors influence an English intern's selection of teaching practice to focus on for purposes of inquiry, recording, and reflection when the audience is not self-selected?

The study extended Rosaen, Lundeberg, Cooper, Fritzen, and Terpstra's (2008) study by comparing an intern's reflections on two video clips, rather than comparing an intern's reflections on one video clip and one based on memory. Similar to Scherff's (2012) work, interns pursued inquiry, with the addition of video recording. I also specifically defined *reflection* and *inquiry*, definitions that are lacking in some studies of video and reflection. See Textbox 7.2 for my definitions.

TEXTBOX 7.2. DEFINITIONS OF REFLECTION AND INQUIRY

While conducting an exploratory case study on using video in English education, I created the following definitions of reflection and inquiry. These definitions guided coding of my data in the study, and I subsequently shared these definitions with my English methods students prior to them recording video and developing inquiry projects.

Reflection. Describing or analyzing one's own practice in a productive way for purposes of better understanding or changing that practice.

This definition of *reflection* is based on Dewey's (1933) and Loughran's (2002) definitions. While I acknowledge that Davis (2006) previously used the concept of productive reflection, here the term *productive* is more closely related to Dewey's (1933) concept of "open-mindedness" (p. 224). In other words, to reflect in a productive way, TCs must be willing to entertain both positive and negative remarks by others about their teaching practice.

Inquiry. Working alone or with others to develop a question or set of questions about practice for purposes of reflecting on or changing that practice.

This definition of inquiry is based on Cochran-Smith and Lytle's (1999) and Scherff's (2012) definitions.

Participants and Data Collection

I engaged in purposeful convenience sampling (Patton, 2007). First, Matt (pseudonym), the instructor of a secondary English methods course for fifth-year interns and one of my colleagues, agreed to participate. Then Matt helped identify an English intern participant, Rachel (pseudonym), who was student teaching at a local rural high school.

Data collected were typical of case studies and allowed for triangulation: observations, course documents, and semistructured interviews (Glesne, 2011; Wolff, 2007). Prior to conducting interviews or obtaining course documents, I observed one 90-minute class session to understand the structure of the course and develop interview questions. I viewed course syllabi and calendars, readings, assignment sheets and evaluation tools, and student responses to course content for the entire year via the Google course platform.

I then conducted one 60-minute interview with the course instructor. During this interview, I asked the instructor broad questions about the curriculum, pedagogy, and structure of the course; additionally, I asked about the video and inquiry assignments, including questions about how interns were prepared to record videos and subsequently reflect on them.

Rachel gave me electronic access to some of her coursework. This included four videos she recorded across the year focused on dialogic instruction (approximately 5 minutes each, shared with a small group of colleagues). Rachel's written coursework included context and questions for her colleagues about her videos, lesson plans for each video, transcripts of the first three videos, and reflections on all four videos (written after reading her colleagues' comments).

After viewing her first three videos and reflections, I conducted one 80-minute interview with Rachel. Again, the interview included general questions about the course and more specific questions about the video and inquiry assignments. Rachel's interview included questions about the definition of *dialogic instruction* (the assigned focus for the first three videos), logistics of recording (e.g., where she placed the camera), and her inquiry topic (the self-selected focus of the fourth video).

Finally, I observed a 2-hour class session in which the interns presented findings from their inquiry projects. Rachel focused on close reading for her inquiry.

Data Analysis, Findings, and Discussion

I created three broad categories of codes for analysis, along with multiple subcodes. The broad codes are the most pertinent to this summary. These included practice (i.e., tasks or types of teaching undertaken or discussed by participants); analysis (i.e., going beyond description to study, decompose, or question practice); and critique by others (i.e., instructor's and colleagues' comments on videos and reflections).

I also line-by-line coded of all of the interns' written reflections as either negative (i.e., the intern was critical of her practice or of a suggestion offered about changing her practice) or positive (i.e., the intern affirmed her practice or a suggestion offered about changing her practice). The purpose of coding the reflections as positive or negative was to see how productively the intern reflected.

Findings included that Rachel reflected more productively on the self-selected inquiry video post than on the instructor-defined video posts. Throughout the three instructor-defined reflections, the intern frequently restated suggestions for practice made by her group members and then evaluated their responses. However, for the self-selected video post, Rachel focused on analysis of her own practice, rather than evaluating her group members' responses.

Rachel's increased focus on analysis in her final reflection may have been due to the questions posed by the instructor for the self-selected post. Rachel's more open-minded final reflection was likely also a consequence of her growth as a teacher across time. Ultimately, this intern realized that teaching is a profession requiring a willingness to revise plans and materials, rather than requiring perfection. See Textbox 7.3 for a summary of Rachel's thoughts about videotaping across time.

TEXTBOX 7.3. SUMMARY OF A TEACHER CANDIDATE'S PROGRESS

While I only interviewed one intern at one university, Rachel's responses and progress (as seen via video, reflections, and other coursework) were relatively typical of most English methods students I have taught across time and two universities.

Rachel's Thoughts About Video 1 (of Four)

"When we had the first video response due, I was like, 'This is silly. I know what's going on in the classroom. I don't need to videotape it.' I remember filming Video 1 and thinking, 'Yeah, that was pretty good. I can find 5 minutes; that'll be easy.' And then I'm looking through the video, and I'm like, 'Oh, this is embarrassing; this is embarrassing; I shouldn't have said that, my students—what are they doing?'"

Rachel's Thoughts About Video 3 (of Four)

"I needed to see myself doing something good and to hear from classmates that I was doing well. Going to Video 3, it's like, 'Ah' [sigh of relief]. Something's changing, and it's getting better. I don't think I've gotten better at, you know, lesson planning or coming up with ideas, but I think I've gotten so much better at the delivery. And that was always my biggest problem, like I would have all these things I want to come out of the discussion, and all these things I want to say, and I just never had the words for it, or the way to go about it, but now it's definitely more natural."

Rachel's Overall Thoughts About Videotaping

"It's such a big deal to record. And sometimes the kids are just like, 'Oh, my gosh, there's a video on . . .' I wouldn't just record myself for fun. . . . I would have never done it if it wasn't required. It's a lot of effort, and it takes a long time to go through it, but once you see that it's not silly, and you don't know what's going on in the classroom, then it becomes more worthwhile, I think."

Revised Video Assignment at Previous University

Conducting an exploratory case study with an English methods instructor and intern helped me revise my own practice. See Textbox 7.4 for my reflection on this revision.

> TEXTBOX 7.4. REFLECTION ON REVISION OF PRACTICE
>
> My research questions focused on the intern's perspective of videotaping and inquiry, but my interview with the instructor also significantly affected my preparation for teaching the course. My findings led me to conclude the instructor highly influenced how the intern took up recording and reflecting on her teaching. In response to this realization, I modified the way I prepared interns for videotaping, reflection, and inquiry.

The following summarizes the ways I altered the original iterations of the English methods video, reflection, and inquiry assignments at my previous institution:

1. Outlined characteristics of dialogic instruction, based on Juzwik, Borsheim-Black, Caughlan, and Heintz (2013)
2. Specifically defined inquiry and reflection, based on my own definitions
3. Prior to videotaping, led interns through a reflection protocol using inanimate objects and classroom photos, based on Hole and McEntee (1999) and Rosaen (2014)
4. Changed questions for reflecting on colleagues' videos to match questions from the in-class reflection protocol

In the paragraphs that follow, I explain these revisions.

Since the focal teaching practice for recording and reflection at this institution had long been dialogic instruction, previous instructors likely also spent time outlining the characteristics of dialogic instruction. However, I considered the altered iteration a revision of previous courses because (a) it was unclear how previous instructors introduced and taught the practice, and (b) my case study elicited this particular revision.

The interview with Rachel, the intern, contributed to how I outlined dialogic instruction for subsequent TCs. Asked to define dialogic instruction, Rachel said, "I'm always like, 'I still don't know what dialogic instruction means.'" She continued, "It's centered on students making meaning for themselves and with each other. . . . I realize it's not just a free-for-all, talk about what you want to talk about." Rachel's apparent discomfort in explaining dialogic instruction was similar to concerns TCs voiced in my class.

Inquiry and reflection were new concepts for TCs. Both are also terms contested in the literature (e.g., Cochran-Smith & Lytle, 1999; Dewey, 1933; Fendler, 2003; Loughran, 2002; Scherff, 2012; and Schön, 1983). Consequently, I aimed for TCs to have a common understanding of the terms.

The case study interviews also affected the alterations of the video, reflection, and inquiry assignments. Matt, the instructor, did not think he prepared TCs well to record and reflect. He elaborated, "What I should have done . . . was to kind of, like, let's watch a video together, and let's try to practice noticing." His realization led me to introduce TCs to a reflection protocol similar to that of Hole and McEntee (1999) and Rosaen (2014).

Rachel's productivity in the final reflection influenced my decision to mirror the questions from the in-class protocol on the assignment sheet for TCs' written reflections. Rachel's final reflection included both description and analysis, and balanced affirmation and critique of her practice. Matt also provided much more directive questions for the final reflection.

VIDEO ASSIGNMENT AT CURRENT UNIVERSITY

Self-reflection is one of the reasons TCs record their teaching at my current institution; however, the primary purpose for video recording is evaluation by teacher educators. TCs at the current institution take one semester of methods, with a 5-week practicum in a local school. TCs then engage in clinical practice, or student teaching, for one semester. Clinical practice at this institution does not include an additional methods course.

To pass their English methods course prior to clinical practice, TCs must earn a particular percentage on a performance-based rubric by the end of their practicum. Teacher educators crafted the rubric around the InTASC Model Core Teaching Standards (Council of Chief State School Officers, 2013). Due to the number of TCs and the geographic locations of their placements, teacher educators are unable to observe TCs in person. Instead, TCs are evaluated on four video submissions during practicum, one of which is peer coached. The videos also inform TCs' evaluations on the performance-based rubric.

To streamline experiences for TCs enrolled in multiple methods courses, instructors across several subject areas have agreed to similar requirements for the assignments. Rather than dialogic instruction, TCs in all methods courses record and reflect on their use of instructional strategies, more broadly. TCs in English methods tend to select literacy-based strategies, such as silent discussions and questioning the author. Across courses, TCs record using College of Education mini-iPads, and they upload clips to LiveText. Instructors require clips to be an average of 10 to 15 minutes; the first two English and social studies clips were 15 to 20 minutes.

Each instructor requires TCs to submit various supplementary documents with the videos. In English methods, TCs submitted the following: a lesson plan, any additional documents or presentations used in the lesson, an English language arts (ELA) video tool, and a reflection. I created the ELA video tool based on the rubric used to evaluate TCs on a common assessment (i.e., instructional strategy presentation) at the end of the semester. TCs looked for video evidence of multiple descriptors within three indicators, aiming to find time stamps for each descriptor in at least one video.

The reflection protocol the author created at this university is different from the protocol used at the previous university. TCs in English methods at the current institution read Garcia and O'Donnell-Allen's (2015) *Pose, Wobble, Flow: A Culturally Proactive Approach to Literacy Instruction*. Prior to beginning practicum, TCs identified poses, or stances, they wanted to work on in their teaching. In their reflections, TCs identified a pose captured in the video, along with ways they wobbled (e.g., experienced challenges) and moments of flow (e.g., briefly achieved their pose).

My exploratory case study and experiences at my previous university influenced the way I prepare TCs for recording and reflection at my current university. First, I continue to provide TCs with my self-created definition of *reflection*. I also specifically define *instructional strategies*, based on previous TCs' challenges understanding *dialogic instruction*. Finally, I show a teaching video to help TCs identify poses, wobbles, and flow in preparation for reflecting on their own videos.

CONSIDERATIONS ABOUT USING VIDEO FOR ENGLISH TEACHER EDUCATORS

As with any methods course assignment, there are both benefits and drawbacks to video recording and reflection. Teacher educators must take the cost-benefit analysis into account for themselves and their teacher candidates to determine the best way to take up this common assignment.

Benefits and Drawbacks for Teacher Educators

Perhaps one of the most apparent benefits of TCs recording their practice is that teacher educators get glimpses into candidates' classrooms without visiting each classroom; however, there are still challenges with time. The 5-minute clips TCs submitted at the previous university were revealing, but they were a drop in the bucket of time TCs spent in the classroom. The 15-to-

20-minute clips TCs submit at the current university capture more time, but they also take more viewing time.

Furthermore, while teacher educators offer guidance selecting particular clips, ultimately TCs decide what to share, possibly avoiding messy teaching moments. Without live observations or lengthy videos, teacher educators may be left wondering about TCs' progress in the classroom. Video alone (i.e., without reflection) provides an efficient but not necessarily holistic picture of TCs.

For video to be helpful for teacher educators, TCs must be prepared to record. As Juzwik et al. (2012) describe, preparation includes technological considerations (e.g., recording device used) and practical concerns (e.g., camera placement). Logistical preparation necessitates time away from pedagogical content knowledge, the typical focus of methods courses (Shulman, 1986). At my previous university, class time for logistics was necessary because TCs did not have previous experience recording their teaching. At my current university, on the other hand, TCs have recorded their teaching in two courses prior to methods and need only a brief refresher (i.e., handout).

Novice teacher educators may bring fresh eyes to an assignment, helping their colleagues consider ways to improve video recording and reflecting. For example, Matt and a colleague streamlined video recording and inquiry by tying the final video to TCs' inquiry projects. However, novice teacher educators have to determine the best ways to take up videotaping and reflection in their own instruction, and their ideas may not align with previous assignment iterations. While the focal practice for recording at the two universities is different, I was able to keep much of my instruction the same.

Video also provides an opportunity for teacher educators to introduce TCs to a theory-practice-research/inquiry-revision cycle. TCs at the previous university engaged in this cycle by reading about and experiencing dialogic instruction in class, attempting to implement dialogic instruction in the field, posing a question about their practice, and gathering data/reflecting using video. Similarly, TCs at my current university read about instructional strategies and experience them in class, attempt to implement instructional strategies in the field, reflect using video, and find research about their strategies. At both universities, candidates then present their findings to colleagues.

Benefits and Drawbacks for Teacher Candidates

Teacher educators often require TCs to videotape to prompt reflection (e.g., Arya, Christ, & Chiu, 2016; Rosaen et al., 2008). The term *reflection* likely means something different to each teacher educator and TC. This might be frustrating to TCs, and simple guidance to reflect may lead to replicating bad practice rather than revising practice (Fendler, 2003). Overall, Rachel referred to reflection as "absolutely necessary because . . . everything happens so fast. Without [reflection], I wouldn't be breaking [my practice] down and analyzing what's going on." Merely viewing video without reflection would not lead to analysis.

TCs benefit from sharing their videos with audiences beyond themselves and teacher educators (i.e., with peers, university supervisors, and mentor teachers). TCs at my previous university shared their videos with three other colleagues, but when they reached the third video post, they performed discourse analysis on one colleague's video and their own video. Focusing intently on only one additional video helped Rachel value the assignment. "The way [my colleague] saw my video . . . was just so much more open-minded and positive [than the way I saw it]."

Conversely, sharing videos with wider audiences presents challenges. Candidates may feel self-conscious about sharing their classrooms with others, especially their peers (Juzwik et al., 2012) and teacher educators (Greenwalt, 2008). Though this assignment is meant to boost morale (e.g., "I have some of the same struggles you do"), sometimes it fosters feelings of competition (e.g., "You have a much easier time getting your students to engage in discussion than I do").

Currently, TCs only share one video with one colleague. The video is typically the third one they record, and they meet in person to view each other's videos. While watching, they complete a peer-coaching protocol developed by another teacher educator. If they peer coached each other more often, TCs might get more out of the assignment, since, as Rachel described, it took discourse analysis to produce a response to her video she found enlightening. Unfortunately, teaching discourse analysis would take much more preparation time in a semester-long, rather than yearlong, course.

Some research suggests TCs reflect differently when they self-select foci for video recording and reflection versus their instructor selecting foci for them (e.g., Rosaen et al., 2010; Sewall, 2009). Though, again, preparing TCs to set their own goals and recording foci takes more time than an instructor making decisions for TCs. At both universities, TCs are given choice within guidelines, in an effort to gain the best of both worlds.

One part of the recording assignment that remained constant at the previous university was the requirement for TCs to transcribe their video clips. While many of them ultimately saw transcribing as a benefit, initially they viewed it as a drawback. According to Matt, "I was nervous to give that assignment, because it's like, shoot, that's asking a lot of them, but now, hands down, they will all say that this is the most helpful part of the video project, is transcribing." I encountered a similar reaction from TCs when I taught the methods course.

Transcription made sense at my previous university, given the dialogic instruction focus and eventual goal of performing discourse analysis. At my current university, I replaced this practice with a self-created ELA video tool.

As previously noted, the main purpose of the tool is to help TCs find evidence of various standards in their teaching in order to prepare them for their final presentation in the course. A secondary purpose is for TCs to analyze their videos before writing their reflections.

Implications for Practice

English methods instructors should keep a few principles in mind (see Textbox 7.5) for video recording and reflection to be meaningful and run smoothly for TCs and teacher educators.

TEXTBOX 7.5. SUMMARY OF CONSIDERATIONS FOR VIDEO RECORDING

- Logistics

  - Video release form
  - Secure site for uploading and sharing video
  - Equipment (not personal devices, if possible)
  - Camera positioning, angles, sound

- Preparation

  - Definition of reflection
  - Guidance to select English-specific foci for recording

- Opportunities to Record, Reflect, and Share

  - Provide multiple opportunities across time to capture growth
  - Video observation or reflection protocol
  - Share beyond teacher educator (mentor teacher, other teacher candidates)
  - Prepare peers to provide appropriate feedback

First, teacher educators must consider logistics. Some school districts are reluctant to allow TCs to record their teaching due to privacy issues, let alone share their videos. At both universities, several steps have been taken to ensure the privacy of secondary students and teachers. Some of these steps include a photo and video release form created by the College of Education; uploading the video to secure, private websites (e.g., Edthena and LiveText);

and requiring TCs to record with College of Education equipment instead of on their own devices.

Additional logistical considerations apply to the TCs themselves. Besides being secure, the platform for uploading and sharing video should be user-friendly. TCs also need direct instruction on recording devices and camera placement. If the point of TCs recording and sharing video is to develop an aspect of their pedagogical content knowledge for teaching English, they should spend more time reflecting than mastering the technology.

Next, TCs need a common definition of reflection, along with a specified reflection protocol. Some may contend such structure lessens the authenticity of reflection. Left to determine their own video-viewing mode, though, TCs tend to notice insignificant details (e.g., the way their voice sounds on the recording). With a common understanding of reflection and a reflection protocol, TCs focus more on their teaching or specific content.

Teacher educators should allow TCs to select their own foci for videotaping, while guiding TCs to focus on English-specific content and practices. Teaching is a complex endeavor. Recording could focus on classroom management, pacing, assessment, or a number of other aspects. However, in order to develop their capacity for teaching English, TCs need opportunities to record and reflect on practices specific to teaching English.

Furthermore, TCs need multiple opportunities to record and reflect on their teaching. One video recorded once in their program will not show growth, nor would it be worth the time needed to properly prepare TCs to record, as outlined in the previous paragraphs. Some TCs have the luxury of spreading four video recordings across a year, while other TCs must record four videos in the span of 5 weeks. Still, all parties are able to see change across time—from managing class and answering questions without consulting their mentors to garnering a wider variety of student participation in discussions. Such growth is especially encouraging to TCs who often wonder if they are making progress.

Finally, just as writing should be shared with multiple audiences to prompt revision, teaching should also be shared with multiple audiences. However, if TCs are going to share their videos with peers, they need preparation to give appropriate feedback. Otherwise, in Matt's words, "there is a sense of the cheerleading aspect . . . but it's kind of the nature of the questions that they're responding to." If TCs are told to respond to their peers' videos without guiding questions or modeling of what responses may look like, TCs often default to overwhelmingly positive comments that lack substance.

In most cases, the benefits of video recording and reflection will outweigh the costs for both teacher educators and teacher candidates. However, teacher educators need to approach the assignment the same way they ask TCs to approach teaching: with careful scaffolding, support, and feedback throughout the recording and reflecting cycle.

NOTE

I wish to acknowledge Cheryl Rosaen, professor emerita of teacher education at Michigan State University, for assisting with conceptualizing this study and providing feedback on an early draft of the write-up.

REFERENCES

Arya, P., Christ, T., & Chiu, M. M. (2016). Video use in teacher education: A survey of teacher-educators' practices across disciplines. *Journal of Computing in Higher Education, 28*(2), 261–300.

Cochran-Smith, M., & Lytle, S. L. (1999). Relationships of knowledge and practice: Teacher learning in communities. *Review of Research in Education, 24,* 249–305.

Council of Chief State School Officers. (2013). Interstate Teacher Assessment and Support Consortium (InTASC). *Model core teaching standards and learning progressions for teachers 1.0: A resource for ongoing teacher development.* Washington, DC: Author.

Davis, E. A. (2006). Characterizing productive reflection among preservice elementary teachers: Seeing what matters. *Teaching and Teacher Education, 22,* 281–301.

Dewey, J. (1933). Why reflective thinking must be an educational aim. In R. D. Archambault (Ed.), *John Dewey on education* (pp. 212–228). Chicago: University of Chicago Press.

Erickson, F. (2007). Ways of seeing video: Toward a phenomenology of viewing minimally edited footage. In R. Goldman, R. Pea, B. Barron, & S. Derry (Eds.), *Video research in the learning sciences* (pp. 145–155). Mahwah, NJ: Lawrence Erlbaum.

Fendler, L. (2003). Teacher reflection in a hall of mirrors: Historical influences and political reverberations. *Educational Researcher, 32*(3), 16–25.

Garcia, A., & O'Donnell-Allen, C. (2015). *Pose, wobble, flow: A culturally proactive approach to literacy instruction.* New York: Teachers College Press.

Gelfuso, A., & Dennis, D. V. (2017). Video as text of teaching: Toward more deliberate literacy field experience supervision. *Teacher Educator, 52*(1), 57–74.

Glesne, C. (2011). *Becoming qualitative researchers: An introduction* (4th ed.). Boston, MA: Pearson.

Greenwalt, K. A. (2008). Through the camera's eye: A phenomenological analysis of teacher subjectivity. *Teaching and Teacher Education, 24,* 387–399.

Grossman, P., Compton, C., Igra, D., Ronfeldt, M., Shahan, E., & Williamson, P. (2009). Teaching practice: A cross-professional perspective. *Teachers College Record, 111*(9), 2055–2100.

Hole, S., & McEntee, G. H. (1999). Reflection is at the heart of practice. *Educational Leadership, 56*(8), 34–37.

Juzwik, M. M., Borsheim-Black, C., Caughlan, S., & Heintz, A. (2013). *Inspiring dialogue: Talking to learn in the English classroom.* New York: Teachers College Press.

Juzwik, M. M., Sherry, M. B., Caughlan, S., Heintz, A., & Borsheim-Black, C. (2012). Supporting dialogically-organized instruction in an English teacher preparation program: A video-based, web 2.0–mediated response and revision pedagogy. *Teachers College Record, 114,* 1–42.

Loughran, J. J. (2002). Effective reflective practice: In search of meaning in learning about teaching. *Journal of Teacher Education, 53*(1), 33–43.

Patton, M. Q. (2007). Sampling, qualitative (purposive). In G. Rizter (Ed.), *Blackwell encyclopedia of sociology online.* doi:10.1111/b.9781405124331.2007.x

Rosaen, C. (2014). *Dewey: Training of thought* [PowerPoint presentation]. Retrieved from ANGEL (Course Management System).

Rosaen, C. L., Lundeberg, M., Cooper, M., Fritzen, A., & Terpstra, M. (2008). Noticing noticing: How does investigation of video records change how teachers reflect on their experiences? *Journal of Teacher Education, 59*(4), 347–360.

Rosaen, C. L., Lundeberg, M., Terpstra, M., Cooper, M., Fu, J., & Niu, R. (2010). Seeing through a different lens: What do interns learn when they make video cases of their own teaching? *Teacher Educator, 45*, 1–22.

Scherff, L. (2012). "This project has personally affected me": Developing an inquiry stance in preservice English teachers. *Journal of Literacy Research, 44*(2), 200–236.

Schön, D. A. (1983). *The reflective practitioner: How professionals think in action*. New York: Basic Books.

Sewall, M. (2009). Transforming supervision: Using video elicitation to support preservice teacher-directed reflective conversations. *Issues in Teacher Education, 18*(2), 11–30.

Shulman, L. S. (1986). Those who understand: Knowledge growth in teaching. *Educational Researcher, 15*(2), 4–14.

Streb, C. K. (2010). Exploratory case study. In A. J. Mills, G. Durepos, & E. Wiebe (Eds.), *Encyclopedia of case study research*. London: Sage.

Whitney, A. E., Olan, E. L., & Fredricksen, J. E. (2013). Experience over all: Preservice teachers and the prizing of the "practical." *English Education, 45*(2), 184–200.

Wolff, K. (2007). Methods, case study. In G. Rizter (Ed.), *Blackwell encyclopedia of sociology online*. doi:10.1111/b.9781405124331.2007.x

A Response to Chapter 7

Christian Z. Goering and Seth D. French

Everyone has probably heard someone 30 or older say something like this: "Gosh, I'm glad there weren't video cameras everywhere when I was growing up." In 2019, society has reached a point where the video camera—usually through the platform of the smartphone—is ubiquitous. Every coffee shop, intersection, school, or convenience store entered is another opportunity to be recorded. The use of video in the preparation of teachers has benefits and drawbacks just as there is a tradeoff with perceived safety and the threats of surveillance. In responding to Julie Bell's chapter, we sought to use the space provided to extend Bell's work by offering multiple protocols for video-recording reflection in the support of teacher development; we also will briefly problematize some uses of video recording in education.

There are legitimate arguments that speak out against video recording in teacher preparation, most notably in response to the proliferation of the Educative Teacher Performance Assessment (edTPA; Au, 2013; Dover, Schultz, Smith, & Duggan, 2015; Madeloni & Gorlewski, 2013). While few would argue against video recordings of teaching in totality, the edTPA provides universities the chance to shift the costs of supervising student teachers to the student teachers themselves, as they pay for an evaluation of their videotaped teaching and sometimes pay tutors additionally (Dover et al., 2015).

In this way, the edTPA becomes a standardized test that allows anonymous noneducator evaluators to assess teaching from afar. As Au (2013) states, the "edTPA effectively sanitized much of our students' work" (p. 22) by creating a standardized—and easy-to-assess—version of teaching. In a similar vein, researchers and computer programmers are working to develop artificial intelligence that can, through videotaped lessons, provide feedback about teacher's lessons (Barshay, 2018).

Criticism aside, we have both video recorded our own teaching and found the process to be beneficial and constructive in nature, allowing for a deep examination of our own practices and the encouragement to reflect on ways in which we'd like to improve. As valuable as the process has been, though, neither of us have engaged in video recording our lessons by being required to do so by some gatekeeping authority (e.g., teacher education program, National Board Certification process).

Typical demands placed on teachers often prevent them from engaging with a depth of reflection unless they are required to do so, suggesting that video reflection's place in teacher education programs is an important one. Bell's chapter provides teacher educators with the necessary guidance for making the video-reflection process with teacher candidates (TCs) as beneficial as it can be. By examining and analyzing the differences between teacher candidates' video-reflection processes at two different universities, Bell helps readers see that the benefits of the video-reflection process are numerous, though not automatic. Without proper guidance, video reflection can become simply another tedious task on the journey to becoming certified.

In the interest of extending the chapter at hand, we thought it would be helpful to consider how the framework Bell used for video reflection compares with those proposed by other contemporary researchers. We are arguing neither for nor against any of the examples of video reflection but simply adding resources to the existing resource provided. Bell herself draws on the work of Garcia and O'Donnell-Allen's (2015) *Pose, Wobble, Flow* for her reflection protocol, implementing a three-step process in which teacher candidates identify (1) "poses" they wanted to improve in their teaching practice, (2) challenges they encountered ("wobbles"), and (3) moments of "flow" in which they overcame challenges to meet their desired goal. McVee, Shanahan, Pearson, and Rinker (2015) base their reflection protocol on Pearson and Gallagher's (1983) gradual release of responsibility (GRR) model, applying a four-step process that gradually develops from the teacher modeling effective reflection to the TCs reflecting on their own. Endacott (2016) discusses the video-stimulated recall (VSR) model, which prompts teacher reflection by posing the following four questions:

1. How was your preparation for instruction reflected in the lesson as you taught it?
2. How did you work to maintain a positive classroom environment for learning?
3. What did you do to facilitate instruction?
4. How are you working to fulfill your professional responsibilities? (p. 36)

Gelfuso (2016), like Bell, places Dewey's (1933) conceptualization of reflection as the foundation of his reflection protocol, which is constructed as a five-step process using a theater metaphor:

1. Setting the stage: PST shares his/her hypothesis for teaching outcomes, connecting teaching demonstration to course content.
2. Opening the curtain: teacher educator poses a question to PST to create dissonance that will engender thoughtful reflection.
3. The play: PST answers dissonance question from previous step while teacher educator pushes for depth in PST's response.
4. The curtain closes: PST and teacher educator write together to create a "warranted assertability" (Dewey, 1986).
5. The bow: PST describes the reflective process through closing conversations with teacher educator. (p. 76)

Finally, drawing from the guidelines for National Board Certification, especially from English Language Arts Portfolio Three, the National Board Certification protocol doesn't specifically cite a theoretical or philosophical underpinning to their approach to having existing teachers video and reflect—through extensive written commentary—on their teaching. Elements of planning, learning environment, feedback, and reflection are present in the questions listed to guide reflection (National Board for Professional Teaching Standards, 2014, pp. 11–12).

In comparison to these other reflection protocols, Bell's is perhaps most similar to that of Gelfuso (2016) in terms of its level of prescriptiveness, structure, and theoretical underpinnings. While the five protocols discussed may differ to varying degrees in these terms, there is a common underlying thread that unites them all: effective reflection does not happen automatically or without careful guidance. Protocols used for reflecting on video-recording episodes of teaching provide additional resources to those of us who prepare English teachers; the usefulness of recording teaching can capture a moment in time that is hard to otherwise document. Recording one's own teaching is an act that teachers find useful and instructive but not something most do without being required to do so. The similarities in the various approaches are not universal, and the benefits teachers could gain by experiencing each approach are naturally different as well.

REFERENCES

Au, W. (2013). What's a nice test like you doing in a place like this? The edTPA and corporate education "reform." *Rethinking Schools, 27*(4), 22–27.

Barshay, J. (2018, July 30). How artificial intelligence could help teachers do a better job. *The Hechinger Report*. Retrieved from https://hechingerreport.org/how-artificial-intelligence-could-help-teachers-do-a-better-job

Dewey, J. (1933). *How we think*. Buffalo, NY: Prometheus Books.

Dewey, J. (1986). How we think: A restatement of the relation of reflective thinking to the educative process, 1933. In J. A. Boydston (Ed.), *The later works of John Dewey* (Vol. 8; pp. 105–352). Carbondale: Southern Illinois University Press.

Dover, A. G., Schultz, B. D., Smith, K., & Duggan, T. J. (2015, March). Who's preparing our candidates? edTPA, localized knowledge and the outsourcing of teacher evaluation. *Teachers College Record*.

Endacott, J. (2016). Using video-stimulated recall to enhance preservice-teacher reflection. *New Educator, 12*(1), 28–47.

Garcia, A., & O'Donnell-Allen, C. (2015). *Pose, wobble, flow: A culturally proactive approach to literacy instruction*. New York: Teachers College Press.

Gelfuso, A. (2016). A framework for facilitating video-mediated reflection: Supporting preservice teachers as they create "warranted assertabilities" about literacy teaching and learning. *Teaching and Teacher Education, 58*, 68–79.

Madeloni, B., & Gorlewski, J. (2013, June 21). Radical imagination, not standardization: Critical teacher education and the edTPA. *Teachers College Record*. Retrieved from http://www.tcrecord.org (ID Number: 17163).

McVee, M. B., Shanahan, L. E., Pearson, P. D., & Rinker, T. W. (2015). Using the gradual release of responsibility model to support video reflection with preservice and in-service teachers. In E. Ortlieb, M. B. McVee, & L. E. Shanahan (Eds.), *Video reflection in literacy teacher education and development: Lessons from research and practice* (1st ed.; pp. 59–80). Bingley, UK: Emerald Group.

National Board for Professional Teaching Standards. (2014). *English language arts component three* (3rd ed.). Retrieved from https://www.nbpts.org/national-board-certification/candidate-center/first-time-and-returning-candidate-resources/

Pearson, P. D., & Gallagher, M. C. (1983). The instruction of reading comprehension. *Contemporary Educational Psychology, 8*, 317–344.

Part III

Beyond English Language Arts: Challenges to Our Profession

Chapter Eight

More Than Left, Right, Up, Down

Teaching Tensions in Non-ELA Literacy Methods Courses

Jeff Spanke and Chea Parton

OVERTURE

They waited for the bell that never came.

The door was shut, the hallway empty, and their classroom packed with stacks of syllabi and less-than-eager student teachers waiting to see what they could glean from the English teachers, who would serve as their instructors, leaning up front. This was these student teachers' last class before student teaching: an intensive, comprehensive 6-week semester centered on mentoring these future educators to teach literacy in their varied content areas.

They came from all corners of the curricular globe: social studies, science, math, technology, and physical education. But no English. *Those* folks had their own methods courses. Literacy was *their* wheelhouse, and those in these whereabouts knew it all too well. This course was an addendum, the class with an asterisk to appease the scholastics and stakeholders—the course they were forced to take because, of course, they'd hopefully make sure to teach not only their content but also how to own it, read it. Yet while the instructors explained their curricular aim, it became clear that nobody thought they would need it.

English teachers, after all, are the ones who teach reading. They love leading students to find deeper meanings. They do writing and grammar and research and speech. They analyze movies and art while they teach. And though none of those students ever put up a fuss, they all seemed preconvinced that literacy was never for teachers "like us."

They soon knew better.

INTERPHASE

Despite these students' preconceived notions of reading and writing as inherently an English endeavor, the historical roots of content area literacy (CAL) instruction go back several decades (Alvermann, Gillis, & Phelps, 2012, p. 4). Herber's (1970) *Teaching Reading in the Content Areas* emerged in an era when the cognitive, process-oriented approaches to learning began eclipsing the previous efforts of behaviorist scholars who insisted that mechanized, rote memorization offered the best ways to achieve student learning.

Indeed, the last 50 years have witnessed a seemingly unprecedented emphasis on content area literacy instruction, spurred, in no small part, by a corresponding increase in national educational mandates, beginning with 1983's *Nation at Risk* report, and perhaps culminating with the 2004 passing of No Child Left Behind (NCLB). Yet, as Riley and Crawford-Garrett (2015) argue, since NCLB was signed into law, "school reform efforts in the United States have been shaped by a neoliberal ideology that has exacted a tremendous toll on students, teachers, and teacher educators" (p. 59).

While this "toll" has certainly manifested in a myriad of complex and wide-reaching implications for teachers, students, and schools, it is also undoubtedly evident in the educational perspectives of the majority of today's preservice teachers, who now enter the profession having "done school" almost entirely in an age of "commodification, marketization, competition, and cost-benefit analysis" (Apple, 2013, p. 6).

As part of this process of marketization and commodification—what the Common Core State Standards (CCSS) have colloquially dubbed "college and career readiness" (CSAI, 2016)—preservice teachers must now learn how to incorporate literacy practices and instruction in their future content-specific classrooms. Granted, a great deal of empirical research supports the notion that CAL courses may enhance or otherwise broaden preservice teachers' *understandings* of literacy (Estrada & Grady, 2011; Freedman & Carver, 2007). But the research also demonstrates, however, that these teachers' responses to the inclusion and application of CAL courses varies widely (Barry, 2012; Daisey, 2009).

Eighty-five percent of Christiansen's (1986) participants, for example, reported that CAL courses should be required in preservice education. Lesley (2014), though, found that preservice teachers ultimately questioned the overall relevance of CAL courses and were skeptical about how they would incorporate such techniques in their non-ELA content areas. Darvin's (2007) study echoes these findings by highlighting how secondary math teacher candidates were "often quite vocal about the fact that they want to teach math . . . not literacy" (p. 247).

Kukner and Orr (2015) add to this tension by noting the "multiple challenges connected to the education of [preservice teachers] and their attitudes towards literacy in general, and to infusing literacy into their instructional practices" (p. 42). These challenges include, among other things, "inflexible attitudes toward literacy; a lack of belief in capability and responsibility in teaching students to read; limited use of metacognitive strategies as part of their own reading practices; and prior school experiences informing [their] identities and expectations for literacy in content area classrooms with an inclination to replicate traditional models of learning" (pp. 42–43).

Complicating matters even further is the more recent trend away from CAL approaches to a more discipline-specific or "disciplinary" literacy (Chauvin & Theodore, 2015; Siebert et al., 2016; Shanahan & Shanahan, 2008). Chauvin and Theodore distinguish between content area literacy and disciplinary literacy by claiming that while the former "focuses on the similarities of literacy in the content area with general strategies . . . that can help students with comprehension and can be applied universally across content areas," *disciplinary literacy* focuses on the "discrete ways reading and writing are used in the specific discipline being studied" (pp. 2–3).

Siebert et al. (2016) further laud disciplinary literacy as a welcome alternative to seemingly antiquated CAL initiatives by positing that the former "are, in fact, the participation literacies for the disciplines" (p. 28). In other words, where once content area literacy courses were thought to promote a culture merely of knowledge *consumption*, those who propose disciplinary literacies now seek a culture of knowledge *production*: a culture that can only exist, ostensibly, alongside literacy instruction that supports student participation and agency within the landscape of a particular discipline.

Still, despite its increasing popularity among teachers and teacher educators, the notion of championing disciplinary literacy over content area literacy—as well as the potential dangers of reducing literacy to such a binary—has not gone unchallenged. Dunkerly-Bean and Bean (2016) argue that "as researchers move past the current contentious claims that proclaim 'content area literacy is dead' and disciplinary literacy the successor," teacher educators should take up calls for innovative interdisciplinary work that "may provide commonalities and connections to be recognized and utilized across approaches to their fullest potential" (p. 469).

These interdisciplinary sites may allow preservice teachers to confront and disrupt their own previous literacy assumptions, examine innovative methods of content area literacy pedagogy, and explore the role of "new literacies such as critical, digital, visual, performative, and alternative texts in literacy instruction" (Kukner & Orr, 2015, p. 43). Nevertheless, despite nearly half a century of content area literacy instruction—and the hordes of methodological, philosophical, and political tensions therein—considerable debate remains about what, exactly, literacy is; how best to teach it; how best to teach others to teach it; and what the nebulous notion of "best" actually means.

It is against this backdrop that we authors, Jeff and Chea, found ourselves, over the course of a semester, re-creating and co-teaching a content area literacy course at our large midwestern public university.

POWER UP

We knew something needed to change. *We* needed to change. In previous semesters, we had each independently taught the course EDCI 309, "Reading in Middle and Secondary Schools: Methods and Problems" with varying degrees of success and apathy. But over the span of only a few years, the class had fallen into disarray: the objectives were muddied; the instructors, inconsistent and lacking direction; and the instruction itself was rooted, at best, in an abstract mess of antiquated assumptions, contradictory research, and unclear, arguably arbitrary, assessments.

Some versions of the course had already moved entirely online and were now "taught" by instructors (which isn't to say literacy experts) housed within the respective content areas. The remaining, traditional courses operated more as hodgepodge catchalls for those non–English language arts (ELA) students needing just *one more course* before entering their own classrooms and starting the real work of teaching.

Needless to say, we had a lot of work to do to ensure that we—both as individuals and representatives of a department—didn't sell out to the increasing demands for expediency and simplicity, and that our students, as the future of literacy instruction, bought in.

As a recent graduate of an English education doctoral program and a doctoral student in the same program, we were (t)asked by our department to breathe new life into the fledging curriculum: to generate some shred of meaning and purpose from amid the existing heap of ambiguous goals, readings, and projects. The machine was still running, so to speak, but we were now charged with applying an alternative source of power.

We began conceiving of the course in a new light. We'd meet at coffee shops, diners, libraries, and park benches to throw ink on pages and see what stuck. As budding English education scholars trained in the modern ways of multimodality, critical literacy, and sociolinguistics, we knew that we'd have our work cut out for us convincing our future science, social studies, and PE teachers that literacy was anything more than grammar and semicolons. We also knew, though, that expanding these students' conceptions of literacy would not only enhance their prowess as future teachers but also broaden the horizons of their future students.

Reframing literacy, we transparently hoped, might also have the added bonus of soldering the curricular relationship between disciplines. Perhaps in the future, we each envisioned, reading and writing wouldn't be culturally relegated to the proverbial English wing but would instead occupy an organic and evolving realm across, around, and among *all* content areas. Maybe even someday, content area literacy courses would cease to exist altogether, and all preservice teachers would forever together learn not only literacy strategies that could apply across contents but also discipline-specific approaches to reading and writing in their own classrooms.

Maybe.

But we were getting ahead of ourselves; we still had a course to make.

And so we began with the old model, stripping the archaic course down to its least common denominator to see if we could salvage any viable components. Once we combined efforts, it didn't take long to identify the kinks in the system. We quickly determined that previous iterations of our course were less than sophisticated in terms of overall content, rigor and range of assessments, and interdisciplinary applicability. Students' grades were derived almost exclusively from a combination of in-class discussions, written responses to readings, workshops, and brief, personal reflections on their prior conceptions of/relationships with literacy.

As a whole, the old version of the course woefully lacked specific applicability to any particular discipline; it relied excessively on printed texts and autonomous conceptions of literacy (Goody & Watt, 1963); was inherently consumptive, as opposed to generative; and, perhaps most damning of all, both in conception and execution, was often transparently framed as "just another hoop" through which students must grudgingly trudge in order to do what they actually wanted to do. Later. Somewhere else.

Through critically deconstructing various elements of the course, we began asking ourselves fundamental questions that ultimately served to guide our conception of a better way to do things.

What are the students really getting out of the experience? we wondered; how does this course challenge/inform/affirm/or privilege their perceptions of literacy? To what extent does (or should) this course implore students to consider both teaching *of* and teaching *as* literacy? How else can we teach this stuff? What other stuff can we teach? Why should we try? How can we make this whole experience better for everyone, and why, after so many semesters of teaching this course, were we both so frustrated with the prospect of teaching this course?

Despite our perhaps selfish pedagogical longing to preserve certain elements of our past labors, we ultimately determined that it was in the best interest of the students and the course to, as Faulkner implores, "kill their darlings" and start anew. The Revamped EDCI 309 course was a far cry from the course we had concluded only a few weeks before. Yet with the wintery, holiday respite behind us and a renewed spark igniting our uncharted path, we both lit into January with polished syllabi, high expectations, and no clue how it would all actually go.

AN ECLOGITE, OF SORTS

The new course featured fresh assignments: multimodal compositions—or "ensembles" (Serafini, 2013)—that invited students to engage with their previous conceptions of literacy while also challenging them to consider how those conceptions would shape the means by which they taught their kids their content. We divided their respective class sections—4-hour blocks that met twice a week, simultaneously—into two distinct parts. During the first portion of class, each of us would meet with our students in our separate rooms wherein we'd discuss the content-specific readings, voice concerns, clarify assignments, make connections, and organically tether the material to our students' future classrooms.

In our own ways, these segregated sessions allowed our respective students and us to dance the dance, in other words, of disciplinary literacy instruction. Since each of our class sections catered to different content areas (Jeff working with preservice teachers in STEM and Chea with social studies and PE), we could devote the first portion of every session to an in-depth examination of how literacy works, looks, sounds, and moves throughout each specific discipline. The readings for any given day were discipline specific, and the discussions and their corresponding assessments addressed the extent to which students understood the discipline-specific implications of literacy.

The second half of class—a period of roughly 2 hours that became affectionately, though somewhat playfully, glibly known as "Together Time"—sought to marble the discipline-specific focus of the first half with a broader, sociocultural view of literacy as it applies across, among, and above all content literacies. During this session, we combined our classrooms and would each take a turn either leading or assisting with the particular day's lesson and activity.

Without exception, Together Time maintained the underscoring theme of teaching as its own form of literacy. All teachers, the course insisted, were not only masters of their respective content and discipline-specific literacies—nor, for that matter, should they also only be masterful in teaching those literacies to their students—but as student teachers engaged in the literate act of teaching, they should also be masters of the literacy *of* teaching. Together Time stressed, perhaps above all else, that all teachers need to recognize and accept their roles in the teaching of, and teaching *as*, literacy.

It's not enough, in other words, to be able to teach content area or disciplinary literacy to one's students; teachers must also embrace their own unique and intimate function in that educative exchange, for the exchange itself very much *is* its own act of literacy. Simply "learning" literacy methods, regardless of their framing as either content area or disciplinarity, without a proper and sophisticated grounding of those methods in some greater literacy landscape, is essentially the same thing as learning letters without having any sort of idea how they sound or what purpose they serve.

And mistaking the sound comprehension of these methods, devoid of teachers' awareness of their role in facilitating their composition, is the same as mistakenly thinking a child who merely recites Dr. Seuss from memory is, in fact, reading about a hat-sporting cat.

In other words, the disciplinary literacies, and their corresponding methods, devolve into first-order symbols: they have value, but only in their limited function as otherwise arbitrary symbols in the imitative act of representation. Without mastering the literacy of teaching literacy, a person can ever only be "playing teacher," just as children may recognize their name in print but can't make sense of or even recognize the individual letters. As an analog to pedagogical practice, the name in this case—the unique and proper combination of sounds and letters—operates as merely an image of the real thing.

To the child, the image of the word *mom* may conjure up a corresponding image of the woman who birthed them, but the individual letters and their corresponding sounds mean nothing. It's just one image. MOM. No different, both in concept and in function, than a photograph or drawing. Still, children point to the image, mumble "mom," and convince the family they can read. Gee (1989) refers to this notion as "mushfake Discourse," meaning the "partial acquisition [of a literacy] coupled with meta-knowledge and strategies to 'make do'" (p. 13). Teacher educators, for example, may very well make a career out of "mushfaking" their mastery of teaching literacy, but as a mushfake, it will never be authentic, and it will never be real mastery.

To combat this reduction of literacy methods to baseless strategies and hollow representation, Together Time also relied heavily on multimodal representations of teachers and teaching, schools and students. As a class combined, the students critically examined cinematic representations of teachers, deconstructing the characters' literacy practices as they related to the practice of teaching. They also explicated TED Talks to engage with nontraditional depictions or conceptions of literacy; analyzed visual art; and composed multimodal narratives to highlight their burgeoning mastery of multiliteracies (Kress & Van Leeuwen, 2001; Leander & Boldt, 2013; New London Group, 1996).

In general, we would begin these sessions by sharing a text (e.g., film, TED Talk, photograph, or comic) that discussed/presented ideas about literacy in some way. After reading the text, students engaged in small- and whole-group discussions across and among content areas to discuss their reading of the texts and how the ideas presented in them affected the way they were thinking about the role of literacy in their classrooms.

And they started to learn that content area or disciplinary literacy is never a unilateral endeavor; after all, good teachers know that the literacy strategies they employ when communicating with students rarely apply when engaging with other stakeholders on the education spectrum. It's one thing to teach a kid to read a technical manual; it's another thing to explain to a parent how and why their student is learning to read that manual.

To these ends, ultimately what the Revamped EDCI 309 (and particularly Together Time) sought to promote was a healthy and productive recognition of all teachers' roles not only as content area/disciplinary literacy instructors but also—and perhaps more importantly—as democratically minded members of complex and evolving local and global communities. Since membership in these communities demands a variety of sophisticated content- and discipline-specific literacies, teachers must therefore be literate as teachers before they can ever hope to teach literacy.

The Revamped 309 included a variety of projects and assessments that served to address this need of fostering sustainable, professional relationships with schools, students, and other stakeholders. Yet perhaps among the most innovative of these projects—and ultimately, the most problematic—was the course's capstone project, which invited students to submit a proposal to a mock academic conference created by us. The conference was designed to simulate students' participation in professional communities of practice through the design and presentation of ideas surrounding narratives and enactments of teaching.

In order to replicate as authentically as possible the very real scenario of being grouped with like-minded strangers at an actual conference, each student submitted an individual proposal in response to the class's Call for Papers, which focused on the use of films as text and narratives of "good" teaching in Tony Kaye's (2012) *Detachment*. We then organized separate panels around groups who had proposed similar presentations. Once grouped, students collaborated with one another to conceive the scope/agenda of their presentation, prepare either holistic or individual papers, and deliver their material to the combined class over two entire, 4-hour class sessions.

The Revamped 309 culminated with an opportunity for content area specialists to cultivate their professional and pedagogical identities by preparing for and presenting at a fictional literacy conference. The presentations were thoughtful; the presenters, for the most part, engaged; and the pervasive, preconceived notions of literacy, presumably erased. Still, while the instructors each felt they had answered several of their initial inquiries regarding the course's aim and agenda, they each equally ended the experience with several more questions, some more pressing and jarring and frustrating than others.

REJECTING THE NULL

While many aspects of the course certainly warranted change (e.g., 2 full days of conference presentations was too much), overall the Revamped 309 seemed to have been a success. The students' formal work, feedback, and course evaluations all indicated that most of them walked away from the class feeling more confident about their ability to teach multiple literacies and enter their future classrooms with an expanded view of literacy's presence in their practice.

Though there were obvious successes, it was clear that Revamped 309 was the first class in which students were given an opportunity to critically examine and wrestle with the interwoven notions of teaching of/as literacy. Because their previous methods classes had centered almost exclusively on their respective content, the Revamped 309 spent considerable time, particularly early on, demonstrating that literacy wasn't just a thing for English teachers.

The battle was arduous and frustrating at times. While most students hopped aboard by the end of the course, the Revamped 309 could've been much more effective had students entered the class with an understanding that literacy *mattered* to them, their teaching, and their content. Rather than spending such a significant portion of the semester anchored in why and how teaching of/as literacy affected a classroom, the course could have attended to how to go about teaching literacy in their content areas.

RECONSTRUCTION

Given that this edited collection seeks to explore the prevalent tensions in ELA methods courses, in our experience, one of the most present and persistent of these tensions involves how teacher educators conceptualize and understand the teaching of literacy. Because content area teachers foreground types of literacy with particular attention to their content (consciously or not), literacy teacher educators, who for the most part, continuously reside in the English content area, must reconsider the overarching purpose of literacy courses, as well as their respective audiences.

Because while the diversity in their students' content areas presented some challenges in our classes, it ultimately opened up discursive spaces about literacy across disciplinary lines in ways that neither of us had previously witnessed or experienced in their English education silo. For example, there seemed to be an underlying and unwritten agreement among students and colleagues in English education that multiple-choice and standardized assessments only test certain aspects of students' literacy, knowledge, and understanding of a skill or topic. In the other content areas represented by the student teachers in EDCI 309, however, this was not the case.

Having challenging discussions about the role of literacy in and the testing of disciplinary literacies through particular types of assessment helped to deepen the class's understanding of how different methods of assessment speak to and examine students' understanding and mastery of various literacies. Of course, these innovative and promising spaces did not come without critical considerations for how, why, and where to move forward.

Why, for example, were there no English students in the class? What assumptions about how English teachers learn about and practice literate/literacy teaching did their absence reveal? Despite the course's relative success in expanding non-ELA students' conceptions of literacy, how did the intentional exclusion of English preservice teachers perpetuate the notion that literacy is, inherently, *not* an integral part of all teaching? Even though our students seemed, for the most part, to subscribe to multiple definitions and applications of literacy, to what extent did their subscription stem from their presumptions that they now simply understand "the English stuff" of their teaching?

English teachers have traditionally and unfairly been charged with teaching students all there is to learn in the realm of literacy. While some changes seem to be appearing on the horizon, there is still a lot to do. If content area teachers are to be teachers of literacy and recognize their own teaching as its own act of literacy, they need more exposure to and experience with both throughout their time in teacher preparation programs.

Ideally, this exposure would begin long before they ever enter their teacher education programs, perhaps even in the earliest stages of their education, when they are taught their contents in conjunction with learning how to read and write that content.

Literacy should no longer be framed or perceived as an augmentation, tangent, or auxiliary to *real* content/disciplinary teaching. And the methods of literacy instruction can no longer afford to fall solely under the purview of English teachers. For indeed, if teachers seek to prepare students for healthy and productive memberships into increasingly complex and global communities, they must begin with introducing concepts of literate membership practice. This means learning to navigate the words of our worlds while also traversing the worlds of our words.

REFERENCES

Alvermann, D., Gillis, V. A., & Phelps, S. F. (2012). *Content area reading and literacy: Succeeding in today's diverse classrooms* (7th ed.). New York: Pearson.

Apple, M. (2013). *Can education change society?* New York: Routledge.

Barry, A. (2012). "I was skeptical at first": Content literacy in the art museum. *Journal of Adolescent and Adult Literacy, 55*(7), 597–607.

Center on Standards and Assessment Implementation (CSAI). (2016). *High school graduation requirements in a time of college and career readiness.* Report funded by grant number #S283B050022A between the U.S. Department of Education and WestEd with a subcontract to the National Center for Research on Evaluation, Standards, and Student Testing (CRESST).

Chauvin, R., & Theodore, K. (2015). Teaching content-area literacy and disciplinary literacy. *SEDL Insights, 3*(1), 1–10.

Christiansen, M. A. (1986). How prospective secondary teachers feel about taking a required course in teaching reading: A survey report. *Journal of Reading, 29*(5), 428–429.

Daisey, P. (2009). The reading experiences and beliefs of secondary preservice teachers. *Reading Horizons, 49*(2), 167–190.

Darvin, J. (2007). Teaching critical literacy principles to math and science educators. *Teaching Education, 18*(3), 245–256.

Dunkerly-Bean, J., & Bean, T. W. (2016). Missing the *savoir* for the *connaissance*: Disciplinary and content area literacy as regimes of truth. *Journal of Literacy Research, 48*(4), 448–475.

Estrada, K., & Grady, K. (2011). Reflective inquiry and preservice teachers' conceptions of content area literacies. *Reflective practice: International and Multidisciplinary Perspectives, 12*(6), 749–762.

Freedman, L., & Carver, C. (2007). Preservice teacher understanding of adolescent literacy development: Naïve wonder to dawning realization to intellectual rigor. *Journal of Adolescent and Adult Literacy, 50*(8), 654–665.

Gee, J. (1989). Literacy, discourse, and linguistics: An introduction. *Journal of Education, 171*(1), 5–14.

Goody, J., & Watt, I. (1963). The consequences of literacy. *Comparative Studies in Society and History, 5,* 304–345.

Herber, H. L. (1970). *Teaching reading in the content areas.* Upper Saddle River, NJ: Prentice Hall.

Kaye, T. (Director). (2012). *Detachment* [motion picture]. United States: Tribeca.

Kress, G. R., & Van Leeuwen, T. (2001). *Multimodal discourse: The modes and media of contemporary communication.* New York: Bloomsbury.

Kukner, J. M., & Orr, A. M. (2015). Inquiring into preservice content area teachers' development of literacy practices and pedagogical content knowledge. *Australian Journal of Teacher Education, 40*(5), 41–60.

Leander, K., & Boldt, G. (2013). Rereading "A pedagogy of multiliteracies": Bodies, texts, and emergence. *Journal of Literacies Research, 45*(1), 22–46.

Lesley, M. (2014). Policy, pedagogy, and research: Three issues affecting content area literacy courses for secondary-level teacher candidates. *Literacy Research and Instruction, 53*(1), 50–71.

New London Group. (1996). A pedagogy of multiliteracies: Designing social futures. *Harvard Educational Review, 66*(1), 60–93.

Riley, K., & Crawford-Garrett, K. (2015, Summer). Reading the world while learning to teach: Critical perspectives on literacy methods. *Teacher Education Quarterly,* 59–79.

Serafini, F. (2013). *Reading the visual: An introduction to teaching multimodal literacy.* New York: Teachers College Press.

Shanahan, T., & Shanahan, C. (2008). Teaching disciplinary literacy to adolescents: Rethinking content area literacy. *Harvard Educational Review, 78*(1), 40–59.

Siebert, D. K., Draper, R. J., Barney, D., Broomhead, P., Grierson, S., Jensen, A. P., . . . Wimmer, J. (2016). Characteristics of literacy instruction that support reform in content area classrooms. *Journal of Adolescent and Adult Literacy, 60*(1), 25–33.

A Response to Chapter 8

Melanie Shoffner

In their chapter, "More Than Left, Right, Up, Down: Teaching Tensions in Non-ELA Literacy Methods Courses," Jeff Spanke and Chea Parton focus on revising and teaching a literacy class designed for preservice teachers outside the English language arts (ELA). Adopting a reflective stance, they discuss the curricular issues driving the course revision, the literacy understandings shaping their reconstruction of the course, their experience teaching the revised course, and the questions that developed from their experience.

At the heart of their chapter are the tensions surrounding teaching and learning literacy. What should a literacy methods course include? How do disciplinary needs shape literacy learning? Why should non-ELA preservice teachers take a literacy methods course? As Spanke and Parton engage with these questions, they encourage us to stop and do the same. How would we address the inherent tensions of literacy teaching and learning if we were to design a course for non-ELA preservice teachers?

In reading their chapter, however, I found myself focusing on a tension swimming beneath the surface: pedagogical discomfort. As Spanke and Parton note, they were familiar with the course, having taught it before; in revising the course, they could easily have retained former assignments or familiar readings. Instead, they embraced the discomfort of starting over: identifying new objectives, adopting a new structure, choosing new readings, and creating new assignments.

In doing so, they (re)created a methods course that required the preservice teachers—and their teachers—to approach literacy from multiple perspectives. Moving beyond academic reading and writing, the course now engaged preservice teachers in the study of literacy as a critical, real-world analysis of purpose and representation. The preservice teachers had no frame of reference for these alterations, of course; they approached the class with the usual level of trepidation reserved for coursework outside their content area comfort zones.

But what about Spanke and Parton? How did their frame of reference for literacy teaching and learning shift because of this work? How were they pushed out of their comfort zones in planning for and teaching non-ELA preservice teachers? In what ways did they benefit from the pedagogical discomfort of starting fresh with a familiar course?

Revision, addition, deletion: Teacher educators expect such actions when we sit down to write, but we may not apply these same principles when we stand up to teach. The apocryphal story of the teacher lecturing from the same yellowing notes, year after year, is one passed along in jest, but we might be surprised by how many of our assignments and instructional practices are also tinged with age. Pedagogical change is uncomfortable; it takes time, it takes effort, and it requires us to reconsider our expertise in the classroom.

Yet we expect our preservice teachers to be uncomfortable every day. We challenge their perspectives and question their understandings; we ask them to read things they've never read and do things they've never done. All the scaffolding we provide doesn't take away from the discomfort of doing something for the first time. As teachers, however, we understand the benefit of having students engage with difficult material and complete challenging assignments. We know that learning is often uncomfortable.

A confession: I was the professor who charged Spanke and Parton with updating the literacy methods course, and I was intentional in choosing them for that work. As recent graduates of and graduate students in the English education program, Spanke and Parton were well versed in literacy content and context; as previous instructors of the course, they were aware of the strengths and limitations of the course structure and outcomes. Spanke and Parton were also former students, so I was familiar with their personalities, teaching styles, and academic interests. They were similar enough to collaboratively create a coherent course yet different enough to struggle with that creation.

As their chapter reveals, Spanke and Parton did struggle to reconcile understandings of and approaches to literacy in order to revise and teach the course. And in doing so, they challenged themselves to rethink their beliefs about and enactments of literacy teaching and learning. By working through the pedagogical tensions inherent in revising and teaching the methods course, Spanke and Parton were able to interrogate and alter the understandings, beliefs, and actions shaping their teaching of the literacy methods course, specifically, and their views on literacy, more broadly.

As teacher educators, we want our preservice teachers to struggle with new material, alternative perspectives, and different understandings. The meaning making that develops through addressing this intellectual (and often personal) discomfort supports their development as reflective practitioners (Dewey, 1960) who are able to manage the constant complexities of teaching.

I believe teacher educators also need the challenge that comes from pedagogical discomfort (e.g., Shoffner, 2016; 2018). As we become more experienced—and more comfortable—we should push beyond our pedagogical comfort zones to acknowledge our strengths and recognize our constraints. At times, this work is likely to be a mixture of the good, the bad, the ugly, and the uncomfortable, but like our preservice teachers, we can grow from the pedagogical discomfort that comes from pushing against the walls of our expertise.

REFERENCES

Dewey, J. (1960). *How we think: A restatement of the relation of reflective thinking to the educative process.* Chicago: D. C. Heath. (Original work published 1933).

Shoffner, M. (2016). From expert to novice: Studying a second discipline. In D. Garbett & A. Ovens (Eds.), *Enacting self-study as methodology for professional inquiry: Proceedings of the 11th International Conference on Self-Study of Teacher Education Practices* (pp. 213–218). Herstmonceux, UK: Creative Commons.

Shoffner, M. (2018). The professor abroad: Crossing the pedagogical border. In D. Garbett & A. Ovens (Eds.), *Pushing boundaries and crossing borders: Self-study as a means for researching pedagogy* (pp. 287–293). Herstmonceux, UK: Creative Commons.

Chapter Nine

Learning From Interns Who Leave the Profession

Emotional Labor and the Limits of the Methods Course

Brandon Sams and Mike Cook

It goes without saying that student teaching is a rapturous and stressful experience. To work, in most cases without pay, for 60 or more hours a week is a supreme test of emotional (and financial) strength. The emotional work that practicing teachers and students learning to teach experience and navigate—well, poorly, and continually—is a crucial factor in teachers' well-being and in student learning. In the contemporary moment of teacher education, you'll find plenty of talk about performance assessment, competencies, and 21st-century skills, but not as much about the complicated emotional work that composes a teaching life, including whether and how teachers can process anger, frustration, or embarrassment with colleagues (Newkirk, 2017).

    I (Brandon, author 1) recently worked with an intern (Beth) whose reaction to workplace emotions suggests how underprepared preservice teachers (PTs) and interns are for the emotional contours of teaching. In a written reflection, Beth reacted to witnessing another teacher express frustration about student apathy in a professional learning community meeting: "One of the teachers came in and told the others how Connor and Megan [Grade 8 students] are 'just not giving an f-word.' She [the other teacher] said it feels like the students are coming up to her and saying 'f-word' you."

    Beth notices, with some surprise, that the other teachers in the room provide encouragement and express similar frustration, albeit lower in degree, at students' lack of engagement and care. Beth, writing in her reflection, was "dumbfounded when [she] heard this [inappropriate] language in a professional setting." She wanted to provide comfort to the teacher but stayed quiet, feeling convinced, as she later wrote, that "it is never appropriate to use foul language in a professional setting" and that teachers "should not be gossiping about students."

Beth views the situation—a professional meeting where teachers are publicly working through the emotions of teaching—as mostly, if not entirely, destructive. Beth interprets the visible emotional work as excessive and indicative of unprofessional behavior. She wants and perhaps assumes she'll be rewarded for adopting a professional persona that is entirely put together with composure and decorum.

Teacher educators have played a role in constructing and making desirable the composed teacher persona. Teachers are nice. Teachers are adult professionals. Beth is not entirely wrong or unjustified in this view. However, Beth needs to recognize and experience the emotional vicissitudes that are a daily part of the profession. Teaching is human, messy, and difficult work. While the difficult emotions that characterize the learning and practice of teaching barely need introduction, naming a few of them—being explicit—might help us collectively recognize, validate, and confront difficulty.

Working with students and families, while tremendously rewarding, can be exhausting. Grading in English language arts (ELA), including carefully marking and conversing with student writing, can be overwhelming. Managing an unruly classroom can make an adult feel like a child. Feeling like a failure or on the verge of failure, as in many stressful professions, can be an almost natural part of the teaching life. If Beth buys into the myth of teacher as savior (Emdin, 2016; Taubman, 2009), she may never feel permission to express her frustrations, embarrassments, or failures, and may be in danger of leaving the profession.

Given that 30% of all new teachers end up leaving the profession within the first 5 years (Ingersoll, 2001) and that emotional competence is a key factor in teacher retention across all content areas (Tait, 2008), it is time to take emotion work and emotional labor seriously in teacher education program coursework. And this work should start well before internship, in ELA methods courses and related professional coursework. Can the difficult emotion work of teaching be simulated in methods courses? Is "talking about it" enough?

LEAVING THE PROFESSION

Both of us have recently worked with two PTs who left internship. One competent and hardworking student quit voluntarily. The second student was asked to leave by her collaborating teacher and was bewildered by the request. For the first student, we puzzled over her choice; for the second, we wondered how we didn't see it coming. This chapter reflects on the purpose and limits of the English methods course, in light of respectfully considering these students as "failure cases."

We write through our own emotional labor, acknowledging our failures as teacher educators to predict how or why teacher candidates fail at this stage, asking how our methods course could have better prepared these PTs to succeed. We also ask whether the methods course in English, generally defined, could have met the needs of these PTs and others like them. Pursuing this question exposes the potential limits of the methods course and what can be taught and learned independent of immersive, professional experience.

The present analysis reframes failure as a productive optic (Halberstam, 2011) that surfaces invisible and unacknowledged problems in English methods and teacher education. The intern who left voluntarily said, "Teaching felt like a prison"—alluding to stacks of grading and standardized curricula that made what she thought she loved intolerable. Focusing on failure cases raises questions about unsustainable features of the profession. What becomes visible about teaching and the systems of education when one acknowledges the failures of PTs and the failures of teacher educators? Can the field design methods courses and programs that somehow honestly engage the unteachable features of the profession?

We address these questions in the context of reflecting on the "failure cases" mentioned above. We begin by noting the present state of the methods course in the field of English teacher education and our own views of the purpose of the methods course. After presenting our narratives about the two PTs mentioned above, we reflect on how we could have improved the methods course to better meet PTs' needs. Then, we present an argument for how the methods course would be challenged to meet their needs, in the process underlining the potential limits of the methods course and the unsustainable features of the teaching profession.

EMOTIONAL LABOR

Researchers in teacher education and English education have explored the emotions of teaching and teaching as emotion work for more than three decades (Hargreaves, 1998; Zembylas, 2003). As Benesch (2017) notes, the work of sociologist Arlie Hochschild (1983) has been instrumental in helping teacher educators and researchers name and explore how emotions are managed, silenced, or channeled in institutional learning contexts. "Feeling rules," for example, refer to appropriate emotions and emotional displays for the workplace, which may or may not be explicit. The "feeling rules" for being a teacher, for instance, may include composure and enthusiasm.

What counts as emotionally appropriate for teaching is influenced by larger, sometimes stereotypical, discourses related to gender and the profession (e.g., women are caring and nurturing). Emotion work and emotion management refer to mismatches between experienced and "appropriate" emotions in the workplace. A teacher might experience anger or frustration because of a student's behavior and engage in emotion management (say, through breathing exercises) and return to a period of composure, thus becoming aligned with expectations for teacher behavior.

Importantly, teachers can use emotional labor to disrupt and potentially rewrite the emotion rules of curricula and their professional context. A popular example is Mr. Keating in *Dead Poets Society* who violates the implicit and explicit feeling rules for curricula and pedagogy at the fictional Welton Academy. He reminds his students that poetry is not something to be counted and measured but is essential to passionate expression and living an authentic life.

Newkirk (2017) has written about the emotional underlife of teaching and learning, calling attention to the silences around the difficult emotion work of the teaching life. Feeling estranged "from much of the upbeat, motivational descriptions of teaching practices, where everything seems to run with machinelike efficiency," Newkirk can't find "the anxieties, hesitancies, frustrations, and yes failures that take up so much of [his] own mental space" (p. 4). Newkirk argues, in effect, that teaching needs a change of feeling rules, that emotions teachers experience need to find expression.

"When, for example, we look at the gruesome statistics of young teachers leaving the profession, how much of that exit is due to a sense of failure, of not living up to expectations, of private embarrassment, that finds no outlet in honest discussion?" (p. 13). Failure is inevitable as we teach and learn. How can teachers, he wonders, create classroom and school cultures where it is safe to fail, and to learn from failure, in our learning journeys?

A related question is more germane to the present chapter: How can teacher educators, in and beyond their methods courses, create classroom and program cultures where a full range of teacher emotions can find honest expression and deliberation? What might a change to the feeling rules of teaching and learning to teach make possible? New teachers (and even veteran ones) will experience a range of emotions working with young people, including anger, frustration, and shame.

Perhaps it's time for teacher education programs to unwind themselves from the moribund languages of audit culture and those accreditation bodies that demand teacher educators and PTs focus on competencies. Perhaps it would be in better service to the profession to focus on what may not be going well, on the emotional vicissitudes of teaching and learning. If PTs and teachers were given more forgiving and capacious "feeling rules," then important conversations could be started before it's too late.

STATE OF THE METHODS COURSE

Traditionally, the methods course, whether geared toward literature or writing or both, has served as an opportunity for PTs to develop teacher identities (Whitney, Olan, & Fredricksen, 2013). Many PTs enter methods coursework feeling "like a student," and one prominent goal of such courses is to help PTs begin thinking like and engaging their work as a teacher. The methods course introduces PTs to the profession by incorporating assignments and field-based activities that allow for the development of teacher knowledge and identity through observation, practice, and feedback.

Many PTs experience methods courses as an integration of university and field experiences, where they work both theoretically and practically to pair subject matter and pedagogy. Yet another way the methods course marries the experience of being a student and that of being teacher is through guided and collaborative experience-based inquiry and evaluation of curricula, standards, and context, which PTs use to design and even implement their own instruction.

OUR VIEW OF METHODS

The methods courses described in this chapter aim to help PTs develop teacher identities in a supportive community of practice. The course organization, assignments, and curricula are designed to provide PTs a variety of experiences and scaffolds that help (and require) them to begin to think like teachers. In the courses and related field experience components, PTs are asked to live two lives simultaneously—that of a student and that of a teacher.

Through readings and class discussions, instructors constantly refer students to these two related lenses and support the notion of teacher-learner, an orientation both teacher educators and PTs benefit from throughout their careers. Both in class and in local schools, PTs have ongoing opportunities to teach and to receive feedback. This is meant to simulate their upcoming internship experiences as closely as possible.

Regardless of the task, the overall goal is to use modeling and engagement to help PTs begin to think about how they will include students in their future classrooms. In our respective methods courses, we establish a collaborative environment where PTs and teacher educators design assignments together, have discussions about assessment criteria, and work together to create a shared classroom body of knowledge.

Following the work of Stock (1993), we have each composed pedagogical anecdotes in order to reflect on two failure cases and, in the process, raise questions about how our version of the methods course could be adapted to better address the needs of PTs. We have told these stories to each other numerous times, each telling filled with wonder, speculation, and learning about how we could have taught, mentored, or responded differently to the situations described. In the written versions presented here, we highlight the potential limits of any English methods course to address everything PTs needs to learn, thus raising questions about the limits of English teacher education.

TEXTBOX 9.1. BRANDON'S STORY: LEARNING FROM AN INTERN WHO VOLUNTARILY LEAVES

I was never a teacher to receive gifts at the end of a semester. On my office desk, I keep a framed print that reads, "Life is like a grapefruit." Emily gave it to me in December 2016. Life being like a grapefruit (and it is) is one of many aphorisms—mostly goofy, sometimes wise—I say to my classes. Emily remembered. I can't recall exactly what I was referring to—perhaps the meaning of a poem or the feeling of studying during midterms. I meant to call attention to a philosophy of life (indeed, a privileged one) that a little bitterness makes life sweet. It stuck with her.

September 2016. We are on the phone, Emily and I, talking about her internship and how she's doing. It's not going well, the internship or the conversation. She wants to leave the whole program and switch degrees. I try to convince her not to. Emily is one of the good ones. She wants to do well—she has for the last two years since I've known her.

"It feels like a prison," Emily says. "I don't want to live to work."

Emily knows that the first few years will be hard, "figuring out who I want to be and how my classroom will work." But Emily didn't anticipate that, despite considerable efficiency on the part of her cooperating teacher, "she [would work] all the time, seven days a week. Are all schools like this?"

I told Emily that, of course, teaching is a lot of work and that, yes, you can find ways to be efficient while teaching in a way that feels authentic. You don't have to spend all your time facing a stack of papers.

Not all schools are like yours. Not all teachers are like yours. It would be foolish to give up something you've worked so hard for because your placement isn't what you'd expected. Teaching is a lot of work.

"I just can't live like that," Emily told me.

* * *

Emily left internship, with a days' notice. On a Tuesday.

I couldn't stop thinking about Emily's refusal. Emily is the earnest one, the hardworking one. Not a "quitter" (I don't like that word), not one to shy away from putting in a hard day's work. I couldn't place her into easy categories: a lazy student, wanting the easy way out? Not Emily. And yet here she was, wanting to leave, leaving and never coming back.

I was troubled that Emily was right. *No one can live like this. Teaching is not for the living.*

I started thinking about the future, Emily's future, our program's future. Emily, so academically talented, so dedicated, had no future in teaching. I remembered Derrida's (1995) notion of a monstrous future, that which is undecided or in excess of categories. He writes,

> The future is necessarily monstrous: the figure of the future, that is, that which can only be surprising, that for which we are not prepared . . . is heralded by a species of monsters. A future would not be monstrous would not be a future; it would be predictable, calculable and programmable tomorrow. All experience open to the future is prepared or prepares itself to welcome the future *arrivant* (pp. 386–387).

I began to think of Emily as a monstrous figure, the arrivant Derrida mentions. What I mean here is entirely serious. Emily managed to destabilize, for me, the categorizes we educators use to organize our curriculum: teacher/student, success/failure, growth/immaturity. As an arrivant, she resides on borderlines, liminal spaces, and calls into question those very constructed borders that she demarcates.

The arrivant, in Derrida's words, causes "dis-ease," rending a hole in everyday logics that preserve the status quo. What, indeed, had Emily torn? What logics of teacher preparation had she put at "dis-ease"? What might Emily's departure teach us? Was she, in fact, the wise one? In sensing the day after day-ness of teaching, did she also sense that which can never be surprising, and this no future at all?

TEXTBOX 9.2. MIKE'S STORY: PERHAPS TEACHING ISN'T FOR YOU

As teachers, our students' struggles are our struggles; their failures are our failures. As teacher educators, I find this an even more complicated proposition—their struggles as students and teachers are deeply connected to our classrooms. More often than I like, some interns simply do not finish and do not become teachers. While this is often a decision they make, sometimes it is a decision made for them. It is in this failure, perhaps more than any other, that keeps me up at night, that causes me to question myself as a teacher educator, and that requires me to interrogate teacher preparation—namely, our methods courses. One recent example continues to weigh on me.

As a student, Katie's grades were fine. She was successful in her coursework and was the kind of student you thought was going to be a good and caring teacher. There had been no dispositional red flags and no real causes for concern.

Once Katie began her internship and I conducted her first observation, things, it appeared, had changed a bit. After watching a lackluster lesson, one that she seemed uncomfortable with, I sat down with her to debrief and offer feedback. Katie became immediately defensive, as if it were the first time she had received constructive feedback.

"It wasn't my lesson," she said. "I did what I was told."

As I prompted her further to think about how she felt the lesson went, she shut down. I talked with her about using her cooperating teacher and me as resources to grow as a teacher. I told her it was okay to have lessons that did not go well. It was early in the semester, and I felt she was simply still transitioning to this new (and quite stressful) role.

As the semester progressed, Katie's response to feedback became an issue between her cooperating teacher and her. Even in this less "academic" way (i.e., from someone other than her professor), she struggled to receive and react to feedback.

What followed was a series of conversations between the cooperating teacher and me, between Katie and me, and among the three of us. The fascinating (and bothersome) part was that her disposition toward feedback never changed. During each conversation, she grew upset and would shut down and not talk to us. The resistance to feedback continued.

On a Sunday, just prior to the midterm break, I received a call from the cooperating teacher. It seemed she and the principal had made the decision to remove Katie from the classroom and the school.

Going through this process and removing the student led me to ask many questions. Why was Katie struggling to receive feedback? What was so different in this context (Katie had been provided regular feedback on teaching throughout her methods courses)? Why were there no red flags? And if there were red flags, why did we not note or heed them? Ultimately, these questions were about the program and the experiences students receive in our two methods courses. The failure, I would argue, lies in the preparation and is simply manifested during internship. I wrestle with this notion regularly, and the more questions I ask, the more questions arise. The answer, perhaps, may be not only in what our methods classes currently are or can be in the future but also in what they cannot.

ALTERING OUR METHODS

Storytelling leads to reflection, and as we composed and read our stories, we reflected on how our methods courses might be improved to meet the needs of students like Katie and Emily and to provide better education for all PTs. While what follows may read as advice for others, it is also advice for us going forward as teacher educators.

Both Katie and Emily could have benefitted from more frequent and authentic feedback on all types of teaching, include teaching simulations completed in methods courses and teaching completed with Grades 6–12 students. Faculty members and teachers need to have shared expectations for the feedback PTs receive, particularly that it be honest and geared toward improvement so that PTs can refine their teaching tool kit, including how they plan, design learning experiences, differentiate instruction, and assess student learning.

PTs also need consistent opportunities to use feedback to improve subsequent teaching; thus they need frequent opportunities to teach in practicum settings before internship, opportunities that are connected to the reflective work they do in methods courses. Process, feedback, and revision are disciplinary cornerstones in English language arts education, and PTs learning to teach need to experience iterative cycles of observation, feedback, and reflection in the methods course.

While we both observed Emily and Katie teach in public schools (practicum settings) before internship, it was, admittedly, only once, due primarily to scheduling conflicts and commitments to observe other students. Authentic feedback from teachers and faculty members presents logistical and labor challenges (e.g., faculty persons must travel to school sites for observations or teachers must provide feedback while juggling the obvious demands on their time), demands that we are both familiar with.

To supplement in-person observation, faculties need to consider incorporating video recording and reflection. Recent research in teacher education suggests that establishing a culture of video reflection as professional practice helps PTs develop critical reflection skills for future self-assessment and improvement (Deeney & Dozier, 2015). While incorporating video reflection will help prepare PTs for high-stakes performance assessments (such as the Educative Teacher Performance Assessment [edTPA]), it will also help PTs in their journey to become 21st-century digital citizens.

Both of us, in hindsight, could have been more honest with students, including Emily and Katie, about teacher workload. The time needed to prepare lessons for multiple preps, the time needed to differentiate instruction, the time needed to provide meaningful feedback on student work, and the time needed to engage meaningfully and purposefully with colleagues, families, and communities—these are significant commitments that require literal and emotional time. To help PTs understand the time commitment of teaching, methods instructors might require that PTs log the time they spend preparing, implementing, and assessing a lesson in their field placement. This may help them begin to understand the rigor of teaching full-time and better anticipate the demands of the student teaching experience.

PTs also need strategies for managing workload and being efficient without sacrificing relationships or quality of engagement. Such a conversation might have helped Emily. At the same time, they need to learn about being an advocate for their profession even as they prepare for the bureaucracy of schooling, especially in the era of reform via standardized testing. Methods instructors might introduce PTs to different ways of being a teacher advocate while they engage in conversation about how to change the structure of schooling to benefit student learning. PTs need to learn how to work within the system while knowing how to change it.

THE LIMITS OF THE METHODS COURSE

In methods courses, can teacher educators prepare PTs for the emotional labor of being 100% responsible for teaching 90 to 150 kids per day? The internship experience is intended to serve as a close approximation of this tall order, a gentle throwing into the fire, complete with a mentor and guide. The *feeling* of being responsible, the literal and emotional time of being responsible and acting on that responsibility—preparing, grading, and communicating with students and parents—cannot be approximated in methods courses.

Consequently, teacher educators cannot coach and mentor PTs as they navigate these feelings.

While giving PTs opportunities to create, try on, and practice teacher identity is important in their development of skills and knowledge (Danielewicz, 2001), these opportunities will likely fall short of approximating the emotional labor of full-time, immersive experience. While the methods course may not be able to approximate the emotional labor of internship, teacher educators and PTs can begin to rewrite the "feeling rules" around what teachers can and cannot talk about. PTs need early opportunities to voice and process their emotions—including joy, anger, fear, and embarrassment—as they learn to teach. Changing the "feeling rules" of learning to teach may have given Katie and Emily permission to voice their frustrations and process their experience before it was too late.

CONCLUSION

Teachers are ultimately human beings asked to do far too much with far too little. Experienced teachers struggle enough with the emotion work of teaching, yet the profession (and the methods course in particular) hasn't developed the appropriate scaffolds and approximate experiences for interns. The methods course, thus, has limits that must be acknowledged and, if not overcome, then worked with to better serve the needs of PTs.

How do teacher educators prepare PTs for the emotion work they'll have to perform? Getting students into secondary classrooms early and often for meaningful experiences seems obvious, as is providing students with regular, critical feedback on their teaching. Teacher educators might also have honest conversations with PTs about their own emotion work and labor. Sharing about the emotional challenges that thread through teaching other people could be a useful way to model vulnerability to PTs and establish the methods course as a space for processing and reflecting on the emotional work of teaching.

Following Newkirk's lead, teacher educators might actively rewrite the feeling rules of teacher education, creating a safe space for explorations of a range of emotions and feelings that accompany failure and working with young people. This work might begin by countering the myth of teacher as savior and making space for honest conversation about the emotional underlife of teaching. Rewriting the feeling rules might also mean that teacher educators redirect the focus of PTs away from idealized cultural scripts of "good teaching" and toward the concrete experiences of the self.

REFERENCES

Benesch, S. (2017). *Emotions and English language teaching: Exploring teachers' emotion labor*. New York: Routledge.
Buchanon, J., Prescott, A., Schuck, S., Aubusson, P., Burke, P., & Louviere, J. (2013). Teacher retention and attrition: Views of early career teachers. *Australian Journal of Teacher Education, 38*(3). Retrieved from https://files.eric.ed.gov/fulltext/EJ1012946.pdf
Danielewicz, J. (2001). *Teaching selves: Identity, pedagogy and teacher education*. Albany, NY: State University of New York Press.
Deeney, T., & Dozier, C. (2015). Constructing successful video reflection experiences in practicum settings. In E. Ortlieb, M. B. McVee, & L. E. Shanahan (Eds.), *Video reflection in literacy teacher education and development* (Vol. 5, pp. 41–57). Literacy Research, Practice, and Evaluation. Bingley, UK: Emerald Group Publishing Limited.
Derrida, J. (1995). Passages: From traumatism to promise. In P. Kamuf (Ed.), *Points . . . Interviews* (pp. 372–395). Stanford, CA: Stanford University Press.
Emdin, C. (2016). *For white folks who teach in the hood . . . and the rest of y'all too: Reality pedagogy and urban education*. Boston: Beacon Press.
Hahs-Vaughn, D. L., & Scherff, L. (2008). Beginning English teacher attrition, mobility, and retention. *Journal of Experimental Education, 77*(1), 21–54.
Halberstam, J. (2011). *The queer art of failure*. Durham, NC: Duke University Press.
Hancock, C. B., & Scherff, L. (2010). Who will stay and who will leave? Predicting secondary English teacher attrition risk. *Journal of Teacher Education, 61*(4), 328–338.
Harfitt, G. J. (2015). From attrition to retention: A narrative inquiry of why beginning teachers leave and then rejoin the profession. *Asia-Pacific Journal of Teacher Education, 43*(1), 22–35.
Hargreaves, A. (1998). The emotional practice of teaching. *Teaching and Teacher Education, 14*(8), 835–854.
Hochschild, A. (1983). *The managed heart: Commercialization of human feelings*. Berkeley, CA: University of California Press.
Ingersoll, R. (2001). Teacher turnover and teacher shortages: An organizational analysis. *American Educational Research Journal, 38*(3), 499–534.
Newkirk, T. (2017). *Embarrassment: And the emotional underlife of learning*. Portsmouth, NH: Heinemann.
Rubin, D. I. (2011). The disheartened teacher: Living in the age of standardization, high-stakes assessments, and No Child Left Behind. *Studies in Culture and Education, 18*(4), 407–416.
Stock, P. L. (1993). The function of anecdote in teacher research. *English Education, 24*(4), 173–187.
Tait, M. (2008, Fall). Resilience as a contributor to novice teacher success, commitment, and retention. *Teacher Education Quarterly*, 57–75.
Taubman, P. (2009). *Teaching by numbers: Deconstructing the discourse of standards and accountability in education*. New York: Routledge.
Whitney, A. E., Olan, E. L., & Fredricksen, J. E. (2013). Experience over all: Preservice teachers and the prizing of the "practical." *English Education, 45*(2), 184–200.
Zembylas, M. (2003). "Structures of feeling" in curriculum and teaching: Theorizing the emotional rules. *Educational Theory, 52*(2), 187–208.

A Response to Chapter 9

Jeremy Glazer

Brandon Sams and Mike Cook's chapter demonstrates that there is a lot to learn from the experiences of teaching interns, particularly those who do not end up choosing to be teachers. The authors' focus on emotions in the lives of teachers, particularly the difficult emotion work required early on, raises the important question of how teacher educators can prepare teachers for this experience. Their work shows that there are real consequences to a lack of such preparation, and that preparation may make a difference between interns choosing to stay or to leave their teaching career before it has even begun. At a moment in our country when teacher attrition rates are incredibly high, the case Sams and Cook are making is an important one. Looking at these cases of preattrition allows the authors to see, in real time, what they call the "unsustainable features of the profession" (p. 151).

Sams and Cook emerge, after having thought through two particular instances of interns who did not become teachers, with some ideas for teacher preparation. The authors ask us to take emotional labor seriously, meaning we must treat the preparation for such labor the same way we treat the preparation to make lesson plans, grade papers, or perform any other task we know that student teachers need to be prepared for. For Sams and Cook, this preparation must include a recognition that teacher interns will ultimately have to learn how to deal with the full range of teacher emotions and that these emotions will need a place for "honest expression and deliberation" (p. 152). Sams and Cook acknowledge that such places aren't often found in the faculty rooms of our schools and that we, as teacher educators, can't just hope that future colleagues provide this kind of space and support. We need to make it part of teacher education. The authors make clear that the feelings these teachers will have in their careers cannot be approximated in their student teaching experience. However, by starting the conversation about emotions and by giving interns "early opportunities to voice and process their emotions" (p. 159) as they learn to teach, teacher educators can introduce a new lens that interns may find useful.

Sams and Cook suggest increased feedback, more cycles of observation that help student teachers understand the rigorous work they can expect, and other strategies for dealing with the workload future English teachers will face. These strategies seem, in some ways, a preemptive strike and a way to help teachers anticipate and understand the emotions they may experience before they actually occur. Thinking of such strategies in terms of emotion work offers a new lens for preparation. In some ways, starting with the emotions teachers will surely experience is a kind of backward planning—a lens that asks teachers to think about how particular things will make them feel. Such a lens helps us move away from thinking of teacher preparation as a kind of cookbook, or way to get teachers to perform the correct moves, and instead asks us to think of teacher preparation in more holistic ways.

We emerge from the chapter with two different, but intertwined, challenges. The first: How do we prepare preservice teachers for the emotions of teaching? The second, and more intractable: How do we deal with the unsustainability of the profession?

Sams and Cook offer suggestions for teacher preparation, but they do not want to put all the onus on early career teachers to deal with the unsustainability of the profession. They do not want to let off the hook those contexts and policies that contribute to feelings of unsustainability. They ask us, as teacher educators, to both prepare student teachers for these feelings and advocate for ways the job can be changed so that these feelings aren't something we take for granted. There will be no easy answers to such challenges, but this chapter makes clear that sustainability must be a priority in teacher education. The problem of attrition starts much earlier than we think.

Chapter Ten

Training for the Unsustainable

The Need to Consider Attrition in ELA Teacher Preparation

Jeremy Glazer

Those who educate English language arts (ELA) teachers face an ever-present swirl of dilemmas, challenges, and tensions. They grapple with issues of standards and "standard" languages, with how much to emphasize various forms of literacy, with teaching about the writing process, and with many other concerns. But there's an additional challenge teacher preparation needs to focus more attention on: teacher attrition.

The teaching workforce in the United States has been transformed by increasing rates of teacher attrition. Now most teachers will no longer be career educators (Ingersoll, Merrill, & Stuckey, 2014). This chapter explores the dilemma this situation poses for education of English language arts teachers by sharing the stories of ELA teachers who left the classroom. Each individual account highlights a different issue linking the teacher's decision to leave with ELA practices. Together, these stories raise the question of how the practice of teaching ELA may play a role in the exit decisions of some experienced teachers and what the implications are for ELA teacher education.

TEACHING: A CHANGING CAREER

Most new public school teachers in the United States will not be in the classroom until retirement. Attrition rates are such that more teachers leave voluntarily rather than remain in the classroom for their career, a radical change from just 30 years ago (Ingersoll, Merrill, & Stuckey, 2014). Teaching has gone from a long-term profession to a short-term profession for most who practice the craft. Teacher educators in general, and ELA teacher educators in particular, need to consider the implications of this shift for our own role in how teachers are educated and developed professionally.

Unfortunately, the attrition problem has not been an area of focus or concern for many teacher education programs. One explanation for this is the lack of clarity about who leaves the field and why they leave. Attrition research often makes contradictory claims about the teachers we are losing. For example, some studies find that worse-prepared, lower-performing teachers are more likely to leave (e.g., Boyd, Grossman, Lankford, Loeb, & Wyckoff, 2008). Other studies find the opposite, namely, that better-prepared, better-educated teachers exit at higher rates (Kelly & Northrop, 2015). There is similar disagreement on other issues as predictors of attrition, including self-efficacy and effectiveness (see, for example, Scheopner, 2010).

One point of general agreement is that attrition rates are high among teachers during the first 3 years of the job, known as the "survival period," when many new teachers realize the career is not for them (Huberman, 1989). Attrition research tends to focus on teachers in this early phase who leave (e.g., Johnson & Birkeland, 2003; Hammerness, 2006).

There is a different group of teachers who leave the profession who should interest the field of teacher preparation, a group referred to as "invested leavers" (Glazer, 2018a; 2018b). These are teachers who were fully credentialed and prepared, who made it through the "survival period," who had reached a level of stability and success in the classroom, and who then decided to leave teaching.

The accounts of this group of well-trained and educated experienced teachers, particularly concerning their decisions to leave, could (and should) have important implications for teacher preparation. This chapter will consider three such teachers, all ELA teachers, and highlight areas of consideration in terms of possible links between ELA teacher education and teacher attrition.

TEACHER ATTRITION CONCERNS GERMANE TO ELA

ELA has a specific set of challenges as a school subject in general. First, it is often less well defined than other subjects. For example, there's less of an agreed-upon sense of what should be taught in a course called "ninth-grade English" than in a course called Algebra 1 or Chemistry (see Applebee, 1974; Christensen, 2011; Probst, 1994; Yagelski, 1994). Second, ELA is often more labor intensive for teachers than other subject areas because of the time demands of grading writing (Baker, 2014; Hahs-Vaughn & Scherff, 2008). Finally, ELA frequently involves more personal involvement between teacher and student than other subjects, as techniques such as reader-response (Galda & Beach, 2001) or personal-narrative (Applebee & Langer, 2013) writing tap into students' lives as the matter of the course itself.

With these understandings in mind, this chapter considers the accounts of ELA teachers who fit in the category of invested leavers, focusing on their decisions to leave the profession. The goal of this chapter is to demonstrate how the particular characteristics of ELA were reflected in the stories of these ELA teachers who had left teaching.

In the accounts of these former ELA teachers, a few important themes that resonate with the particular nature of teaching ELA emerged, including curricular freedom, overwhelming workload, and involvement in the personal lives of students. Each theme will be illustrated here through the account of an individual former teacher.

CASE ONE: CURRICULAR FREEDOM

After receiving his master's degree in education, Roger (all names used are pseudonyms) taught high school English for 8 years in a diverse, urban school in a large metropolitan school district. He was well regarded by colleagues and was appointed department head at his school for several years. He decided to leave teaching when his district began moving toward mandated scripted lesson plans. Roger said, "[Previously,] I was used to being creative and having the freedom to teach what I wanted to teach. It was all things that were supposed to be taught, or [things] it was OK to teach based on the curriculum, but it was my choice what novels I taught, what plays I taught, where I wanted to stop and discuss, what vocabulary I wanted to use, what questions I wanted to use—all of it."

Such freedom in designing the curriculum that he taught had allowed him to practice the skills he had learned in his master's program to engage students, offer authentic writing assignments, use a variety of discussion formats, integrate a range of works, incorporate current events, and implement other techniques. He experienced the scripted plans, however, as the antithesis of the kind of teaching he had previously practiced. The scripted plans dictated to him what to read, when to pause, and even when to ask particular questions. He recalled, "I can remember teaching 'The Most Dangerous Game' [a short story by Richard Connell] and just . . . it's not that I hated the story, it's just the having to stop and here's your red dot and this is where you stop and pause and ask this question about irony or . . . it's just . . . it was just against my nature." Roger told me, "That was not the kind of teaching I was used to, that I was comfortable with, that I wanted to do."

Roger found the lesson plans interfered with his curricular autonomy and did not allow him to practice the skills he had learned in his teacher education program and developed in his first several years in the classroom. While planning autonomy is not only an issue for ELA teachers, it may be particularly salient in the discipline of ELA because there is less of an agreed-upon core, and teachers, particularly as they gain experience, become accustomed to developing their own sense of the discipline and what they will or will not cover in class.

Techniques used in ELA teacher education, such as those found in the work of Lee (1995), Nystrand and Gamoran (1991), and Smagorinsky (2008), encourage creativity in material and methods, and within these works is the assumption that teachers will have the curricular freedom to employ such creativity. Roger was a true believer in such methods but was then confronted with a new district policy, and thus a situation in which he was not allowed to do the kind of teaching he was prepared for. This was one of the reasons he decided to leave the classroom.

CASE TWO: STUDENT LOAD

Steve also taught high school ELA for 8 years in a major metropolitan area after receiving a master's degree in teaching. He experienced an important structural change at his school as he entered his seventh year. Due to budget cuts, each high school teacher would be teaching six classes, instead of the five classes he had been used to. This completely changed the teaching experience for Steve. He said, "[There was also an] increased student load and then as an English teacher, less time to grade the work you're collecting, and you're collecting more work. . . . And I could tell you, I worked in that schedule for one year, and it was already, what I said was a challenging job, a tiring job, but that put it over the top substantially."

Steve felt that having more classes had an extremely negative impact on the classroom environment he wanted to create.

> All the things that went into creating a just, positive experience in the classroom, it requires time, energy, effort, planning. All that. So, all that starts to dry up because you lose the time during the day. . . . You need to spend more time on assessment so there's less time for planning. . . . You are less likely to create those types of assessments that are going to require a lot of grading time because you know that you don't have that. You know I already said those are some of the real great opportunities to engage students. . . . So I think the classroom experience definitely takes a nosedive.

Workload is obviously not exclusively a concern for ELA teachers, but it is a particular kind of issue for ELA teachers. The education of ELA teachers extols the virtues of a variety of forms of writing, of attention to the writing process, following the work of scholars such as Hillocks (1995), Smagorinsky (2008), Lee (1992), and others. The simple fact of responding to the volume of writing students produce is daunting, but we also educate ELA teachers to respond in particular ways with a variety of considerations (e.g., Christensen, 2011; Daiker, 1989; Delpit, 1988; Sommers, 1982; VanDeWeghe, 2004).

Grading essays or other types of writing is labor intensive, and so any increase in load, such as Steve experienced, is magnified for ELA teachers who rely on assignments that in Steve's words "require a lot of grading time." In Steve's case, his increased student load was one of the major reasons he left the classroom.

While National Council of Teachers of English (NCTE) guidelines recommend smaller class sizes for ELA teachers, such policy suggestions may not be followed by many districts. According to Baker (2014), here referring to the NCTE guidelines, "neither I nor any of the secondary teachers I know or worked with in the last 10 years had class sizes consistently that small or a total load that low." Even if there is compliance with NCTE recommendations, the workload of teachers grading writing is "well over the 40-hour workweek" (Reyes & Imber, 1992). Thus, an increased student load may have a bigger impact on ELA classrooms than the classrooms of teachers of other subjects.

CASE THREE: DEALING WITH THE SOCIAL/EMOTIONAL NEEDS OF STUDENTS

Karen taught high school ELA and humanities for 4 years after receiving a master's degree. She appeared to be a teacher who was keenly aware of the emotional needs of her students and knew about their personal lives, which she often became aware of through her work as an ELA teacher. Dealing with these emotional situations and trying to be aware of and respond to the socioemotional needs of her students was manageable for Karen when she felt supported by her administration. But when the assistant principal who was supervising her changed, things became more difficult, ultimately prompting Karen to leave the classroom.

Karen recounted the story of two students in her English class who were good friends and who were struggling with mental health issues. One of these students became suicidal. When the other reported it, the friendship ended. Then, according to Karen, the second student "ended up developing really a very serious depression and anxiety episode, and he was out of the school for two months very shortly after that. [And] that same year I had a student whose mother had lost her job and [the student was] suicidal."

Through her role as an English teacher, Karen became aware of the challenges these students were facing. These incidents all occurred at a time when Karen had lost a supportive administrator who, for three previous years, had helped Karen as she was dealing with the social/emotional needs of her students in her students' lives that emerged in class. Karen had a new administrator during this particularly challenging year involving the suicidal students. She told me, "I was dealing with all this emotional stuff and [the administrator] was very . . . she was very cold." The absence of support, in part, led to her decision to leave the classroom.

Again, while engagement with students' personal lives is not solely the province of ELA teachers, the work of those such as Ladson-Billings, Rosenblatt, Elbow, Rose, Hull, Christensen, and others connect effective pedagogy with techniques that draw on the lives of students. Such pedagogy often involves students responding to literature and expressing themselves through a variety of types of writing that often mine issues and situations from their own lives.

Inevitably, ELA teachers educated in such practices become more aware of the issues and conflicts students are facing, and many ELA teachers, like Karen, lack sufficient support to deal with the issues of students' lives. Karen did not have the training of a mental health professional or the information with which to make appropriate referrals for her students, and she did not feel that the administration in her school helped her fill in the gaps. In the absence of such support, she chose to leave.

IMPLICATIONS FOR ELA TEACHER EDUCATION

Each of these accounts raises a particular challenge facing ELA teachers, and it's important for English educators to consider how we deal with the issues highlighted. Roger's account raises the concern that, while teacher candidates are educated in what the field sees as worthwhile curricular practices built on both a theoretical and research base, many teachers may not be able to implement such practices in schools where they are not given the freedom to do so. Steve's case challenges the field to somehow account for teacher workload and sustainability in the consideration of the classroom writing experiences of students.

Karen's story questions the effects that the emphasis on students' use of the personal as a way of connecting to ELA reading and writing may have a detrimental effect on the persistence of ELA teachers if these teachers do not have the support system in place to deal with ensuing revelations. Each of these teachers felt a conflict between the work their situation allowed them to do and what they felt was necessary to do in order to be a good ELA teacher.

"Craft Conscience"

Santoro (2017) writes about the conflicts faced by teachers like those described above using the concept of a "craft conscience," which she defines as "the manifestation of norms that guide the members of a profession" (p. 751). A craft conscience is basically a teacher's sense of what it means to be a good teacher. Santoro notes that a key question guiding this craft conscience is, How is one "meeting the needs of those served by the profession?" (p. 752). Santoro has studied teachers, some she terms "conscientious objectors" (2011), who left because they were not comfortable with the ways they had to do their job. They did not feel they were able to meet the needs of the students.

The former ELA teachers above faced challenges and dilemmas as they were attempting to follow norms of the ELA profession they had learned during their teacher education. This friction, the tension between their craft conscience and what they were able to do in their classrooms, contributed to their decisions to leave.

Such accounts challenge us to think about how the very practices the field of ELA teacher education tries to encourage may contribute to the exit decisions of experienced teachers. This is not to say that these practices should be abandoned or discontinued, or that the norms of the English education field should be blamed for attrition. Clearly there are other structural issues contributing to attrition as teachers of all different subjects are leaving the field at a high rate (Ingersoll et al., 2014). But it is important to acknowledge that ELA practices in schools may make the career unsustainable for some. Teacher educators of ELA teachers must grapple with this fact.

Acknowledging the Reality of Schools

In each of the accounts above, it is not the practices of ELA teaching themselves causing friction but the conflict between these practices and the characteristics of actual schools. Smagorinsky (2018) raises this important point in regard to ELA teaching, reminding us to remember, when thinking about teacher practices, "it's the context, stupid." In Roger's context, the friction is between his curricular training and the restrictions of his district. In Steve's context the friction is between the ways he has been taught to provide students opportunities for writing and meaningful feedback and the number of students his school requires him to teach. In Karen's context, the friction is between the connections she has been educated to make with the lives of her students and the lack of support for dealing with this emotional work at her school.

ELA teacher preparation must acknowledge the variety of contexts in which teachers will be practicing, and as teacher educators we must consider the implications for the norms we are establishing. While teacher education programs may draw from the latest research and theory to inform and shape the teaching practices they advocate, these education programs may be ignoring the future context for the student teachers being educated. It is difficult to deny that many teachers will not have the kind of freedom we wish they had, that many will have too many students, and that many will not have a supportive administration for most or even some of their careers.

Sometimes there is a simplistic response to such concerns. At a recent NCTE conference, a panelist said, somewhat flippantly, that if teachers were being told what to teach and were uncomfortable with such demands, they should find a new district to teach in. Setting aside the implications of putting the onus for resolving the conflict on the teacher—rather than the administration or the policy makers—this option is not even available for most who work in regional districts and would have to travel a long distance just to reach a new district (and thus, potentially, a new curricular policy). And if neighboring districts are subject to the same state mandates, such travel wouldn't even make a difference as there would be little policy variation.

One can imagine similarly dismissive, and similarly insufficient, responses to teachers with the challenges of high student loads or of having an administration unsupportive of the emotional needs of students and teachers. It's easy to tell teachers to just find a different school, but this avoids a fundamental question that ELA teacher educators must consider: Do we prepare teachers for the schools that exist or the schools we want?

A facile response to this question tries to have it both ways: We prepare teachers to advocate for and help achieve the kinds of transformation our schools may need. But as the teachers chronicled above demonstrate, if teachers are not prepared in ways that help them have sustainable careers in the schools that exist, it is hard to imagine how they will stay long enough to have the opportunity to transform schools.

Sustainability as an Important Part of Preparation

There are a few concrete ways ELA methods courses could be reimagined, particularly in response to the concerns articulated here:

- Sustainability could be frontloaded in discussions about pedagogical tasks such as commenting on student papers and planning. Instead of purely focusing on the effects on students of various practices, the effects on teachers could be considered as well.
- Student teachers could be educated both to create their own curricula and to tailor and work within existing curricula in order to achieve pedagogical goals within the curricular constraints they may face in their own particular situation.

- Student teachers could be educated explicitly in how to deal with students' personal revelations, including some immediate "triage" techniques as well as heuristics to figure out when to refer students and to whom when certain issues are revealed.

Beyond these suggestions, teacher education programs have a great resource to help student teachers: former students. If alumni of teacher education programs, both those who have stayed in the classroom and those who have left, are brought in and used as a resource in methods courses, they may help teacher education programs foster generative discussions about teacher practice grounded in the actual experiences of their own graduates. Sustainability will inevitably be a part of these discussions.

CONCLUSION

This chapter raises more questions than it answers, but the purpose is to highlight the need to make attrition and sustainability serious considerations throughout teacher preparation, here particularly in the case of ELA methods courses. Concerns and tensions important to ELA teachers, including curricular freedom, workload, and dealing with personal issues in students' lives, are reflected in the stories of the invested leavers chronicled above. As the field continues to evolve and develop and refine our philosophies of good ELA teaching methods, the kind of teaching we need to prepare new teachers for, we need to think carefully about the sustainability of these methods as well. If new teachers are trained in methods they can practice only in certain places or only for a few years, we are serving neither our profession well nor our children.

REFERENCES

Applebee, A. N. (1974). *Tradition and reform in the teaching of English: A history*. Urbana, IL: National Council of Teachers of English.

Applebee, A. N., & Langer, J. A. (1983). Instructional scaffolding: Reading and writing as natural language activities. *Language Arts, 60*(2), 168–175.

Applebee, A. N., & Langer, J. A. (2013). *Writing instruction that works: Proven methods for middle and high school classrooms*. New York: Teachers College Press.

Baker, N. L. (2014). "Get it off my stack": Teachers' tools for grading papers. *Assessing Writing, 19*, 36–50.

Boyd, D., Grossman, P., Lankford, H., Loeb, S., & Wyckoff, J. (2008). Who leaves? Teacher attrition and student achievement. National Bureau of Economic Research. Retrieved from http://www.nber.org/papers/w14022

Christensen, L. (2011). Finding voice: Learning about language and power. *Voices From the Middle, 18*(3), 9–17.

Daiker, D. A. (1989). Learning to praise. In C. M. Anson (Ed.), *Writing and response*. Urbana, IL: NCTE.

Daiker, D. A. (2011). Learning to praise. In I. Clark (Ed.), *Concepts in Composition: Theory and Practice in the Teaching of Writing* (p. 168). Hoboken, NJ: Taylor & Francis.

Delpit, L. (1988). The silenced dialogue: Power and pedagogy in educating other people's children. *Harvard Educational Review, 58*(3), 280–299.

Galda, L., & Beach, R. (2001). Response to literature as a cultural activity. *Reading Research Quarterly, 36*(1), 64–73.

Glazer, J. (2018a). Learning from those who no longer teach: Viewing teacher attrition through a resistance lens. *Teaching and Teacher Education, 74*, 62–71.

Glazer, J. (2018b). Leaving lessons: Learning from the exit decisions of experienced teachers. *Teachers and Teaching, 24*(1), 50–62.

Hahs-Vaughn, D. L., & Scherff, L. (2008). Beginning English teacher attrition, mobility, and retention. *Journal of Experimental Education, 77*(1), 21–54.

Hammerness, K. (2006). *Seeing through teachers' eyes: Professional ideals and classroom practice*. New York: Teachers College Press.

Hillocks, G. (1995). *Teaching writing as reflective practice*. New York: Teacher's College Press.

Huberman, M. (1989). The professional life cycle of teachers. *Teachers College Record, 91*(1), 31–57.

Ingersoll, R., Merrill, L., & Stuckey, D. (2014). Seven trends: The transformation of the teaching force. CPRE Report RR-80. *Consortium for Policy Research in Education*.

Johnson, S. M., & Birkeland, S. E. (2003). Pursuing a "sense of success": New teachers explain their career decisions. *American Educational Research Journal, 40*(3), 581–617.

Kelly, S., & Northrop, L. (2015). Early career outcomes for the "best and the brightest" selectivity, satisfaction, and attrition in the beginning teacher longitudinal survey. *American Educational Research Journal, 52*(4), 624–656.

Lee, C. D. (1992). Literacy, cultural diversity, and instruction. *Education and Urban Society, 24*(2), 279–291.

Lee, C. D. (1995). A culturally based cognitive apprenticeship: Teaching African American high school students skills in literary interpretation. *Reading Research Quarterly*, 608–630.

Nystrand, M., & Gamoran, A. (1991). Instructional discourse, student engagement, and literature achievement. *Research in the Teaching of English*, 261–290.

Probst, R. E. (1994). Reader-response theory and the English curriculum. *English Journal, 83*(3), 37–44.

Reyes, P., & Imber, M. (1992). Teachers' perceptions of the fairness of their workload and their commitment, job satisfaction, and morale: Implications for teacher evaluation. *Journal of Personnel Evaluation in Education, 5*(3), 291–302.

Santoro, D. A. (2011). Teaching's conscientious objectors: Principled leavers of high-poverty schools. *Teachers College Record, 113*(12), 2670–2704.

Santoro, D. A. (2017). Teachers' expressions of craft conscience: Upholding the integrity of a profession. *Teachers and Teaching, 23*(6), 750–761.

Scheopner, A. J. (2010). Irreconcilable differences: Teacher attrition in public and Catholic schools. *Educational Research Review, 5*(3), 261–277.

Smagorinsky, P. (2008). Teaching English by design: How to create and carry out instructional units. Portsmouth, NH: Heinemann.

Smagorinsky, P. (2018). Literacy in teacher education: "It's the context, stupid." *Journal of Literacy Research*, 1086296X18784692.

Sommers, N. (1982). Responding to student writing. *College Composition and Communication, 33*(2), 148–156.

VanDeWeghe, R. (2004). "Awesome dude!" Responding hopefully to peer writing. *English Journal, 94*(1), 95–99.

Yagelski, R. P. (1994). Literature and literacy: Rethinking English as a school subject. *English Journal, 83*(3), 30–36.

A Response to Chapter 10

Jeff Spanke

> The return to consciousness, the escape from everyday sleep represent the first steps of absurd freedom.
> —Albert Camus, *The Myth of Sisyphus* (p. 59)

I remember thinking they were frauds.

By the time I enrolled in my first education methods course in my mid-20s, I had already graduated from college with a double major in psychology and English and was finishing my master's degree in American studies. I'd always found a certain inspiration in my college literature professors. Despite my various, oftentimes conflicting opinions of their respective classes and styles, I remember always admiring them, if only as professionals, because as literature professors, they, quite literally, practiced what they preached. They taught literature *while also* studying, reading, and writing about literature. Their pedagogical aims, it seemed to me, mirrored directly their personal aspirations and professional agendas. And if nothing else, I found comfort in that.

My methods instructors in teacher education were different.

In my limited worldview at the time, I always thought they were simply teaching us to do the very thing that they themselves, for whatever reason, quit doing. It was as if they were spending all their time making sure the deck chairs looked nice and shiny right before they got off the *Titanic* and waived bon voyage from the safety of port. As a preservice teacher, I remember feeling suspicious about teacher education, similar to the way I still sometimes feel whenever the dentist flees the room before zapping my face with an undisclosed amount of radiation. Why not stick around, I think to myself; what happens when they flip that switch, and why aren't they ever in the room when it's buzzing?

So, as a teacher educator myself now, I find an odd, discomforting solace in the disruptive yet poignant argument laid out by Jeremy Glazer. I quit teaching while very much on the cusp of becoming what Glazer calls an "invested leaver" and thus, in my current capacity as a teacher educator, have found my infant career wrought with the same anxieties and absurd tensions that Glazer interrogates in his chapter.

By indirectly addressing Glazer's guiding inquiries—namely, do we prepare teachers for the schools that exist or the schools that we want?—I've chosen to frame my career through the lens of Albert Camus's (1955/1991) *Myth of Sisyphus*. As someone who's seen his own share of "invested leavers," I can think of no greater connection to teacher attrition than the text that begins by proclaiming, "There is but one truly serious philosophical problem, and that is suicide" (p. 3). As I explain to my students before reading Camus's existential treatise, if we replace the word *suicide* with *quitting*, then *Sisyphus* evolves into a recipe for transcending the absurdities of American public education and, as teachers, becoming absurd heroes in our own right.

Indeed, the principle dilemma Glazer investigates in his chapter marks the beginning of the absurd in education, for as Camus notes, it is "born of this confrontation between the human need and the unreasonable silence of the world" (p. 28). Whether this absurdity manifests as lack of curricular freedom, excessive student load, or the pressures of dealing with the various social/emotional needs of students, Glazer's work highlights the degree to which all teachers—not just the invested leavers—must grapple with becoming the rocks they themselves push up the hill.

When teacher educators fail to prepare students for the realities of real teaching, "when the images of earth cling too tightly to memory, when the call of happiness becomes too insistent, it happens that melancholy arises in man's heart" (p. 122). Teachers quit. They resign to their hills and just stop pushing. And this, says Camus, "is the rock's victory; this is the rock itself" (p. 122).

Rather, as both Glazer and Camus suggest, we must teach our future teachers that there is, indeed, "no sun without shadow, and it is essential to know the night" (p. 123). As Glazer rightfully suggests, simply finding *another district* is often not (and perhaps should never be) an option. Sisyphus can't choose another hill. "One always finds one's burden again" (p. 123). And yet Camus suggests that "the struggle itself towards the heights is enough to fill a man's heart" (p. 123).

Still, Glazer's governing purpose to "highlight the need to make attrition and sustainability serious considerations throughout teacher preparation" (p. 171) gives me pause. Just as Camus leaves his Sisyphus "at the foot of the mountain" (p. 123), I too am left wondering what role my story plays in my students' consciousness of the absurd. Like Sisyphus, our moment of enlightenment lies in the descent from the mountain, for if in that descent—that return to our task—we can find happiness, then it is within each of us (and our students) to achieve that "higher fidelity that negates the gods and raises rocks" (p. 123). We too can conclude all is well and live conscientious, sustainable, productive professional lives, despite the rocks we inevitably heave.

But as teacher educators, we must be aware of our place on the hill, of our competing functions as both Sisyphus and the gods. Our students trust us to guide them up the same mountain that ironically once challenged us yet whose existence we maintain by the nature of our profession. How do we reconcile that? How transparent should we be with our students about why we left our classrooms? What do we risk by erring on the side of opacity and facades?

Can we ever really teach the reality of schools without accepting and disclosing the reality of our own circumstance as invested leavers?

Perhaps this then becomes the new truly serious philosophical problem: not simply preparing our students not to quit but coming to terms with the fact that most of us already did. If we can find happiness in that and share it with our students, we can teach them to become heroes.

Otherwise they may just think we're frauds.

REFERENCE

Camus, A. (1955/1991). *The myth of Sisyphus, and other essays.* New York: Vintage.

Index

A Nation at Risk (1983), 58, 96

AACTE. *See* American Association for Colleges of Teacher Education
academic language, 17, 59, 63, 65, 73
accreditation, 111, 152
activity theory, 22
Adichie, Chimamanda Ngozi, 17
agency, 135, 184
American Association for Colleges of Teacher Education, 59
appreciative stance, 6, 9
antideficit theory, 5; antideficit approaches, 19; antideficit classroom practices, 4, 10, 17; antideficit English educators, education, 6, 12; antideficit perspectives, 12; antideficit stance, 5

Bird by Bird, 10
Black Lives Matter, #BlackLivesMatter, 46

Camus, Albert, 174
CCSS. *See* Common Core State Standards
CEE. *See* Conference on English Education
CEE Methods National Study, 99, 100, 101
Christensen, Linda, 168
classrooms: for the 21st century, 78, 81, 91, 97
classroom management, xiii, 17, 25, 42, 43, 45, 82, 123
cooperating teacher, 32, 44, 154, 156–157
Common Core State Standards, 58, 96, 97, 99, 100, 101, 107, 134
communities of practice, 140, 153
Conference on English Education, 77, 78, 80, 96, 98, 99–100, 108
constructivism, constructivist, xv, 26, 32
counternarrative, 5, 19
craft conscience, 169
critical lenses, 63
critical literacy, 136
critical reflection, 12, 158
critical stance, xvii, 10–11
cultural assets, 3
culturally relevant pedagogy, 10
cultural responsiveness, 42

Dead Poets Society, 152
deficit thinking, 3, 4, 5, 12; deficit-oriented ELA teaching, 3
Detachment, 140
dialogic curriculum, 6
dialogic instruction, 112, 113, 114, 117, 118, 119, 120, 121
dialogic stance, 6
digital, 135; digital citizens, 158; digital environments, 78; digital learning, 80, 84; digital literacy, 83; digital reflection, 112; digital tools, 5–6, 19

differentiation, 8, 9, 27, 82, 157, 158
disciplinary literacy, 135, 138, 139, 140
diversity, 4, 5, 8, 11, 42, 47, 141

edTPA. *See* Educative Teacher Performance Assessment
Education Testing Services, 58, 60, 67, 71
Educative Teacher Performance Assessment, 57, 58, 59–61, 62, 63, 64, 65, 66, 71–72, 73, 127, 129
Elbow, Peter, 168
Emanuel African Methodist Episcopal Church (South Carolina), 47
English Journal, 39
English language learners, 40
English language arts (ELA) methods course, xiii, xiv, 5–6, 8, 10, 17, 18, 21, 36, 41, 51–52, 57, 60, 61, 62, 64–65, 66, 68, 80, 83, 85, 86, 87, 91, 93, 95, 96–97, 98, 99, 101, 102, 107, 111, 112, 114, 118, 119, 120, 133, 141, 145, 146, 150–151, 152, 153, 156, 157, 158, 159, 170, 171, 173
English Language Arts Teacher Educators (ELATE). *See* Conference on English Education
ensembles, 138
e-portfolio assessment, 79, 81, 82
equity, xv, 4, 6, 18, 19, 45, 47, 59
ETS. *See* Education Testing Services
exposure model, exposure, 142

field experience, field work, xiv, 4, 21, 23, 28, 36, 37, 85, 86, 101, 103, 153; tensions with, 111
funds of knowledge, 3

Google Classroom, 93
Google Drive, 85
Gradual Release of Responsibility model, 128
GRR. *See* Gradual Release of Responsibility model

heteronormativity, 43
heuristics, 171
Hull, Glynda, 168

identity, 5, 22, 31–32, 153; gender identity, 45, 46; identity formation, 22, 23, 30, 31, 32; identity paradigm, 32; identity theory, 22; identity work, 23, 30; teacher identity, xiii, xiv, 30, 31, 92
inequity, 85, 86
inquiry, xiii, 4, 7, 8, 9, 10, 11–12, 18, 113, 114, 117, 153; inquiry assignments, 40, 112, 114, 115, 117, 120; inquiry, community of, 19; inquiry revision, 120; inquiry stance, 9, 37
in-service teachers, xiii, 105, 108
invested leaver, 165, 171, 174, 175

Kansas Performance Teaching Portfolio, 71, 72
KPTP. *See* Kansas Performance Teaching Portfolio

Ladson-Billings, Gloria, 10, 168
literary analysis, 26, 65
literary study, 62
literary texts, 61
literary vocabulary, 62, 63, 65

Marjory Stoneman Douglas High School (Florida), 47
Me Too Movement, #MeToo, 47
mentor, mentor teacher, xiv, xv, 17, 21, 27, 28, 29, 30, 31, 43, 93, 112, 121, 122, 123, 158; mentoring, 6, 23, 24, 30, 36, 133, 158; mentoring relationships, 28, 37
Missouri Pre-service Teacher Assessment, 57
MoPTA. *See* Missouri Pre-service Teacher Assessment
motivation, 3, 42, 43, 152
multicultural, 24
multimodal, xiii, 78, 79, 80, 136, 139; multimodal composition, 138, 139; multimodal literacies, 78, 100; multimodal texts, 78, 100
mushfake Discourse, 139
Myth of Sisyphus, 174
myth of teacher as savior, 150

National Board of Professional Teaching Standards, 73

National Council of Teachers of English, xi, 57, 58, 63, 64, 65, 66, 67, 77, 100, 101, 167, 170
National Writing Project, 19
NBPTS. *See* National Board of Professional Teaching Standards
NCLB. *See* No Child Left Behind (2001)
NCTE. *See* National Council of Teachers of English
new literacies, 77, 78, 135
New London Group, 7
Night, 46
No Child Left Behind (2001), 58, 96, 134
NWP. *See* National Writing Project

OAS-ELA. *See* Oklahoma Academic Standards for English Language Arts
Oklahoma Academic Standards for English Language Arts, 99, 101, 105
Oklahoma State Department of Education, 100, 102
OSAT. *See* Oklahoma Subject Area Test
Oklahoma Subject Area Test, 103
On Writing: A Memoir of the Craft, 10
out-of-school literacy practices, 3, 10

PACT. *See* Performance Assessment for California Teachers
pedagogy, pedagogies, xiii, 4, 24, 39, 81, 85, 114, 152, 153, 168; culturally relevant pedagogy, 10; subject specific pedagogy, 61, 63, 135; writing pedagogy, 61, 62, 63
Performance Assessment for California Teachers (PACT), 57
personal practical theory, 41, 45
positioning, 5, 7, 60, 93
PowerPoint, 81, 83
PPAT. *See* Praxis Performance Assessment for Teachers
practicum, practicum experiences, 23, 24, 25, 27, 28, 29, 31, 91, 118, 119, 157
practitioner problems, 40, 41, 42, 43, 45, 46, 47, 51, 52
praxis, 24, 45, 58, 60, 64, 71, 103
Praxis Performance Assessment for Teachers, 58, 60, 72
preservice teacher, xiii, 4, 17–19, 22, 28, 30, 35, 39–40, 51, 57, 58, 61, 64, 77, 79, 83, 91, 92, 93, 96, 107, 134–135, 142, 145–146, 149, 162, 168, 173; dispositions, 24, 41, 42, 156. *See also* teacher candidates, PSTs, PTs
Prezi, 81
professional development, 57, 93
PSTs. *See* preservice teachers; teacher candidates
PTs, 4, 51, 149, 150. *See also* preservice teachers; teacher candidates

racial diversity, 11
racial stereotypes, 43, 46
racial identities, xv, 5, 11, 18
racial literacy, 5, 6, 19
racism, 4, 5, 6, 12, 17, 18, 46
reader-response, reader response theory, 164
reciprocity, 103
recursive planning, 26, 27, 28
reflection, 5, 12, 18, 23, 24, 26, 27–28, 36, 64, 73, 100, 111, 112, 113, 115, 120, 121, 122, 123, 128, 129, 137, 149, 157, 158
reflection protocol, 117, 118, 119, 122, 123, 128, 129
relational teaching, 42
resource pedagogies, 3, 5, 8, 10, 17, 18, 19
Rosenblatt, Louise, 168
rural, 46, 93, 114

SCALE. *See* Stanford Center for Assessment, Learning, and Equity
Schoology, 83
Secondary English Teacher Education in the United States (2018), 96, 98
service-learning, 6
Skype, 92
sociocultural, xviii, 138
social justice, xv, 17
social memoir, 40
standardization, standardized testing, standardized curricula/scripted curriculum, xvi, 17, 58, 61, 63, 64, 67, 87, 127, 141, 151, 158, 165
Stanford Center for Assessment, Learning, and Equity, 59, 60
The State of State English Standards (2005), 98

systemic racism, 12

TCs. *See* teacher candidates
teacher candidates, 18, 19, 22, 30, 35, 57, 58, 60, 62, 64, 65–66, 72, 77, 79, 82, 87–88, 91, 93, 96, 103, 104, 107, 111, 122, 123, 128, 151, 168. *See also* preservice teachers; PSTs
teacher licensure, 71, 81, 95, 103
Teacher Performance Assessment (TPA), 57–58, 59, 60, 61, 63, 64, 65, 66, 67–68, 71
teaching approach: differences, 3, 4, 5, 6, 11, 18, 19, 36, 39, 45, 51, 52, 61, 62, 65, 66, 78, 82, 99, 123, 129, 134, 135, 137
Teaching Reading in the Content Areas, 134
testing, 58, 61, 67, 68, 71, 158; high-stakes testing, 57
TED Talk, 17, 139, 140
TPA. *See* Teacher Performance Assessment
tutor, 6, 127; online tutoring, 79

two-world pitfall, 21, 26, 31, 32

video, 6, 79, 82
video reflection, video reflection assignment, 111–112, 113, 114, 116, 117, 118, 128, 158
Vimeo, 112
Voices from the Middle, 39
VoiceThread, 112

warranted assertability, 129
Wiesel, Elie, 46
wobble, 119, 128
workshop, 9–10, 83, 137
Writing Life, 10
writing purposes, 64; writing as an argument for teaching, 64; writing as a tool for thinking, 67; writing to reflect, 64; writing to advocate, 64
Writing Teacher Educators, 58, 60, 65
WTEs. *See* Writing Teacher Educators

young adult literature, 92
Youtube, 82, 112

About the Editors and Contributors

Heidi L. Hallman is professor of English education in the Department of Curriculum and Teaching at the University of Kansas. Hallman's research interests include studying "at-risk" students' literacy learning as well as how prospective English teachers are prepared to teach in diverse school contexts. Her work has appeared in *English Journal, Teaching Education, English Education*, and *Equity and Excellence in Education*, among others. In 2018, she was a corecipient of the National Council of Teachers of English's (NCTE) English Language Arts Teacher Educators (ELATE) Richard A. Meade Award for her coauthored book *Secondary English Teacher Education in the United States* (2018).

Kristen Pastore-Capuana is assistant professor of English education at Buffalo State College where she teaches undergraduate English language arts methods courses and coordinates field experiences and community partnerships. A former high school English teacher in western New York, Pastore-Capuana's 14 years of experience informs her work as a researcher and teacher educator. Her research interests include critical literacy pedagogy, secondary English language arts teacher development, and teacher advocacy. She is also the assistant director of the Western New York Network of English Teachers.

Donna L. Pasternak is professor of English education and director of the University of Wisconsin–Milwaukee Writing Project. She studies the integration of technology into the teaching of English and English language arts teacher education in urban contexts. Pasternak's scholarship has been published in a variety of journals and edited volumes. In 2018, she was a corecipient of the National Council of Teachers of English's (NCTE) English

Language Arts Teacher Educators (ELATE) Richard A. Meade Award for her coauthored book *Secondary English Teacher Education in the United States* (2018).

* * *

Julie Bell is assistant professor of teacher education at the University of Nebraska at Omaha. Prior to earning her PhD from Michigan State University, she taught high school English, speech, and theater in Indiana and Illinois. Currently, Bell teaches undergraduate and graduate courses in content area reading and disciplinary literacy, English methods, and young adult literature. Her research interests include exploring the implementation of content area reading and disciplinary literacy strategies in secondary classrooms and the mentoring of preservice and in-service teachers.

Mike Cook is assistant professor at Auburn University, where he teaches undergraduate and graduate courses within the English education program. His research interests include multimodal literacy and teacher identity development, particularly PTs' development as teacher-activists and socially just educators. He embeds this work in his preparation of preservice and graduate-level ELA teachers and has done research, presented, and published on comics and graphic novels as literacy and identity sponsors and the experiences and perceptions of PTs as they plan and work toward examining and interrupting inequality and oppression. His scholarship has appeared in *ALAN Review*, *Literacy Research and Instruction*, the *Journal of Language and Literacy Education*, and the *Journal of College Literacy and Learning*, among others.

Katharine Covino, assistant professor of English studies, teaches writing, literature, and teacher-preparation classes at Fitchburg State University. Her research interests include critical pedagogy, gender, and identity. Three areas of current scholarship focus on (a) examining the implications of including critical pedagogy in elementary literacy classrooms, (b) applying indigenous lenses to critically examine and retell cultural myths, and (c) exploring the disconnects that can arise for novice secondary English teachers as they begin their teaching careers. Additionally, she has published and presented on a variety of issues related to literacy praxis, entwining theory and practice to support English teachers in their classrooms. Guided by her interest in promoting critical, collaborative, and reflective pedagogy, she has served for multiple years as a faculty mentor at Fitchburg State University. Prior to teaching at the university level, she taught middle school and high school in Austin, Texas. In addition to her work as a teacher and researcher, she is also a children's book author with two upcoming projects in the works.

Michelle Fowler-Amato is assistant professor of English and English education at Old Dominion University. In addition, she has worked as a teacher, literacy coach, and staff developer in urban and suburban K–12 public schools. Fowler-Amato's research interests include adolescent literacy, anti-deficit English education, and inquiry-based approaches to teaching and learning. She has published articles in *Teaching Writing: The Journal of Writing Teacher Education, Voices From the Middle,* and *Literacy Research: Theory, Method, and Practice.*

Seth D. French is a distinguished doctoral fellow studying curriculum and instruction at the University of Arkansas, where he also works with preservice teachers. His recent work includes coauthored book chapters "Reinterpreting Revolutions: An 'Encoding/Decoding' Analysis of *Animal Farm*" (2018) and "Fiction or Reality? The Reciprocity of School Film Literacy Representations and Educational Policy, 1955–2017" (2018). French's research interests include new literacies and student engagement, with special emphasis on critical media literacy and gamification.

Jessica Gallo is assistant professor of English education in the College of Education at the University of Nevada, Reno. Before becoming a teacher educator, she taught high school English in rural school districts in Wisconsin. She has been a National Writing Project teacher leader since 2008 and is a former codirector for the Rural Wisconsin Writing Institute, a site of the Fox Valley Writing Project. Her current research focuses on rural education and English teacher preparation.

Jeremy Glazer is assistant professor of English education in Rowan University's College of Education. He taught high school English and social studies in Philadelphia and Miami. His areas of research include ELA curriculum and instruction, teacher retention and attrition, teacher preparation, and classroom discussion. His work has appeared in *Teaching and Teacher Education, Teachers and Teaching: Theory and Practice,* and *Kappan.*

Christian Z. Goering is professor of English education at the University of Arkansas where he directs the Northwest Arkansas Writing Project and works with the licensure programs in English education and theater/communications. Goering taught high school English in Topeka, Kansas, and is a nationally board certified teacher. In 2018 he coedited *Critical Media Literacy and Fake News in Post-Truth America* and in 2016 coauthored *The Arkansas Delta Oral History Project: Culture, Place, and Authenticity.* He's currently chair of the English Language Arts Teacher Educators (ELATE). A singer-songwriter in his spare time, Goering organizes a monthly Songs in

Progress event in the community. A father to Katie and Zach and partner of Emily, he and his family live in Fayetteville, Arkansas.

Sarah Hochstetler is associate professor of English education at Illinois State University where she teaches preservice and in-service teachers in the department of English. She edited *Reform and Literacy Education: History, Effects, and Advocacy* (2018) and has recent publications in *Voices From the Middle* and *English Journal* on topics related to teacher agency. Hochstetler is a former secondary English teacher and National Writing Project fellow.

Melinda J. McBee Orzulak is associate professor of English at Bradley University in Peoria, Illinois, where she teaches future teachers and serves as the English education coordinator. Her research focuses on equity and language in English language arts teaching. Her recent work includes *Understanding Language: Supporting ELL Students in Responsive ELA Classrooms* (2017), and she has appeared in *Research in the Teaching of English*, *English Education*, *English Journal*, and the edited volume *Teaching English Language Arts to English Language Learners*. She is a former secondary English, writing, and humanities teacher.

Chea Parton is a dean's scholar at the University of Texas at Austin where she is pursuing her doctorate. Before beginning her graduate studies, she taught high school English at a rural school in East Central Indiana. Her experiences in the classroom inform her research interests, which include adolescence as a cultural construct, rural teacher education, and the impact of place on teaching and learning.

Brandon Sams is assistant professor of English at Iowa State University. He teaches undergraduate and graduate courses on writing and literature methods in the English education program. Much of his current work focuses on the potential of aesthetic and contemplative reading practices to interrupt and renew "schooled" reading practices shaped by the epistemologies of audit culture. His work has recently appeared in the *ALAN Review*, the *Journal of Language and Literacy Education*, and *Changing English*.

Lara Searcy is assistant professor, English education specialist, at Northeastern State University (NSU) in Tahlequah, Oklahoma, where she teaches English teacher candidates. She is a former high school English teacher and middle school literacy resource specialist and is nationally board certified in AYA-ELA. In 2018, she was awarded the Circle of Excellence in Teaching from NSU. Her research interests include teacher efficacy, standards-based reforms, and English teacher professional development. She is a proud member of the National Council of Teachers of English (NCTE) and is currently the president elect of the Oklahoma affiliate OKCTE.

Melanie Shoffner is associate professor of English education at James Madison University. Her recent work includes the edited book *Exploring Teachers in Fiction and Film* and articles published in the *Teacher Educator* and the *Journal of Language and Literacy Education*. Her research and writing focus on the dispositional and reflective development of preservice English teachers. A former high school English teacher, Shoffner recently spent a year in Romania as a Fulbright Scholar, teaching courses in adolescent literature, pedagogy, and American culture.

Jeff Spanke is assistant professor of English at Ball State University where he teaches courses in introductory composition, young adult literature, and English teaching methods. Prior to Ball State, he earned a PhD in English education from Purdue University where he served as a university supervisor for secondary ELA student teachers and taught courses in content area literacy and introductory composition. Before Purdue, he taught high school English in Crawfordsville, Indiana. Spanke's current scholarship focuses on the various social constructions of schools, teachers, and learning, as well as the extent to which narrative constructions of education may help preservice teachers negotiate their roles in their future classrooms.

Connor K. Warner is assistant professor of education at the University of Saint Mary in Leavenworth, Kansas. Prior to moving into higher education, he served for almost a decade as a department chair and English/social studies teacher in western Montana. Warner's primary scholarly agenda centers on the interplay of teacher education policy, curriculum, and assessment. His most recent article, "Navigating Mandates and Working Toward Coherence: Our Journey With a High-Stakes Teacher Performance Assessment," coauthored with colleagues, will be published in 2019 in the *Educational Forum*.

Amber Warrington is assistant professor of English education at Boise State University where she teaches in the undergraduate and graduate programs and codirects the Boise State Writing Project. She is a former high school English language arts teacher, member of the National Council of Teachers of English, and editorial board member of the blog *Teachers, Profs, Parents: Writers Who Care*. Warrington's scholarship focuses on teacher inquiry, teacher/researcher collaboration, and antideficit English education, particularly related to writing instruction and assessment.

www.ingramcontent.com/pod-product-compliance
Lightning Source LLC
Chambersburg PA
CBHW022013300426
44117CB00005B/162